ADDRESSING STUDENT SEXUAL VIOLENCE IN HIGHER EDUCATION

ADDRESSING STUDENT SEXUAL VIOLENCE IN HIGHER EDUCATION

A Good Practice Guide

Second Edition

BY

CLARISSA J. DISANTIS
University of Galway, Ireland

AND

GRAHAM J. TOWL
Durham University, UK

emerald
PUBLISHING

United Kingdom – North America – Japan
India – Malaysia – China

REVIEWS

The second edition of *Addressing Student Sexual Violence in Higher Education: A Good Practice Guide* by Clarissa J. DiSantis and Graham J. Towl is a crucial and timely resource for higher education providers committing to combatting sexual violence in their communities. The authors provide actionable advice and guidance on critical areas such as policy development, prevention education and institutional responses, paving the way for a comprehensive, institution-wide, survivor-centred and trauma-informed approach. DiSantis and Towl's intersectional approach ensures that their guidance is practical and effective across diverse educational settings. This book is a must-have for higher education professionals working towards safer and more supportive environments for all students.

—*Sharna Bremner* **is the Founder and Director of End Rape on Campus Australia**

The first edition of this book has become indispensable to anyone working to combat gender-based violence in UK higher education. This second edition, with cutting-edge new material and case studies, is also set to become an instant classic. Its recommendations on good practice should be read and acted on by everyone – activists, practitioners, researchers, and leaders – trying to change their university for the better.

—*Anna Bull* **is a Senior Lecturer at the University of York and a Co-Director of the 1752 Group**

This is a very timely new edition of a book that should be essential reading for anyone seeking to tackle sexual misconduct in universities. New chapters on matters such as the impact of technology provide vital new evidence and guidance. This includes setting out the growing prevalence of technology-facilitated sexual misconduct, as well as the benefits of using technology to investigate cases and support students. This balanced approach infuses the whole book, working towards a system and policy approach that works fairly for all.

—*Professor Clare McGlynn KC (Hon)*, **Professor of Law at Durham University, Expert on Violence Against Women & Girls**

A necessary and critical blueprint for Higher Education Institutions to incorporate in their efforts to tackle sexual violence and to change culture and attitudes. Socially relevant, this guide will be useful to anyone committed to embracing and normalizing safety, security, accountability and equality for those who are vulnerable to sexual predatory behavior. It is a comprehensive guide on what to do and what not to do with respect to preventing and responding to sexual violence written in the best interests of the student and without shying away from the gendered realities of who is more likely to be a victim. At the same time there is an explicit call to action that provokes a sense of urgency to reduce the prevalence of sexual violence coupled with a sober assessment of measured progress against the backdrop of resistance, stubborn biases and institutionalized failings. The broad scope of this guide makes this a useful tool for leaders, practitioners, policymakers, student services administrators, case managers, educators, investigators, adjudicators, activists. Additionally, its narrow focus makes this updated guidance an essential lifeline to those responsible for receiving sexual violence disclosures and those drafting and revising the policies.

—*Furaha-Joy Sekai Saungweme*, **Founder of the Africa End Sexual Harassment Initiative (AESHI)**

In *Addressing Student Sexual Violence in Higher Education*, DiSantis and Towl draw on their extensive experience to provide this thorough and practical guide for universities looking to improve campus safety. The book offers insights into best practices for prevention, intervention and support in relation to gender-based violence, making it an essential resource for anyone working in this field. I highly recommend it as a vital tool for all practitioners aiming to create lasting, meaningful change on campuses.

—*Fiona Drouet MBE*, **Founder and CEO of EmilyTest**

Emerald Publishing Limited
Emerald Publishing, Floor 5, Northspring, 21-23 Wellington Street, Leeds
LS1 4DL

Second Edition 2025

Reprints and permissions service
Contact: www.copyright.com

British Library Cataloguing in Publication Data
A catalogue record for this book is available from the British Library

ISBN: 978-1-83797-786-4 (Print)
ISBN: 978-1-83797-783-3 (Online)
ISBN: 978-1-83797-785-7 (Epub)

INVESTOR IN PEOPLE

The RSACC was established in 1990 and is the only free and specialist provider of services for survivors of sexual violence in Darlington and County Durham. RSACC is a feminist, women-led charity working to end rape and sexual violence by supporting and empowering survivors.

Support for survivors of sexual violence is desperately needed within Darlington and County Durham. Sexual violence has significant and lasting consequences on survivors, including impacting individuals' mental and physical health, leaving women feeling isolated and disconnected from their community. Other long-term consequences can include posttraumatic stress disorder, anxiety and panic attacks, depression, social phobia, substance abuse, obesity, eating disorders, self-harm and suicide. Often survivors are involved in the criminal justice system, which has the impact of increasing stress and anxiety, even re-traumatisation, as clients describe not feeling believed or experiencing victim-blaming.

Over the decades, demand for RSACC's support has grown, and they now support more than 1,000 survivors each year. RSACC's services include specialist counselling, group support and an anonymous telephone and email support line. They also offer Independent Sexual Violence Advisors, who support survivors going through the criminal justice system.

RSACC is an accredited member of Rape Crisis England and Wales National Service Standards and actively supports campaigning both locally and nationally to end violence against women and girls.

RSACC

Rape and Sexual Abuse Counselling Centre
Darlington and County Durham

All author royalties for the 1st and 2nd Edition of this book are donated in full to RSACC.

CONTENTS

Resources

LIST OF FIGURES

LIST OF TABLES

LIST OF ABBREVIATIONS
AND ACRONYMS

AHRC	Australian Human Rights Commission
AMOSSHE	The Student Services Organisation
ATIXA	Association of Title IX Administrators
BLOG	Believe, Listen, Offer Options and Resources, Get Support for Yourself
BRAG	Blue, Red, Amber, Green (Traffic Light System)
CJS	Criminal Justice System
CPS	The Crown Prosecution Service
CUC	Committee of University Chairs
DARVO	Deny, Attack, Reverse Victim and Offender
DfE	Department for Education
EHRC	Equality and Human Rights Commission
FE	Further Education
FOUR	Fixated, Obsessive, Unwanted, Repeated
FT/FTE	Full-Time/Full-Time Equivalent
GBV	Gender-Based Violence
GDPR	General Data Protection Regulation
HE	Higher Education
HEI	Higher Education Institution
IDVA	Independent Domestic Violence Advisor
ISVA	Independent Sexual Violence Advisor
MOU	Memorandum of Understanding
NASPA	Student Affairs Administrators in Higher Education
NUS	National Union of Students
OfS	Office for Students
OIA	Office of the Independent Adjudicator for Higher Education (England and Wales)
ONS	Office for National Statistics
PTSD	Posttraumatic Stress Disorder
RJ	Restorative Justice
RMA	Rape Myth Acceptance
RSE	Relationships and Sex Education
SAMHSA	Substance Abuse and Mental Health Services Administration
SARC	Sexual Assault Referral Centre
SLII	Surveillance, Life Invasion, Intimidation, Interference
SU	Students' Union
SVLO	Sexual Violence Liaison Officer
TFSV	Techology-facilitated Sexual Violence
UUK	Universities UK
VAW/VAWG	Violence Against Women/Violence Against Women and Girls
VLE	Virtual Learning Environment

ACKNOWLEDGEMENTS

In the 4 years since we wrote the first edition of this book, we have watched the higher education sector recognise that sexual violence cannot be ignored. Student activism has remained strong, practitioner networks to share good practice and seek guidance have developed and more resources have been dedicated to addressing sexual violence within university communities. We take this time to thank each person who has supported this development and kept sexual violence on the agenda. Thank you to the students, staff, activists and advocates from external organisations who have worked diligently to ensure that university leaders could not ignore this issue.

There are key people within our personal and professional networks that have helped develop our own thinking in this area, that have been sounding boards for evolving our ideas and practice, and who have supported us to sustain this work. With too many to name, we know you know who you are – we say thank you.

Finally, we wish to acknowledge the victims and survivors whose human rights were violated at university. We hope this second edition will aid in this fight for the basic human rights of safety and equality. We see and hear you, and most importantly, we believe you. Thank you.

PART 1

WHY

All students have the right to live and study in an environment of dignity and respect, free from the fear of harassment or violence.

~Olivia Bailey
NUS National Women's Officer, Hidden Marks, National Union of Students, 2011

1

1

INTRODUCTION

Sexual violence in higher education (HE) is pervasive. It is akin to a wildfire burning through the HE forest causing students to leave their universities and for some lose their lives. It is destructive, devastating and costly both in human and financial terms. Without prevention measures in place, sexual violence will keep happening, destroying any semblance of safety, especially for women, in universities. Without the proper tools, those working to put out the fires might as well only have a small fire extinguisher in their hand. Maybe they can help put out one fire, but the trauma and devastation has occurred. Putting out one fire is good, but we strongly argue that preventing the fire to begin with is better. We must put prevention measures in place. In the same way that higher education institutions (HEIs) dedicate resource and training to the prevention of real fires, we need to dedicate resource and training to prevent sexual violence.[1] Universities appoint fire officers with expertise on fire safety. Given the potential for harm and relatively high risk of occurrence of sexual violence in HE, we invite university leaders and governing bodies to employ those with expertise in addressing sexual violence. Just as fire safety is a specialist area so is addressing our challenging problem of sexual violence at universities. We need proper tools and resources to respond when

---

[1]Throughout this book, we use the terms 'higher education institution (HEI)', 'university' and 'institution' interchangeably to represent all types of institutions of higher learning or tertiary education.

sexual violence occurs. We need to address sexual violence from a comprehensive institution-wide approach to prevent harm in our communities.

A root cause of sexual violence is power and domination (Linder et al., 2020). Sexual violence is gendered and markedly so. In terms of occupational groups most likely to be subjected to sexual violence, there are no other groups with a higher level of risk than students and especially young women students (ONS, 2023). Gender inequality and rape culture play large roles in terms of the environmental backdrop to a culture which largely protects perpetrators while doing comparatively little to support those subjected to sexual violence (Linder et al., 2020). In terms of risks to student wellbeing, we would hope that sexual violence in a university community would be high up on institutional risk registers.

We wrote the first edition of this book because shockingly but unsurprisingly, there was an absence of practical and detailed guidance on how to address issues of sexual violence in universities. Four years later, we see limited change, resourcing and enforcement of preventing sexual violence in HE. In fact, our current assessment from our combined experience is that universities may be happy to do tick box exercises to appear to be addressing sexual violence, without resourcing or attempting meaningful change. This was partly what has inspired us to renew our efforts in contributing to addressing the problem. We decided to provide updated guidance and tools to support the ever-evolving landscape that is HE with the same goal – to prevent and respond to sexual violence. We hope this edition is of use to the sector and particularly to the activists who have led the way in pushing this on university governing bodies' agendas. Whereas in the first edition we very much focused upon practical solutions in a handbook format, this second edition goes beyond that. We go into more detail on the contextual nature of the problem – in other words how the HE environment contributes to enabling sexual misconduct and how the reliance on student and staff activists for leadership in this area seems to us to reflect an abrogation of responsibility from highly paid senior leaders whose role it is to – lead. Chapters 6 and 13 of this book give more detailed coverage on the nature of some of our key problems, but as with the first edition, we focus on solutions too.

But our solutions are predicated on leaders wishing, authentically, to reduce sexual misconduct at universities and to ensure that those subjected to sexual misconduct receive the care and support that they deserve.

This book is intended for leaders, practitioners, policymakers, student services administrators, case managers, educators, investigators, adjudicators, activists and all of us who may receive a disclosure of sexual violence. We want this to be a useful resource and tool for all of us who care about making a difference in reducing sexual violence in HE.

Although there has been some progress in addressing sexual violence in HE, it seems to us that at very best it has stalled, and there remains much to be done, and that as a sector, we have done little more than take the first few steps needed to address this pervasive issue in HEIs. Some have gone backwards. One illustration of this is when senior leaders make the implausible claim that one reason for a lack of progress is a lack of funds. We think that this may more accurately be described as a lack of prioritisation. Compared with other areas of the public sector, such as Further Education (FE), universities seem comparatively well funded and overall relatively wealthy notwithstanding current concerns around the financial viability of the sector. One concern that we have is that with the current talk of difficult funding models, there is a danger that tackling our problem with sexual violence will be relatively low on the list of institutional priorities. We argue that executive leaders and governing bodies can make the choice to prioritise investing in this work. Indecision is not neutral. Indecision supports the existing situation, which is that young women students, in particular, are likely at the highest level of risk of their lifetimes of being subjected to sexual violence while enroled in our courses. Indecision maintains the status quo. Or we can choose to address the problem.

The lack of sufficient HE senior leadership prioritisation in this area continues to be a part of the problem and can reflect a narrow view of the potential of HE communities. Successive generations of HEI governing bodies and executive leaders have not seen fit to make fundamental changes to address sexual violence. Increasingly, we are seeing the human cost of such failures of leadership (Towl & Paske, 2017). Research and teaching are key to HE and so are broader notions of education, learning and making a positive impact in wider societies.

The UK Criminal Justice System (CJS) seems to us to be a very blunt, and largely ineffectual, system in tackling sexual violence, although we note recent improvements through Operation Soteria (2024). In 2018/19, rates of rape prosecutions and charges in England and Wales were at the lowest levels in a decade with only 1 in 65 rapes reported to the police resulting in a charge or summons (Barr et al., 2019). In 2022/23, charges for sexual offences increased by 18% (National Police Chief's Council, 2024). Despite this slight improvement, we note that there are still many barriers to reporting to police and/or universities for student victim-survivors (NUS, 2011; Revolt Sexual Assault, 2018).

This is a key point that we would pick up as tapping into the broader educational purpose of HEIs to do something good and useful in wider society sometimes viewed as our 'civic duties'. We are uniquely well placed to contribute to addressing the problem where the CJS has historically failed victims and continues to do so. We have the ability to get our own house in order in the academic world.

We need to invest to increase reporting, support victim-survivors and ensure the quality of internal investigations and decision-making processes. We need to create environments where students and staff can access education and employment free from the fear of sexual violence. A central argument of this book is that if disclosing and reporting becomes the 'new norm', this may very well contribute to prevention through deterrence for some, alongside a robust comprehensive prevention programme. Every year, university communities have the opportunity to share what we are doing to address our problem with sexual violence when we have prospective students with their parents' visiting on our much vaunted 'open days'. Talking about our problem with sexual violence and what we are doing to address it at open days sends out clear and positive messages to prospective students. To those who may be subjected to sexual violence, it conveys the values of the institution and in particular that if they come forward, they will be believed and supported. For prospective perpetrators, it lets them know that we want reporting to become the 'new norm' in HE, and we will hold perpetrators accountable for any such behaviours, including using sanctions like expulsion. Above all what it conveys to prospective students and their parents alike is that we are transparent about our problems, and we are doing something about it. And that may be a question that they can ask at other university open day visits they have planned. They may well conclude that it is surely safer to be at a university that is transparent about the problem and taking it very seriously in tangible ways that can be articulated on open days along with any other student safety issues.

If we can make a real and tangible difference to the prevention of sexual violence in HE and potentially within wider society, why would we not do it? We argue that we can and should do what we can as a sector to make a difference. In doing so, we are seeking to protect the long-term interests of all of us.

As we will discuss throughout the book, it is important how we discuss and frame these issues. In this book, we use the term 'sexual violence' as an umbrella term to capture a range of non-consensual, unwanted, forced and/or coerced sexual behaviours including, but not limited to, rape, assault by penetration, sexual assault, sexual harassment, indecent exposure, image-based sexual abuse, stalking and domestic abuse, including coercive and controlling behaviour. These are all forms of gender-based violence identified as part of what is considered the 'sexual violence continuum' (Kelly, 1987, 1988). In Chapters 2 and 4, we highlight why sexual violence is considered gender-based violence. We note that internationally, particularly in the United States and Scotland, the term 'gender-based violence' is preferred in HE prevention efforts. For the purposes of this book, we have chosen to use 'sexual violence', as sector guidance in England and Wales predominently uses this language.

We use the following terms to refer to those subjected to or perpetrating sexual violence:

- **Victim-survivor/Survivor:** individual subjected to any form of sexual violence.

- **Perpetrator/Offender:** individual who committed any form of sexual violence.

- **Reporting Party:** individual disclosing or reporting to an HEI that they have been subjected to any form of sexual violence.

- **Responding Party:** individual reported to have committed any form of sexual violence within an HEI.

- **Subjected to (Sexual Violence):** we prefer the epithet 'subjected to' rather than 'experienced' because it more accurately reflects the power dynamic involved. The term 'experienced' implies a level of neutrality that does not reflect this power dynamic and ignores the aggressor of the violence.

The language is purposeful in that we choose not to use 'victim' as a standalone label even though 'victim' along with 'injured party' or 'witness' are used in the CJS. HEI administrations may enact civil justice-based procedures and processes but not criminal justice-based investigations, and we aim to reflect this in our language. Where appropriate, we would use 'survivor' as a standalone label; however, from our joint clinical experience working with victim-survivors, we recognise that the labels of 'victim' and 'survivor' take on different meanings and purposes at different points in recovery. Therefore, out of respect for the autonomy of individuals to choose a label that supports their recovery at a specific point, we have chosen this double-barrelled label to use throughout our book only abbreviating to 'survivor' on occasion. The use of victim-survivor takes on the meaning of moving from victim to survivor and on to thriving in the recovery process highlighting an individual's resilience and strength. In our experience, excluding the use of the term 'victim' may have the impact of individuals feeling as if their victimisation by the perpetrator was ignored or minimised, and that they were only asked to survive or pull themselves up by their bootstraps. In addition, we acknowledge the brutal reality that not all individuals subjected to gender-based violence survive. The sobering, but necessary, tragic truth is that in England and Wales, an estimated 1 in 10 women subjected to sexual violence attempt suicide (Office for National Statistics, 2021). In the United Kingdom, 'the number of women and girls killed by men every year remains depressingly consistent. The average number of women and girls killed annually since 2009 is 142' (Allen et al., 2024, p. 6).

We use the term 'Reporting Party' as a label for an individual who reports to an HEI they have been subjected to sexual violence. This is a neutral term for the purposes of an internal investigation. We find that using 'victim', 'survivor' and 'victim-survivor' within an internal investigation creates a perceived bias that will encourage Responding Parties to appeal decisions. The term 'complainant' is problematic too as it implies the individual is complaining, whining or in some way potentially viewed, albeit erroneously, as a problem.

The term 'Responding Party' is, again, a neutral term to refer to an individual who has been reported to have committed sexual violence. Other terms, which may be viewed to hold bias, but hold the same meaning, would include accused party or alleged perpetrator. Both terms are in common use in the CJS, but we would reiterate the need to not use CJS-based terms but rather to recognise the civil legal nature of university proceedings.

This book is a modest and in places emotive, but we hope, helpful contribution to this growing field. Notwithstanding the above, what distinguishes this book is its firm focus on the practicalities of addressing sexual violence in HE; in that sense, it is more of a handbook offering case studies, tools and resources to practitioners and policy makers. We have structured this book into two parts. Part 1 focuses on why HEIs must address sexual violence in their communities. The short answer – it is the right thing to do. However, if the moral argument is not strong enough, in Part 1, we demonstrate the overarching need for the work to be done due to the immeasurable harm currently occurring in our communities, alongside the legal, financial and reputational risks of not addressing sexual violence. In Chapter 2, we consider the landscape for addressing sexual violence in HE internationally. In Chapter 3, we highlight learning from changes made in the sector due to the COVID-19 pandemic and identify a key area of focus on universities' need to address technology-facilitated sexual violence. To close Part 1, we offer a call to action for senior leaders to invest in and lead in, this area. In Part 2 starting in Chapter 5, we offer practical how-to guidance beginning with a model for a comprehensive institution-wide approach alongside discussions of how to resource this work. In Chapter 6, we consider how HEIs can resist, stall or dismantle prevention and response initiatives aimed at addressing sexual violence and offer strategies to overcome this resistance. In Chapter 7, we detail how to develop robust policies in this challenging area. This is followed by a discussion on how to develop comprehensive prevention and response training across the institution. In Chapter 9, we describe how to respond to disclosures of sexual violence from a first-aid lens. In Chapter 10, we discuss the importance of specialist case management and practitioner safety. In Chapters 11 and 12, we discuss how to run trauma-informed investigations and disciplinary procedures. These chapters are followed by a hard-hitting but necessary discussion on when universities fail victim-survivors to help HEIs avoid making the same mistakes. In Chapter 14, we return to speaking directly to university leaders discussing the importance of leadership and partnerships for any of this work to be successful. Finally, in Chapter 15, we offer concluding thoughts and recommendations. In addition, we provide a set of resources and templates for practitioners at the end of this book.

Little of what follows in terms of practical advice and proposed policies and practices may be achieved if there are insufficient financial resources being prioritised to support such work. We recognise that students, increasingly, are talking about sexual violence more openly. We hope this dialogue is welcomed by university executive leadership teams and governing bodies. We are keen that the second edition of this book is a useful contribution to those conversations and aids in addressing sexual violence in higher education.

2

SEXUAL VIOLENCE IN HIGHER EDUCATION: AN INTERNATIONAL ISSUE

Sexual violence at universities is an international, widely recognised and well-documented problem (Towl & Walker, 2019), and sexual harassment is widespread internationally too (Saungweme et al., 2024). Recent work in this area has sought to outline the extent of the problem while also having a focus upon the core requirements to successfully address this issue (UN Women, 2018a, 2018b). However, although there has been much work in this area internationally, there overwhelmingly remains much more to do than has been done to date. And much of what has been done does not appear to have been successful (e.g. Office for Students, 2022). There are concerns internationally about a lack of adequate regulation and oversight of our problem of sexual violence at universities internationally (Baird et al., 2022; Henry, 2023). Some have compellingly argued that there is a degree of regulatory ritual around the regulation of sexual misconduct at universities, e.g. in Australia insofar as regulation lacks legal teeth. Much of regulation seems more characterised by exhortation rather than legal direction. While we think that it is important to acknowledge some progress, in some areas, we are mindful of the scale of the tasks ahead for higher education institution (HEI) leadership teams, including governing bodies, and wider HEI communities nationally and internationally.

In April 2021, the Office for Students (OfS) published their *Statement of Expectations for Preventing and Addressing Harassment and Sexual Misconduct Affecting Students in Higher Education* herein 'Statement of Expectations' which only encouraged HEIs in England to have the most basic level of service in place for students. As a sector, we have not even managed to meet such comparatively modest expectations as evidenced in a national study where the authors were quite so lacking in faith that the sector would meet the expectations that they strongly recommended a move towards firmer regulation (Baird et al., 2022). The OfS acknowledged this evidence and exhortation in their consultation with English higher education (HE) on whether a condition of registration to ensure that students are protected from harassment and sexual misconduct be imposed. At the time of writing, the decision on this has not been released.

In Chapters 4 and 14, we look closely at why HEI leadership teams and communities more widely need to be much more pro-actively involved in addressing sexual violence. This chapter draws together some international commonalities in our understanding of sexual violence in HE. Whereas there are differences in terms of the legal context of such work across, and sometimes within, countries, there are some key commonalities in terms of the specific problems to be addressed. Indeed, there are some ubiquitous lessons about our understanding of sexual violence across societies more generally, which are also evident when reviewing the international evidence on sexual violence in HE. We will note the differences where relevant.

PREVALENCE IN HIGHER EDUCATION

Major reviews and related surveys have been undertaken in several countries where there is an increasing acknowledgement of the problem of sexual violence in HEIs. In the United Kingdom, the National Union of Students (NUS) has perhaps been most forth-right and proactive in ensuring that this is an area that HEI executive leadership teams and governing bodies need to address (2011) and, refreshingly, the influence of the union has extended to HE and Further Education (FE) provision in UK Colleges (2019). That said, current work in HE seems more developed than that in FE, and the focus of this book is addressing sexual violence in HE.

'University campuses create a unique set of risks for women including exposure to, and experience of, violence such as sexual assault, stalking, intimate partner violence/dating violence, and sexual harassment' (UN Women, 2018a, p. 5). Women between the ages of 16 and 24 are at heightened risk for sexual violence and domestic abuse (Ministry of Justice et al., 2013; Office for National Statistics, 2023; Rennison et al., 2017). Research conducted by the NUS (2011) in the United Kingdom revealed that women respondents experienced the following while students: 1 in 7 women were subjected to a serious physical or sexual assault, 68% reported being subjected to some form of verbal or non-verbal harassment, 12% were subjected to stalking and 1 in 10 victim-survivors were given alcohol or drugs against their will before an assault. In the United States, 1 in 5 women students and 1 in 14 men reported being subjected to sexual assault (Krebs et al., 2016). For women who are bisexual, the rates of sexual assault appear higher (1 in 3), and to a lesser, but still inflated degree, for transgender students (1 in 4) (Krebs et al., 2016). A study conducted with university students in Ireland found 49% of women student respondents were subjected to non-consensual sexual touching, 34% were subjected to non-consensual vaginal penetration, and 9% were subjected to non-consensual anal penetration (MacNeela et al., 2022). In the same study, LGBT+ students and students with disabilities also reported high rates of sexual violence. The position at other European universities shows broadly comparable results in terms of the prevalence of sexual violence. Some European universities are beginning to address sexual violence on campus actively, but progress is varied much like in the United Kingdom (Towl & Walker, 2019). A content analysis of 10 years of research into campus sexual violence identified that many studies found perpetrators target minoritised students at high rates: 'students with disabilities, queer and trans students, and women of color all experience higher rates of campus sexual violence than their able-bodied, heterosexual, cisgender, and white peers', (Linder et al., 2020, p. 1037).

A recent report by the National Police Chief's Council (2024) that reported on rape and serious sexual offences reported to the police in England and Wales found that 38% of perpetrators were a current or ex-partner of the victim-survivor and 29% were individuals known to the victim-survivor. A study by Revolt Sexual Assault in partnership with The Student Room (2018) found that in 57% of cases, the perpetrator was known to the student victim-survivor. The highest rates of sexual assaults appear to be in the first few months of university attendance (Kimble et al., 2008). This appears to be the case in several countries internationally as well (Towl & Walker, 2019). The US research indicates that students are less likely to report to the police than non-students. These data are drawn upon in arguments about why we need to have a particular focus upon tackling sexual violence in HE. The aim is to make disclosing to the university the 'new norm', thus reversing the previous trend so that more victim-survivors can access support. If they can access support, they may feel more empowered to make a choice to report should they want this. For student victim-survivors, friends or acquaintances are the most likely perpetrators followed by 'existing sexual partners' (Bureau of Justice Statistics, 2014). Interestingly, and this is perhaps a commentary on the socialisation of students, a greater proportion of students said that they did not report because they did not view the rape/sexual assault as serious enough (Bureau of Justice Statistics, 2014).

The major source of evidence for significant under-reporting of sexual violence in the United Kingdom is the Crime Survey for England and Wales, where the numbers who report having been subjected to sexual violence are far greater than the numbers recorded by the police (Towl & Walker, 2019). The marked under-reporting of sexual violence in societies across the world seems to be an international phenomenon (Towl & Walker, 2019). This is key to informing how we may make progress in this challenging area. Just as there is under-reporting in society, there is, it seems, significant under-reporting to university administrations. Reporting rates among students to university administrations in the United States seem to be at around 7% of those subjected to rape (Krebs et al., 2016). The Criminal Justice System (CJS) requires a 'beyond reasonable doubt' standard of proof. Civil justice requires 'a more likely than not' standard. HEIs address misconduct (including sexual misconduct) with a civil standard of proof. Such actions in the case of the CJS are through the courts; whereas civil justice is used at universities primarily through disciplinary processes. It may be that a barrier to reporting is that victim-survivors do not realise that HEIs use the civil standard of proof to determine breaches of policy, and in fact that not all forms of sexual violence covered by policy would constitute a criminal offence.

It is not unusual for media coverage of sexual violence at universities to conflate reporting rates with prevalence rates. Prevalence rates would represent the number of people who have or have not been subjected to sexual violence in the community; whereas, reporting rates would represent the number of people who have disclosed or reported incidents of sexual violence. Prevalence rates may include, for example, the percentage of women in their first year at university who are not subjected to sexual harassment. It may also include the numbers and proportion of women not subjected to rape and/or attempted rape. This needs to be distinguished from the reporting rates. Headlines scream at, rather than welcome, high reporting rates. We would, of course, want the prevalence levels to be zero, with no students subjected to sexual violence. However, in our current reality, such a state of affairs seems highly improbable to us. Thus, there will be a percentage of individuals who will be subjected to some form of sexual violence. In view of that, we have a marked preference for such individuals to feel empowered, enabled and supported to disclose and/or report. Again, if reporting becomes the 'new norm', more students can access support and potentially would-be perpetrators may be deterred.

Thus, contrary to ill-informed journalistic coverage of this challenging topic, high reports at universities are far more plausibly an indicant of student trust than a meaningful measure of actual prevalence rates. Indeed, we would strongly argue that those institutions with the lowest levels of reports (or those HEIs declining to record and report incidents) may well be some of the more dangerous institutions in terms of the risk of sexual violence. In the United Kingdom, 33 universities declined to report to a BBC survey of sexual violence reporting rates in HE (Jeffreys, 2019). It is highly unlikely that, for example, no reports equate with no incidents of sexual violence. However, no reports may very well mean that students simply do not trust their institutions (Ghani & Towl, 2017). Often such distrust may be well founded, and this is what we need to change if we are to make significant progress in this challenging area.

The number of reports reflect the number of students who reported to their university that they were subjected to sexual violence. Collecting prevalence data is important and potentially very useful, too, for at least three reasons. First, it provides university communities with baseline data to measure any implemented interventions to tackle sexual violence against, allowing evaluation of interventions. Second, conducting such a survey can raise awareness about sexual violence on campus, and in that respect increased visibility of a problem may serve to increase the chances of reporting and arguably potentially deter some would-be perpetrators. This, as noted earlier, is because a message is being sent out that sexual violence is something taken very seriously with a (new) normative expectation of reporting. Third, if carefully designed, such surveys may inform the precise nature of any strategies to reduce the risk of sexual violence. For example, if there are a disproportionately high number of first-year women students being subjected to sexual violence or if there are particular times or places where sexual harassment is more likely, resources may thus be targeted to maximise impact.

In the United States, there has been ever-changing guidance to address sexual violence at universities based on the government in power. A great deal of progress was made under the Obama Administration through key guidance such as the *Dear Colleague Letter* which set out expectations of implementation of Title IX – a law to safeguard students from sex-based discrimination (Office for Civil Rights, 2011). The Dear Colleague Letter was later repealed under the Trump Administration. However, in April 2024, the Biden Administration's final Title IX rule went into effect expanding protections for LGBT+ and pregnant students, eliminating cross-examinations in university disciplinary hearings, extending jurisdiction to off-campus and international incidents, expanding the sexual harassment definition and clarifying protections against sexuality and gender identity discrimination (American Council on Education, 2024). We note in the United States that The White House Task Force, which commenced in 2014, focused upon campus climate surveys. This positions US universities ahead of the United Kingdom in terms of having undertaken prevalence studies at individual universities. Regrettably, this is not a discipline which has been widespread in the United Kingdom. As alluded to earlier, we would very strongly advise that university leadership teams undertake prevalence surveys and will discuss this further in Chapter 5.

PERPETRATION IN HE

When considering risk of sexual violence, most often the focus is on the risk of victimisation. Although we will touch on those risks as well, we feel it is vital to frame the conversation around the risks of perpetration. Historically, sexual violence prevention has been framed by the former with limited effectiveness. It is noted that protecting oneself from becoming a victim will not stop an assault from occurring, as a perpetrator will move on to target the next person who is potentially more vulnerable. The majority of sexual violence does not occur in the 'risky' situations that women are taught to avoid, but by men they know in spaces where they feel comfortable, e.g. their own home. Furthermore, focusing solely on the risk of victimisation places the responsibility of stopping sexual violence on the potential victims rather than holding potential perpetrators accountable. This reinforces rape culture. Therefore, we choose to consider the risks of perpetration first and foremost.

The focus of this book is addressing student sexual violence, so we will focus this section on student perpetrators. However, we note that staff perpetrators also target staff and students (NUS, 2018). What we know about perpetration comes from research with detected (and subsequently convicted) and undetected perpetrators (but reported in surveys) in the wider community. In HE, some of the characteristics, risk factors and motivations of staff perpetrators may well be similar to student perpetrators, although we would anticipate that there will be new learning too.

Overwhelmingly, perpetrators of sexual violence in HE are men, which is representative of perpetration in the wider community (Murphy & Van Brunt, 2017). In a study by the Office of National

Statistics (2021) that looked at the years ending in March 2017 and March 2020 combined, data showed that respondents in England and Wales who had been subjected to rape or assault by penetration since they were 16 years old reported in 98% of cases that their perpetrators were male. In the same study, 65% of victim-survivors identified the perpetrator as a man aged between 20 and 39.

Researchers look at the characteristics of perpetrators, risk factors of perpetration, motivations for perpetration, theories of causation and typologies in offending (Quadara, 2014). Adult perpetrators are a heterogeneous group which makes covering the characteristics of perpetration too broad for the scope of this book (Greathouse et al., 2015; Swartout et al., 2015). For our purposes, we will focus mainly on risk factors, which are also referred to as 'predictors' or 'determinants' in the literature.

We note that most research done with perpetrators has been conducted with detected sexual offenders (Greathouse et al., 2015; Quadara, 2014). However, uniquely in university settings, undetected perpetrators who admit to perpetration in anonymous surveying have also been studied. Although anyone can argue that more research is needed to understand perpetration of sexual violence in HE specifically, the current research gives us some basis to inform our judgements upon.

There are common themes in risk factors among detected and undetected perpetrators (Quadara, 2014). These factors are not causes of sexual violence but rather increase the probability of perpetration (Fletcher, 2014). We divide the risk factors into two categories: (1) individual and (2) community and pull from multiple sources which consider student perpetrators for our summary of risks below (i.e. Busch-Armendariz et al., 2016; Murphy & Van Brunt, 2017; Quadara, 2014). It is necessary to understand these risk factors, as prevention efforts will be focused on reducing or mitigating for these risks. We will discuss this further in Part 2.

The most cited individual risk factors include Rape Myth Acceptance (RMA), a lack of empathy for rape victim-survivors, the personal use of alcohol, hostility towards women and hyper-masculinity (Busch-Armendariz et al., 2016; Murphy & Van Brunt, 2017; Quadara, 2014). Perpetrators tend to have hostile views towards women and hold rigid gender role beliefs including that men are entitled to sex. Perpetrators often associate with peers who approve of 'forced sex' (N.B., this is rape). They lack empathy towards others, but in particular towards women and victim-survivors. They accept rape myths, meaning they believe in societal misconceptions about rape used to minimise or justify rape while blaming victims. This can be seen in their behaviour after an assault. 'Following the assault, sexual assault perpetrators commonly display cognitive distortions, or thought processes, that provide justification or excuses for their behaviour. These may include blaming the victim or denials that the act was planned' (Greathouse et al., 2015, p. xii).

The most common community risk factors found for sexual violence within HE are communities which lack effective deterrents, fail to have effective guardians and promote and endorse or tolerate rape culture (DeKeseredy, 2017; Fletcher, 2014; McPhail, 2017; Murphy & Van Brunt, 2017; Powers & Leili, 2017). Deterrents can come in the form of a policy specific to sexual violence with actual consequences for breaching the policy, e.g. expulsion. Guardians may represent active bystanders, university officials who enact the policy or student groups who campaign against sexual violence. The term 'rape culture' refers to 'the social, cultural, structural discourses and practices in which sexual violence is tolerated, accepted, eroticised, minimised and trivialised' (Powell & Henry, 2014, p. 2). It is characterised as a culture where victim-survivors are not believed and are blamed for their assaults, while perpetrators' behaviours are excused or justified. In the United Kingdom, this is closely linked to what is euphemistically referred to as 'lad culture' (Phipps & Young, 2012). Lad culture is characterised by sexist beliefs, excessive alcohol consumption and violence (Phipps & Young, 2012; NUS, 2013). This can lead to such beliefs and behaviours being viewed more widely as the prevailing social norms of an institution. There are parallels with the term rape culture whereby sexist beliefs may be widely held and comparatively rarely challenged; the notion that what an individual (usually a young woman) wears may impact upon their culpability for being subjected to sexual violence is one of many examples of such a belief.

In addition, there are some distinctive features of university environments, which may add to the level of risk (Murphy & Van Brunt, 2017). In the United Kingdom, where the legal drinking age is 18, the first few weeks at university may be a time of increased alcohol consumption; perpetrators may view this as an opportunity in one of at least two ways: first, through disinhibition, as there are fewer personal controls on behaviour with potentially greater impulsivity. Some students arriving at university may not have been accustomed to drinking alcohol in the quantities of some of their peers. High levels of alcohol consumption may sometimes contribute to making potential victims more vulnerable in combination with making potential perpetrators more disinhibited and thus potentially more likely to engage in sexual violence or misconduct. Second is a more calculated approach where perpetrators target prospective victims based on their perceived vulnerability.

There is debate over the type of perpetrators in the HE setting, with some arguing that university sexual violence is often perpetrated by a small number of serial perpetrators (Lisak & Miller, 2002) and others arguing that serial perpetration is not as common in university settings (Swartout et al., 2015). In the wider community in England and Wales, evidence from the National Police Chief's Council (2024) is clear that serial perpetration is common – with those prosecuted for rape in 2011, having committed on average 2.3 rape offences and up to 45.6% of sexual violence suspects linked to more than one sex offence. 'VAWG perpetrators cause significant harm, often offending repeatedly' (National Police Chief's Council, 2024, p. 23).

Risks for victimisation include the perpetrator knowing the potential victim, the potential victim being isolated from others and prior consensual activity between the perpetrator and potential victim (Quadara, 2014). Alarmingly undetected perpetrators report a tendency to use nonphysical coercive tactics rather than physical tactics, e.g. physical violence (Quadara, 2014).

As the overwhelming majority of perpetrators are men, we have presented information about perpetrators who are men. Women are much less likely to perpetrate sexual violence, and there is less research on women who perpetrate against adults, especially in HE (Greathouse et al., 2015).

So, in university communities, this illustrates the need to target men students rather than women students as men are very much more likely to be perpetrators of sexual violence towards other students than women. This can inform programme designs to reduce the risk of men subjecting women, trans students or men to sexual violence. This is an important focus for any such safety campaigns. There are some potential sensitivities around men not wishing to be unduly targeted for such initiatives. But this is a sensitive subject, and equally, there are some sensitivities around women not wishing to be subjected to sexual violence too. Younger men are more likely to be perpetrators, and hence, we would anticipate potentially high rates of sexual violence at universities, and this seems to be supported by the empirical data to date (Office for National Statistics, 2017). Again, this appears to be the case internationally.

On a positive note, what we know about the potential impacts of alcohol upon both potential perpetrators and victims suggests we have the opportunity to effect positive change. Communications aimed at potential perpetrators about the problems of disinhibition and their impact on others may be a starting point in addressing individual behaviour. It is important, however, not to mix messages when discussing sexual violence prevention and alcohol safety awareness; these messages should never be victim-blaming. There is evidence that men who frequently go to nightclubs have higher rates of perpetration compared to men who do not attend such venues (Towl & Walker, 2019). Bars and nightclubs clearly have a role in terms of policing the behaviour (including risk regarding spiking) of potential perpetrators who tend to be, although not exclusively, young men. Management teams at pubs and clubs have an important role in showing an intolerance towards sexual violence on their premises. Work may be undertaken with young men (and all) students to learn the skills of spotting inappropriate behaviour and responding to it through bystander interventions.

COMMONALITIES IN ADDRESSING SEXUAL VIOLENCE INTERNATIONALLY

Universities UK (UUK), a membership-based organisation for around 130 Vice-Chancellors, produced a key document for the sector in the United Kingdom with its *Changing the Culture* report (2016) followed by multiple related reports reviewing progress with tackling sexual violence at universities or in some case the distinct lack thereof and offering additional guidance regarding data sharing, online harassment and staff-to-student sexual misconduct (2016–2022). The question of what is meant by progress has proved an interesting one internationally. For example, Cambridge University and De Montfort University openly declared that an increased number of reports of sexual violence are deemed a measure of success (UUK, 2017). Two criticisms of the generally positively received UUK's report in 2016 were the lack of nationally enforceable standards and the focus exclusively upon students subjected to sexual violence at universities. These two concerns are reflected internationally to differing degrees. In short, the material impacts include a great degree of variability around how sexual violence is, or is not, tackled at universities internationally. On the second point, UUK released guidance on addressing staff-to-student sexual misconduct in 2022. We note that addressing perpetration by staff for our purposes would require a book of its own due to the inherent complexity and scale of the challenges; therefore, in this second edition, we mention a few specific issues regarding staff sexual misconduct but do not intend to address this area in full through this book. One such challenge is associated with the structures of universities as institutions with different sets of regulations for staff and students, sometimes as if they are mutually exclusive groups. Traditionally, at HEIs, the inappropriate behaviour of staff falls under the remit of HR departments and the inappropriate behaviour of students is addressed organisationally elsewhere within, for example, a student services directorate of some kind. In policy and practice, there is a need to apply the same underlying principles to address sexual violence through a comprehensive institution-wide approach; however, there may be some differences to procedure as the legal framework will be different in the student (consumer) relationship and staff (employee) relationship. The materials and suggestions in this book are focused on student-to-student sexual violence, but there may be some overlap when considering prevention and response of staff sexual misconduct.

In this section, we draw heavily upon two key sources when considering our international lens: one published by the United Nations (UN Women, 2018a) and the other a UK book on tackling sexual violence, which brings an international perspective to the problem (Towl & Walker, 2019).

One key international commonality in the way in which sexual violence is, or is not, being addressed is in the great variation and range of responses at individual universities. This is, in that respect, an international phenomenon (Towl & Walker, 2019). In Chapter 7, we will discuss the nuts and bolts of how to draft and develop a policy and related procedures. It is probably axiomatic to state that unless there is a policy in place explicitly indicating that sexual violence will be robustly addressed, then little is likely to happen. No policy would have been broken!

There seems to be increasingly widespread agreement that we need to increase reporting at universities and respect the Reporting Party's decision about how far to progress such reports. This is important because respecting the autonomy and decision-making of Reporting Parties is likely in and of itself to increase confidence in reporting processes and thereby increase reporting overall. It is also important in supporting the mental health and wellbeing of the Reporting Party.

The White House Task Force produced a guide for university leaders on how to tackle sexual violence at their universities. Unfortunately, the take-up on this appears to have been highly variable. This reflects the earlier problem we mentioned in terms of critical feedback around the UUK's report on tackling sexual violence (UUK, 2016, 2017). If university leaders undertook regular campus climate surveys, then both 'failures' and 'successes' could be measured.

Many university communities are particularly well resourced with researchers. This basic truth positions university communities to do so much more to address sexual violence. For example, undertaking research in the area of sexual violence at universities could potentially make a contribution to prevention and also the gauging of progress. RMA questionnaires are one way of measuring attitudinal change, which may be linked to the propensity to an increased risk of sexual violence. One recent study in the United States has shown some changes in RMA among undergraduates from 2010 to 2017 with a decrease in RMA albeit with male students and younger students being significantly more likely to endorse rape myths (Beshers & DiVita, 2019).

There is some similar learning for the sector internationally from extensive survey work (e.g. through the Australian Human Rights Commission [AHRC], 2017) undertaken in Australia. There seems to be a very broad commonality in terms of the percentages of young women subjected to sexual violence at university whether in Australia, the United States, Canada or the United Kingdom. One key publication in Australia for the sector is the Department of Education (2023) – a government commissioned report with five priorities for action. It is a general review of ways forward for the sector, and one of its five key priorities includes student and staff safety. This provides a clear government strategic framework to populate work on addressing sexual violence. So, there is much promise there, but we have been here before in the sector with grandiose assertions about tackling sexual violence only to fail on delivery. We will watch developments in Australia with a keen interest especially in relation to any regulatory changes and how they compare and contrast with developments in the United Kingdom. At the time of writing, we understand that an announcement from the OfS regarding potential for regulation is 'imminent'.

University leaders have already had countless opportunities to estimate likely levels of the numbers of students having been subjected to sexual violence at their institutions. Most appear to have chosen not to find out. We do not think that that sits especially well with claims, often made after media coverage of such incidents, of 'taking all cases of sexual violence very seriously', far from it. There is an easy fix to this aspect of the work in addressing sexual violence. We recommend ascertaining more locally accurate figures through campus climate surveys, but we are aware that some institutions may initially, and entirely understandably, wish to prioritise investing resources in victim-survivor services, staff training and prevention programmes. In one of the most recent and substantive assessments of how Australian universities are doing in delivering their responses to the growing awareness of the scale of the problem of sexual violence, the authors share their palpable frustration that there is a lack of consistency across the sector in how the issue is addressed, e.g. with data collection (Australian Human Rights Institute, 2024). Internationally, it seems to us that there is a case for greater regulation and consistency of approach. Not only does this have the potential to reduce the number of such cases, but it gives us better quality data to make comparisons over time and across institutions. Interestingly, China appears to have made more progress than most when it comes to establishing a national approach, with, for example, a national register of incidents of staff-on-student sexual harassment (Packer, 2024). Such a national register is not a silver bullet, but it is one potential tool to contribute to addressing the problem of passing the perpetrator where individuals move from institution to institution without a record of their behaviour following them.

Recommendations for tackling sexual violence at universities seem to be increasingly characterised by their commonalities rather than their differences. For example, there is a need for a standalone policy to address sexual assault and harassment. There is a need for staff training on how to receive disclosures. Embedded in policy development is the need to minimise the number of times students need to recount their traumatic experience.

There is some Canadian evidence that the risk of sexual assault is highest earlier into a degree programme. What is sometimes termed the 'red zone' for young women students in particular is the first few weeks of the semester or term (Kimble et al., 2008). These findings have clear implications for universities the world over. It is perhaps unsurprising that this would be a time of vulnerability in view of the adaptive stresses associated with switching to a new environment. More generally, the psychological backdrop of change is the need for a period of adaptation to a new environment, and that is when a range of vulnerabilities may be most manifest. So, such vulnerability may well be twofold. First, there may well be a greater vulnerability to sexual violence in the new university environment with perpetrators specifically targeting those who they perceive as more vulnerable. Second, individual mental health and related adaptive resources may be diminished in any period of transition such as would be likely to be the case in adapting to a university environment.

Readers interested in a case study of how to enact a positive change in addressing sexual violence at universities have a number of potential resources (e.g. see Towl, 2016). The paper outlines some key steps successfully undertaken at Durham University, UK, to shift the culture, including increased reporting, implementing widespread staff and student training and paying for specialist counselling support services too.

Another international theme has been the importance of ensuring that university services are appropriately linked into local services, e.g. health, support and criminal justice services. We discuss the importance of developing partnerships in Chapter 14.

One pervasive theme with such work is the need to have an awareness of the impacts of an intersectional understanding of sexual violence. Due to structural inequalities, there will be differential vulnerabilities to being subjected to sexual violence and also its perpetration. Thus, an intersectional understanding is important in informing our understanding both from a Reporting Party perspective and that of the Responding Party.

One good test of policies is whether they are used by students in practice. A policy is, by definition, not a good policy if it remains largely unused in practice.

Investigations need to enjoy the trust of Reporting and Responding Parties. This may be achieved by having appointed and trained internal staff or bringing in external investigators to undertake any such investigations. Timings are key for any reporting process. We need to recognise that Reporting Parties may well not come forward immediately after they have been subjected to some form of sexual violence. It is important to understand the potential impacts of trauma whereby an individual may take time to be ready to make such a report.

Confidentiality is important to the process. However, it is important not to keep matters so confidential to the point of secrecy. We think that broadly, the right balance is to provide individual confidentiality but to produce regular statistical information and a narrative on the numbers of cases reported, actions taken and outcomes. The culture of universities can be important as a wider context to any such decision-making. It is important what messages, overt and covert, are being shared across the institution, especially perhaps from senior leadership team members.

We now move on to looking at the international learning. The #MeToo movement has been global in its influence bringing to the fore structural power inequalities that have for too long perpetuated sexual violence. Catherine MacKinnon highlights this power dynamic well:

> *Power is being believed no matter how little sense you make and how little evidence you have. Powerlessness is not being believed no matter how much evidence you have and how much sense you make.*
>
> *(quoted in, UN Women, 2018b, p. 10)*

Catherine MacKinnon developed guidance on core elements of policy and practice in addressing sexual violence as captured in the following principles:

(a) *Sexual harassment is a matter of sex and gender inequality and a violation of human rights.*

(b) *In non-criminal proceedings, e.g. workplace procedures, criminal standards and procedures are not appropriate.*

(c) *Equality of treatment for those who report and those who are accused.*

(d) *Gender inequality sits alongside and across other forms of inequalities, such as race, disability, sexual orientation and age. How these intersect to shape sexual harassment, responses to reports or avenues of redress needs to be woven through all work on sexual harassment.*

(MacKinnon, C. in UN Women, 2018b, p. 7)

The United Nations under the auspices of UN Women has helpfully produced a guidance note on campus violence prevention and responses as part of the work of their *Ending Violence Against Women Section* (UN Women, 2018a). There were advisors and expert contributors from around the world drawn upon to inform the guidance. The UN Women report helpfully draws upon the principles presented by MacKinnon and outlines the scope of the problem and how to address it. UN Women lists 10 essential actions universities must take to address sexual violence including (1) assess the situation,

(2) implement a policy, (3) assign a dedicated university coordinator, (4) create protocols and procedures, (5) identify interim and supportive measures, (6) monitor and evaluate, (7) create a budget, (8) create a provision of essential services, (9) embed awareness raising and active bystander programmes and (10) promote respectful relationships and challenge harmful masculinities (2018a).

The authors make the fundamental point that approaches to ending violence against women need to be comprehensive and not merely responsive to when reporting takes place, however welcome at one level.

In the guidance, the centrality of a survivor-centred approach is emphasised. The key takeaway message here is to preserve the personal autonomy of the victim-survivor – a pervasive and oft, and unapologetically, repeated mantra in this book. The authors persuasively argue for the importance of involving those likely to be affected by violence in the design of prevention methods.

The report is helpfully action focused, with 10 recommended actions explicated. Assessing the existing situation is recommended by the authors with a view to undertaking a campus survey and/or engaging with focus groups. Crucially, any such emergent data need to be used to inform planning for prevention and actively encouraging and addressing reports in a timely fashion when made. In the guidance, it is stressed that victim-survivors should not be blamed in the event that they have engaged in substance abuse. We take that as axiomatic.

Action two in the guidance is to put a policy in place, which has been informed by the first action point of assessment of the situation. One of the key recommendations under this section of the proposed action points is the appointment of an 'End Violence Against Women' coordinator. Some universities in the United Kingdom have sent staff on training courses to become 'Sexual Violence Liaison Officers' (SVLOs). This title is derived from similar roles of Independent Sexual Violence Advisors. These are often not full-time posts; nonetheless, the point we would make is that it is not sufficient simply to send a group of staff on a training course. If they are to work effectively with reporting students and others, then time needs to be freed up to do so. Also, the central role of a coordinator of such activities and processes seems central to us. The other key point made, it seems to us, is the importance of ensuring that there is an allocated resource, and that the coordinator has budget authority to use it, for example, for staff and student training.

There is a need to put in place protocols that outline the appropriate procedures for the handling of reports of sexual violence. There needs to be detailed guidance on the conduct of investigations, appropriate training for investigators, and we need to ensure that members of disciplinary panels have received appropriate training on cases of sexual violence too.

One often overlooked aspect of work on tackling sexual violence at universities is the need to monitor and evaluate progress, or in some cases the lack of it. The guidance emphasises the importance of taking such actions along with having a dedicated budget. When university media offices assert that their institution takes sexual violence very seriously, this can seem like a hollow or meaningless assertion if not accompanied with a list of actions taken and commensurate resources invested. The setting up of the services, which are needed to support addressing sexual violence, needs to be addressed prior to policies going 'live'.

Prevention is another key strand of the recommendations for action. One opportunity for awareness-raising activities is at open days, and we would strongly recommend that sharing with prospective students work that has been and is done to tackle sexual violence needs to be covered within a context of the importance of student safety and wellbeing. The final set of actions proposed in the guidance is the promotion more generally of respectful relationships and a routine challenge of what the authors refer to as 'harmful masculinities'. The approach includes consent education and also mainstreaming issues of gender into courses across the university.

So, we have seen how sexual violence at universities is an international problem both beyond and within universities. Despite knowing for decades that sexual violence is a problem in universities internationally, the problem does not appear to be declining. We may be at the stage where it is a case of the problem simply being more widely recognised and acknowledged rather than there having been a particular growth in the problem – what we know for sure is what we have now is a far more visible problem. We invite readers to take some hope from this in that at least our problem with sexual violence is increasingly not underground and unspoken about. It puts university leaders in the spotlight as to what leadership they are showing in addressing the problem across the globe. We have noted the high degree of commonalities across different countries about the substantive problems in terms of the high prevalence rates of sexual violence at universities. In this chapter, we have drawn heavily upon some of the international guidance on how we may improve what we do to tackle sexual violence at our universities. As we continue Part 1 of this book, we look next at technology-facilitated sexual violence in HE and then on to the fundamental question of why university leaders should address sexual violence within university communities.

Related Resources

- Hales, S. (2023). Sexual violence in higher education: Prevalence and characteristics of perpetrators. In C. J. Humphreys & G. J. Towl (Eds.), *Stopping gender-based violence in higher education: Policy, practice, and partnerships*. Routledge.
- Towl, G. J., & Walker, T. (2019). *Tackling sexual violence at universities: An international perspective*. Routledge.
- Saungweme, F. J. S, Ngang, C. C., & Towl, G. J. (Eds.). (2024). *Sexual harassment and the law in Africa*. Routledge.

3

TECHNOLOGY-FACILITATED SEXUAL VIOLENCE AND TECHNOLOGY-BASED SOLUTIONS: LEARNING AFTER COVID-19

Sadly, sexual violence is not only perpetrated in person. And this reality was exacerbated during the coronavirus (COVID-19) pandemic. Not only did we see significant increases in rates of domestic abuse (UUK, 2020), but we also saw a rise in technology-facilitated abuse, arguably with perpetrators learning new ways to harm through the forced use of technology to communicate due to lockdown (UN Women, 2020). Online sexual harassment, image-based sexual abuse (or so-called 'revenge porn'), cyber-stalking, cyberflashing, fakeporn, sextortion and gender-based hate speech on social media are all examples of technology-facilitated sexual violence impacting university communities and the safe access to education for students.

We remind readers that young women at universities in the United Kingdom have been reported as the group most likely to be subjected to sexual violence while at university, and evidence demonstrates that this is true for online sexual harassment too. This is an important point because it can be too easy for some to simply indicate that sexual violence is a problem across society and is by no means exclusive to university communities. Of course, there is truth to that, but what is both untrue and unhelpful is the use of such general statements to hide the truth that our problem is most likely worse than most, as we shall see later in this chapter when referring to the evidence base. Indeed, our academic culture of secrecy may well have a distinct role in the continuation and enablement of sexual violence at universities. And, as ever, we can perhaps find it most difficult to look at ourselves as in any way a part of the problem.

Technology is in one sense value free. But how it is used is far from value free. In this chapter, we will present how perpetrators use technology to harm victim-survivors and discuss the impacts identified on university students. But we also discuss ways technology can be used to prevent and respond to sexual violence. We discuss the potential for seizing and understanding some of the learning from what were initial adaptations to the new reality of COVID-19 and its impacts on how we may best address our problem with sexual violence at universities.

TECHNOLOGY-FACILITATED SEXUAL VIOLENCE (TFSV)

The online world has much that is positive to offer, but in terms of sexual violence, it is simply another environment where this can be manifest and enacted. When technology is used to harass, stalk, coerce, control or sexual exploit another person, this is what is referred to as technology-facilitated abuse. Universities UK (2019b) defines online harassment as 'The use of information and communication technologies by an individual or group to repeatedly cause harm to another person with relatively less power to defend themselves' (p. 7), noting that these behaviours are also referred to as cyberbullying, cyberharassment, cyberaggression, cyberhate, cyber-victimisation and deviant online behaviour. For our purposes, we will focus on TFSV which is most broadly defined as 'harmful sexual behaviours that have been enabled, assisted, prompted, or promoted by communicative technology' (Powell & Henry, 2014, p. 3). This commonly includes online sexual harassment, image-based sexual abuse, cyberstalking, cyberflashing and related forms of abuse.

In Chapter 7, we provide example policy definitions for six forms of TFSV: (1) online sexual harassment, (2) cyberstalking, (3) image-based sexual abuse, (4) upskirting, (5) fakeporn and (6) cyberflashing. In this chapter, we discuss these forms in more detail. We note that like technology, TFSV is ever evolving; as technology evolves, sadly, so do ways in which perpetrators use technology to harm victim-survivors. Therefore, we recommend that in any policy, TFSV is not limited to only specific examples; a policy statement can say 'TFSV can include, but is not limited to, …' as a useful way to allow for flexibility as new forms of TFSV inevitably evolve.

Online sexual harassment can be defined as 'offensive, degrading, intimidating and/or humiliating unwanted conduct of a sexual nature through social media, email, or group/private online messages. This can include gender-based hate speech, "slut-shaming," denigration, threats, and cyberbullying' (Humphreys, 2021, p. 37). This commonly intersects with other forms of hate speech, often targeting someone's protected characteristics. Online sexual harassment can be perpetrated by individuals or groups of students and involves **internet pile-ons** 'where large numbers of people are encouraged to target one individual with numerous messages' (UUK, 2019b). We have seen online sexual harassment in recent years at universities when a group of students who were men made degrading and offensive sexual comments about their peers who were women on an online group chat (Batty, 2020) and when a group of men who were prospective students planned a competition to have sex with the poorest undergraduate women alongside other misogynistic, homophobic and racist comments on an online group chat (Halliday, 2020).

UUK (2019b) defines **cyberstalking** as 'repeated and deliberate use of the internet and other electronic communication tools to engage in persistent, unwanted communication intending to frighten, intimidate or harass someone, or to spy on someone' (p. 16). Cyberstalking is a way perpetrators can stalk victim-survivors. There are two useful acronyms that help clarify stalking behaviour; the first is 'FOUR'. The four warning signs of stalking are if a perpetrator's behaviour to a victim-survivor is:

1. Fixated.

2. Obsessive.

3. Unwanted.

4. Repeated.

(Police.uk, 2024)

Additionally, 'SLII' helps identify common stalking tactics.

- Surveillance: The perpetrator watches and gathers information about the victim-survivor in-person, online and/or by using spying technology.

- Life Invasion: The perpetrator shows up in the victim-survivor's life without their consent through physical or electronic means.

- Intimidation: Behaviour that is intimidating (when considered in context of all the stalking behaviours).

- Interference: Often through sabotage or attack impacting the victim-survivor's employment, reputation and/or physical safety.
(Stalking Prevention, Awareness, and Resource Center, 2022)

UUK (2019b) defines **image-based sexual abuse** as 'online disclosure of sexual or intimate photos or videos, without the consent of the person pictured' (p. 16). Image-based sexual abuse can include a range of behaviours including, but not limited to, the act of capturing, disseminating or threatening to disseminate nude or sexually explicit images or videos without the subject's consent (McGlynn & Rackley, 2017). Colloquially, this is referred to as 'revenge porn'; however, this term is problematic as it (1) does not fully capture the full range of abusive behaviours, i.e. sexual violence, (2) inaccurately assumes the motivation of perpetrators and (3) is victim-blaming as the implication is the victim has done something wrong to deserve the revengeful act by the perpetrator (McGlynn et al., 2019). Included as forms of image-based sexual abuse are **voyeurism** (recording a sexual image without knowledge for the purpose of sexual gratification) and **upskirting** (filming or photographing under the victim-survivor's clothes without their consent to capture images of their body or underwear).

Fakeporn is digitally altering images or videos to represent the victim-survivor in a sexual way. The development of 'deepfake pornography' facilitated with the use of digital technologies remains a real problem and one where the law is slower than technology. In April 2024, the Ministry of Justice announced a new criminal offence regarding sexually explicit deepfakes would be introduced (EVAW, 2024). We note here that 'pornography' is also an unhelpful term as sexualised deepfakes are sexual violence.

Cyberflashing is sending an unsolicited genital image to another person(s). This can include what are colloquially referred to as unwanted 'dick pics' – most commonly when men send photos of what is presumed to be their penis to another person without consent (McGlynn & Johnson, 2020). Cyberflashing can be perpetrated by someone known to the victim-survivor or by a stranger in a nearby location using Wi-Fi, Bluetooth or AirDrop technology or through someone making contact through a dating app, private messaging through social media or a website (Humphreys, 2021). During lockdown, cyberflashing through 'zoombombing' occurred at universities during lectures and events held online. **Zoombombing** is when someone or a group of individuals disrupt a video-conference call by displaying or saying lewd, obscene, racist, homophobic and/or other abusive material or remarks. For example, LGBT students were attacked by a group of individuals during an online university event during lockdown who shouted homophobic slurs and displayed sexually explicit videos (Coughlan, 2020).

Concerns about the apparent growth of online sexual harassment appear on the increase internationally (e.g. Tan et al., 2024) as do concerns more generally about sexual harassment (e.g. Saungweme et al., 2024). In England and Wales, from August 2022 to July 2023, the police recorded 123,525 Violence Against Women and Girls (VAWG) offences which had an online element; stalking and harassment made up 85% of all online and tech-enabled VAWG offences (National Police Chiefs' Council, 2024). The demographics of those most impacted upon by online sexual harassment are especially germane in the context of the higher education (HE) sector. One study indicated that among 19–24-year-olds, 39% had been subjected to online sexual harassment compared with 21% among 45–60-year-olds (Gamez-Gaudix et al., 2015). A study in Ireland found the 50% of the university student respondents reported they had been subjected to 'the display, use or distribution of sexist of suggestive materials (for example, offensive pictures, stories or pornography)' (MacNeela et al., 2022, p. 15). In the same study, 42% of student respondents had been subjected to someone sending or posting unwelcome sexual comments, jokes or images through technology. UUK (2019b) is clear in stating that online harassment is a gendered issue and is 'considered a digital extension of traditional sexual violence' (p. 19). Women are more likely to experience TFSV, and this is exacerbated for women of colour, lesbian and bisexual women and women with disabilities (UUK, 2019b).

Impact of TFSV

The impact of being subjected to TFSV can be significant. It is important not to underestimate the extent of such potential problems. Those subjected to TFSV can experience negative impacts to their mental health including low self-esteem, depression and anxiety (Kamal & Newman, 2016). They can also experience practical impacts particularly when private content has gone 'viral', thus losing their anonymity as a victim-survivor; these impacts include withdrawing from university and/or losing their job (Citron & Franks, 2014; UUK, 2019b). Students' academic progress is greatly impacted due to online harassment, and those subjected to online harassment are more likely to withdraw from university (UUK, 2019b).

Although some may minimise TFSV believing it is 'not as bad' as physical sexual violence, it must be noted that online harassment and TFSV can have substantial impact on the victim-survivor. Some argue that TFSV can impact victim-survivors to a greater extent than the impact of in-person harassment as online harassment can seemingly be never-ending, with an unlimited audience, longevity of how long a private image/video may be available online and on multiple sources (UUK, 2019b).[1] Although we do not advise comparing severity of forms of sexual violence, we do agree that it is important not to minimise TFSV based on it being virtual. To expand on this point, consider in the case of image-based sexual abuse, if a perpetrator records a sexual act without the consent of the victim-survivor and then uploads this to a pornographic website. This can be viewed by hundreds of thousands of people in only a short period of time. Although there are organisations that can help remove this content from a website in some cases (Worthington, 2021), if someone or multiple people have downloaded the video to their own devices, the video can be reuploaded at any time. Organisations can continue to remove the content as it appears; however, a whack-a-mole approach to removing content can do little to relieve a victim-survivor's anxiety of a non-consensual video of them being shared publicly with no estimated timeframe for when it will stop. Unsurprisingly, studies show that those who have been subjected to image-based sexual abuse can experience posttraumatic stress disorder, suicidal ideation, anxiety and depression (McGlynn et al., 2021) along with many other life-changing harms.

As TFSV is hugely impactful on students and impacts their ability to access their education safely sometimes leading to dropping out of university, it is obvious (to us) that higher education institutions (HEIs) must include TFSV within their approach to addressing sexual violence. We note here that like most sexual violence, TFSV may not occur on university campus or on the virtual learning environment (VLE) used by the university. However, the impact of TFSV, like rape, means that the student victim-survivor may not be able to access their education safely. Therefore, universities need to actively prevent and respond to TFSV impacting students. The UUK (2019b) guidance on online harassment sets out seven principles to support HEIs in addressing online harassment:

---

[1]Each individual is impacted by sexual violence in ways that are deeply personal; we do not recommend comparing forms of sexual violence as severe or less severe.

1. *Sustain commitment and accountability from senior leaders*

2. *Implement a whole-institution approach*

3. *Engage students in a shared understanding of online harassment and in the development, delivery and evaluation of interventions*

4. *Develop and evaluate prevention strategies*

5. *Develop and evaluate response strategies*

6. *Promote online safety and welfare*

7. *Share knowledge and good practice*

(p. 8)

University administrators may wish to use the *Higher Education Online Safeguarding Self-Review Tool* that defines 23 features of online safeguarding policy and practice with four levels for self-assessment (Bond and Phippen, 2019). This may be a good auditing tool for university leaders who are looking at online safety for students and want to determine where there may be gaps or areas of improvement to safeguard students. University leaders may also consider building partnerships with schools on addressing online harms, given many of these behaviours begin with school-age children (Phippen & Bond, 2023).

For the remainder of this chapter, we will look to how universities can use technology to aid in addressing sexual violence, particularly highlighting what universities learned due to COVID-19.

ACCELERATED ONLINE LEARNING FROM COVID-19

Despite the global tragedy and continued suffering especially perhaps among those with 'long COVID', there have been some positives for student support services in universities which have emerged in the aftermath of the pandemic (Franklin-Corben & Towl, 2023). First, we acknowledge that a whole cohort of students missed out on what may be termed the broader educational experience so commonly promised by university marketeers. However, there is much learning to be gleaned from this unique time and set of responses to a pandemic.

Whereas previously, primacy had been placed upon in-person meetings throughout much of any processes in response to reports of sexual misconduct at universities, this changed with a move towards online discussions and interviews. Such an acceleration in the use of such communications technology would surely have been unlikely to have progressed anything like so quickly without the advent of COVID-19 and consequent in-person contact restrictions, i.e. lockdown. We note again that some of the restrictions themselves contributed to a rise in intimate partner violence with fewer escape routes from such abuses.

The Impact of Technology

Some have looked at specific online tools to try and support victims, but there is little in the way of rigorous evaluations of their efficacy. And social media corporations have been slow to try and clamp down on the world of sexual violence on social media. In the HE sector, governing bodies have been slow to get a grip of some of the implications of the latest manifestations of the digital age – and we highlight some of the burgeoning problems in this chapter. However, one change that does seem to be acknowledged now at the highest levels of university governance is in relation to the recognition that students are at a high level of risk of being subjected to sexual violence when compared with other occupational groups (CUC, 2022). Thus, governing bodies can no longer indulge the dismissive fantasy that sexual violence is not a particular problem in universities but simply a problem in society more broadly. The evidence seems to indicate that it is indeed more of a problem at universities (ONS, 2020). This is important because it is linked to the motivation for change and can help justify the allocation of resources. Governing bodies and executive teams make decisions about resource allocation.

In the counselling and support worlds in HE, there has long been a privileging of in-person one-to-one sessions with concerns that 'something' would be lost with the advent of any online alternatives. Similarly, investigative interviews for the purposes of establishing whether on the balance of probabilities, there has been a breach of university policy in the case of sexual misconduct were thought to require in-person interviews, certainly as the preferred practice.

Initially, when COVID-19 restrictions were announced, there was, in many institutions, a hiatus in activities to appropriately manage cases of reported sexual misconduct. Initially, this led to a backlog of cases. But this could not last as it became evident that there was no immediately foreseeable point at which we would return to any sort of 'normality', meanwhile cases were not progressing for Reporting or Responding Parties. The position became untenable, and hence, initially out of expediency, the casework moved from an in-person-based system to an online system. This, along with many other parts of university services, was delivered online and in some universities continues to use technology for these activities, e.g. lectures, seminars and university meetings,

The learning associated with the adaptations to COVID-19 has shone a light on some of our prejudices, and it is notable that many appear to have kept the option of online meetings even when such meetings could be in person. Below, we discuss some of the benefits and disadvantages of exercising such choices.

Benefits of Technology

A recent paper reviewed and reflected on the changes in how sexual violence at universities is addressed; as a function of COVID-19, several notable benefits and limitations to the increased use of technology in the effective management of sexual misconduct at universities were identified (Franklin-Corben & Towl, 2023). In terms of the potential benefits giving Reporting and Responding Parties the choice of whether to have in-person or online meetings at every stage of the process can be mutually beneficial. The notion of choice is arguable especially important in a field where the supporting and reinforcing of personal agency is quite so important for Reporting Parties. Without the pandemic, it is unlikely that universities would have been equipped to offer online meetings readily, yet with the benefit of hindsight, it seems that now, such choices are axiomatic for good practice. In short, both parties can now have a say in the environment in which they engage. In general, a sense of personal agency is associated with improved mental health outcomes.

Related, but distinguishable from, the opportunity to undertake interviews in person or online – a net impact of such choices – has been the potential to markedly speed up such processes, particularly if room bookings are not available. Slow justice is no justice. So, a speeding up of our processes in addressing our problem with sexual violence at universities is again another positive contribution to such work. It also serves to lower the probability of responding parties having graduated before the outcomes of any such investigations have been undertaken.

For some universities, moving investigation meetings online meant they also utilised technology to take notes of the meeting, either by keeping audio/video recordings of the meetings or using the transcribe function on a video-conferencing platform (e.g. Microsoft Teams) to capture notes. Note-taking in investigation meetings when using a note-taker is resource intensive say compared with using transcription software. Note-takers can also make errors that change the meaning of what was said, e.g. noting 'pants' when they should note 'trousers'[2] as the American author of this book once did – a particularly relevant difference in sexual misconduct cases. Additionally, note-takers add another person in the physical or virtual room in an investigation meeting, which can impact a Reporting Party, Responding Party and/or witnesses engagement in the interview. We do note, however, that transcription software is some way from perfect, but it is more than good enough to capture much of such exchanges – alongside having a recording of the interview to cross check any aspect of the details in terms of precisely what was said. Again, this serves to markedly improve the speed of our processes.

Perhaps one of the most overlooked benefits for Reporting and Responding Parties is in the changes that have been made to germane student support services. For some students, they may find

---

[2]In the UK, 'pants' refers to underwear.

engaging with counselling online offers an additional layer of privacy. This can help students (Reporting and Responding Parties) engage more with support. On a broader level, when we look at how teaching has changed in HE as a function of management responses to COVID-19, lectures are now, in large part, routinely recorded which gives students the opportunity to hear the lecture at a time that suits them; thus, they are less restricted in terms of when they can engage with student support services of whatever type but crucially to include participation in investigations into reports of sexual misconduct. Previously, teaching timetables were more of a limiting factor for the organisation of relevant interviews than is the case post-COVID-19 management measures.

We also saw a marked increase in using videoconferencing to deliver training courses to students and staff during lockdown. With the risk of sexual violence in a training being present, specifically through zoombombing, technology can actually aid trainers in delivering training safely for participants. On platforms such as Zoom, trainers can set up security when scheduling the training meeting virtual room. Security can include the use of a passcode to enter the virtual room, a waiting room to allow the host to control who comes into the room and when, and only allowing authenticated users to join the virtual room. Meetings hosts, i.e. the trainer or a technology administrator supporting the training, can control whether participants are on mute or have their cameras on and who has permission to share their own screen, as this can be limited to the host only. Using technology to keep participants safe and mitigate for the zoombombing is helpful in preventing sexual violence in virtual learning spaces.

Along with changes and benefits we gained through the adaptations due to COVID-19, we also want to note how technology more widely can be used. HEIs can use technology positively in prevention and response initiatives to address sexual violence. A key recommendation we make in Part 2 is to provide victim-survivors multiple pathways to disclose and/or make a report. Online reporting tools can help reduce barriers to reporting and often offer other benefits too. In the United Kingdom, some universities have created their own online reporting tools. Some use a tool called *Report + Support* which is an online reporting platform for multiple forms of bullying, harassment and sexual violence (see Chapter 10 for more details). A reporting tool used by some US universities is *Callisto* which allows university survivors to have a safe alternative to reporting with an aim on matching cases of serial perpetrators so that serial offenders can be held accountable (Project Callisto, 2024).

Similarly, but not necessarily for making reports for investigative action, we see online tools used to help map sexual violence for specific locations and/or anonymously capture experiences of sexual violence online to empower victim-survivors and raise awareness of these issues. In Egypt, *HarassMap* is used to pin on a map when sexual harassment occurs. In the United States, *Right to Be* formerly called Hollaback gives survivors a place to document harassment online, in the media or in the survivor's personal life. In the United Kingdom, *Everyone's Invited* offers survivors an anonymous place online to share their stories with the aim to 'expose and eradicate rape culture with empathy, compassion and understanding' (Everyone's Invited, 2023, p. 4). It must be noted that more than 80 UK universities have been named on this site in survivor testimonials. At Durham Students' Union, they have a tool called *Pincident*, where students can pin on the map the type of harassment, bullying or sexual violence a survivor is subjected to or any active bystander intervention.

We can see that there have been some significant changes to our process and procedures in the management of investigations into reports of sexual misconduct at universities, and that universities can use technology to aid in prevention and response work. Technology can also be used to empower survivors, raise awareness and aid in campaigns. We next consider some of the disadvantages or risks that technology can bring.

Risks in Using Technology

For some students, there are barriers to completing a meeting online, depending upon their individual circumstances (AMOSSHE, 2020), e.g. neurodivergent students who may prefer in-person meeting to online meetings. From the perspective of interviewers, it can be more difficult to pick up non-verbal cues from a screen rather than in the presence of the interviewee. So, for example, an interviewee could be becoming distressed when recounting their account of events in relation to sexual violence without the investigators being able to see this, e.g. wringing hands off camera. Although technology is becoming more neuroinclusive, which can help for online trainings, the same tools and strategies, like allowing participants to leave their camera off or use an avatar, non-verbal reactions tools and using the chat box, may not assist in an investigation meeting.

Whereas as noted previously, there are numerous advantages in having the capacity to interview online, the technology comes with its frustrations such as the potential loss of internet access for either attendee, prior to commencing any such interviews or during them. This can be especially distressing in view of the sensitive content of such interviews.

Another technology related risk is in relation to an ethical issue – the preservation of confidentiality. With in-person interviews, we can be sure of who is and is not in the room and able to hear what is being said. However, with online interviews, it is not always clear if someone else is within earshot of the discussion. But the risks go beyond the preservation of confidentiality. For example, it is normative not to have legal representatives in such interviews. Particularly where legal representation has been requested, usually by the Responding Party, when declined the Responding Party may still seek to have a legal representative in the room which they may or may not declare to the interviewer. In cases of student misconduct across the piece, we would not tend to have legal representatives involved in the enactment of internal university policies and procedures. Additionally, concerns of students recording the interviews themselves, rather than following the instructions set by university regarding what will be recorded, how this is shared, how it is stored and for how long.

These potential issues can be raised early with anyone exercising the choice as to whether to opt for an online or in-person interview. If the option is available, then students should be permitted to make an informed choice.

As we conclude this chapter, we highlight that technology is always developing. Thus, as perpetrators evolve with technology to use this to harm our students and impact their safe access to education, universities, too, must evolve with technology to be responsive to harm that is being caused but also to harness the advantages that technology allows for in the prevention and response of sexual violence. As we saw during lockdown, what we thought was the only way we could do something (like hold an in-person counselling session) has actually been wrong. Much of the learning has helped call into question previous assumptions about what we thought may reflect student preferences. Some of the contingencies put in place for the management of COVID-19 have either simply not returned to the previous ways of working or with the legacy of such changing work patterns having changed in at least some ways. And we have seen how this has impacted upon changed ways of working in related areas such as student counselling services too.

📖 Related Resources

- Franklin-Corben, P., & Towl, G. (2023). Responding to gender-based violence in higher education: Changes as a function of Covid-19. *Journal of Aggression, Conflict and Peace Research*, 15(3), 216–220. https://doi.org/10.1108/JACPR-06-2022-0721
- Humphreys, C. J. (2021). Technology-facilitated sexual violence in higher education: Impact on victim-survivors and recommendations for universities. In N. Akdemir, C. J. Lawless, & U. Türkşen (Eds.), *Cybercrime in action: An international approach to cybercrime*. Nobel.
- Bond, E., & Phippen, A. (2019). *Higher education online safeguarding self-review tool*. University of Suffolk.

4

THE CALL TO ACTION: HIGHER EDUCATION INSTITUTIONS' ROLE IN ADDRESSING SEXUAL VIOLENCE

In this chapter, we argue that it is a civic duty for university communities to contribute to the reduction of sexual violence. Broadly the role is twofold: (1) prevention and (2) addressing the needs of those subjected to sexual violence. For those colleagues not necessarily persuaded by arguments such as these, we outline the (UK) legislative underpinnings of the need for such work for students in terms of the Human Rights Act 1998 and the Equality Act 2010. We also cover the risks for not doing this work, which include the risk of harm to students and/or staff and legal, financial and reputational risks to the institution. Finally, we note that in an ever more competitive environment to secure the recruitment of students, some university leaders may wish to promote excellence in tackling sexual violence at their institutions partly because it makes such good business sense. We note that increasingly students and parents are interested in what university communities are doing to address student safety, including the broad rubric of mental health, which is directly connected to sexual violence.

In the United Kingdom, universities are usually publicly funded. There is more of a mix between public and private institutions internationally. Both types will find major problems with sexual violence within their communities, and both, we would argue, have the civic duty to address this problem. By common consent, the Criminal Justice System (CJS) has not been as successful as any of us would wish in addressing the broader societal problem of sexual violence. In July 2024, the National Police Chief's Council published a 70-page report that began by stating, 'Violence Against Women and Girls (VAWG) has reached epidemic levels in England and Wales, in terms of its scale, complexity and impact on victims', noting that 'at least 1 in every 12 women will be a victim of VAWG every year (2 million victims) and 1 in 20 adults in England and Wales will be a perpetrator of VAWG every year (2.3 million perpetrators)', (p. 4). The Office for National Statistics (ONS) has long highlighted that women who are full-time students are subjected to sexual violence at higher rates than any other occupation and gender (Ministry of Justice et al., 2013; ONS, 2023).

University communities are uniquely well placed to address our problem with sexual violence and in so doing help address sexual violence in a way that to date the CJS has been unable or unwilling to do. We know that a disproportionate amount of societal sexual violence happens at our universities, and this gives university executive leaders and governing bodies a further incentive to address the problem. Part of the uniqueness of the opportunity afforded to universities is that not only do we have the scope, if there is the will, to address our problem of sexual violence, but we also have the opportunity to shape the narrative with future leaders across broader society. This gives us the promise of the potential to influence a whole range of workplaces and roles across society. As a sector, we are used to dealing with both academic and non-academic misconduct. One benefit, which should perhaps be given greater emphasis in the sector and student movement more widely, is that we make, our judgements regarding non-academic misconduct based on a balance of probabilities rather than the CJS threshold of beyond all reasonable doubt. Of course, we rightly do not have the opportunity to issue the range of sanctions familiar to the CJS, but we do have a greater potential to give victim-survivors some level of closure in view of the level of evidence required in such civil cases. We also do have a range of possible sanctions including educational based interventions, suspension of studies or expulsion. We still have some way to go as a sector in terms of being more joined up about such work. For example, we would anticipate that the sector may wish to have a dialogue with the University and Colleges Admission Service (UCAS) about how we may improve in this area, e.g. looking at applications for further studies from those who have been found to be in breach of a particular university's policy on sexual misconduct.

Education is about more than simply the study of specific academic disciplines, important though they are. Those benefiting from the privilege of a higher education (HE) are disproportionately likely to eventually take leadership roles in society. As indicated previously, we cannot overstate this distinctive contribution; those in positions of power are highly likely to have opportunities to make a difference with the prevention of sexual violence in society more widely. So, even simply the promotion of a greater awareness of issues of sexual violence at universities may result in some long-term public benefits and thereby contribute at a broader level to prevention.

To reiterate, because it sometimes seems to go below the radar in statements issued from universities on the problem – students are at a higher risk of being subjected to sexual violence than, on average, others. The evidence in support of such assertions is chiefly drawn from two key sources.

First, official figures on sexual violence are largely derived from the crime survey for England and Wales where students are explicitly identified as being at an inflated risk of being subjected to sexual violence (ONS, 2023). Young women students are at an especially high level of risk of being subjected to sexual violence and domestic abuse. Perpetrators frequently exhibit such sexual violence towards young women (students) at, and around, nightclubs. Such official figures, which allow the comparison between reporting rates to the police and disclosure rates to the crime survey for England and Wales, form an important part of the evidential basis for the widely recognised problem of under-reporting. So, such data expose a measure of the overall prevalence of sexual offending across society in England and Wales.

Second, when we compare the rates cited from the above resources, it is evident that they are, overall, lower and sometimes much lower than that reported in a range (internationally) of surveys of experiences of sexual violence within university communities. One particularly disturbing and widespread finding is that students with disabilities are more likely to be subjected to sexual harassment (63% compared with 50% of non-disabled students reported in the AHRC, 2017 report). The National Union of Students' groundbreaking *Hidden Marks* study focused on women students' experiences of harassment, stalking, violence and sexual assault and therefore informs our understanding of sexual violence at universities as noted in Chapter 2. One in four women students reported being subjected to unwanted sexual contact. Around one-third of respondents of the survey reported feeling unsafe when visiting university or college buildings in the evening. This contrasts with feelings of safety during the day, which enjoyed positive levels at around 97%. Around 16% of respondents had been subjected to unwanted kissing, touching or molesting during their time as students and the majority of these experiences had taken place in a public place. This perhaps speaks for university governing bodies and Vice-Chancellors to ensure student (and staff) training as detailed in Chapter 8.

The majority of perpetrators are already known to the victim-survivor, and the majority are other (men) students. They are likely to be studying at the same institution and may be on the same course and even in the same lecture or residence hall as the victim-survivor. Hence, this can be a difficult and especially sensitive area for university communities to tackle. Prospective students do not on the whole wish to think of themselves as sex offenders, nor do parents wish to think of our children in such terms. Nonetheless, the brutal and deeply uncomfortable truth is that a significant number of prospective, chiefly young men, students will go on to perpetrate acts or an act of sexual misconduct in breach of university policies. It is young women who are chiefly the victim-survivors in such cases.

Common reasons for not reporting sexual assault include feelings of shame and embarrassment. Nearly half of those not reporting indicate that they are concerned that they will be blamed (as the victim)! Such findings could helpfully inform university-wide campaigns to give clear messages that those coming forward will not be blamed. And it is the behaviour of would-be perpetrators that we need to target for change. Too often in the past, the focus has perhaps been upon young women to change their behaviour. Whereas we recognise the importance of young women having self-awareness of personal including sexual safety; this is by no means an indication that we in any way 'blame victims', far from it – we want all that can be done to be done to reduce the risk of the enactment of sexual misconduct at universities.

It may well be simply lazy thinking or misplaced complacency that simply repeats the defensive institutional mantra that sexual violence happens everywhere in society, and thus, it is not, so the argument runs, a particular concern for universities but rather for society more generally. Such assertions will often come across as, at best, defensive of untenable policies and practices and, at worst, as an explicit or implicit collusion with perpetrators that is oriented against victim-survivors. Nonetheless, this exemplifies there is no such thing as a neutral position when it comes to tackling sexual violence at universities. We need to be in no doubt that doing nothing protects perpetrators and further victimises survivors. The argument that we should do no more than anyone else simply because it is a problem everywhere is empirically and ethically untenable. There is however room for further research on whether sexual violence is more or less prevalent at different types of universities. We would strongly advise that the best working assumption on the empirical evidence is that there will be high levels of sexual violence at universities, and that most of it will go unreported.

IMPACT OF SEXUAL VIOLENCE ON VICTIM-SURVIVORS AND THE COMMUNITY

The social harms of sexual violence are potentially significant for students. These may be both personal and educational with individuals not achieving or contributing to their full potential. We should not underestimate the potential impacts of sexual violence.

These impacts cut across individual and community levels and can have lasting effects.

At the community level, we recognise that as sexual violence is gender-based violence (GBV), the community impact is gendered too. The fear of sexual violence may restrict everyday activities for victim-survivors, but particularly for women. For example, one might avoid particular places because of such safety concerns. Having to think constantly about such personal safety concerns especially and disproportionately for women students is surely an undue emotional labour. For women students, such considerations are highly socialised parts of everyday life. Susan Griffin said, 'rape and the fear of rape are a daily part of every woman's consciousness' (1971, p. 27). Liz Kelly coined the term 'safety work' to describe behaviours where women change their movements, appearance and activities for fear of violence. The invisible or hidden nature of safety work that women do is almost subconscious:

> ... *responsibility for preventing sexual violence is embedded in who women are, not only in what they do. This means that we can know on one hand that women should be able to act in any way they want to, while on the other still feel responsible if anything should happen. This highlights something that researchers have referred to as the difference between feeling safe from and feeling safe to. The gendered expectation of women's safety work means that we learn that keeping ourselves safe from violence is more important than feeling safe to express and expand ourselves freely in the world. (Vera-Gray, 2018, p. 83)*

Ultimately, what we can learn from Kelly's and Vera-Gray's work is that women students are already taking actions to protect themselves from sexual violence or more specifically **men's violence against women**. Therefore, this issue already disproportionately affects women students, even if they themselves do not identify as a victim or survivor, as their daily lives and choices are impacted.

On an individual level, we see impacts for victim-survivors that can have a profound effect upon the rest of their lives. Some may be short term, but many impacts have lasting or long-term effects. We categorise these effects as physical, psychological, emotional, behavioural and practical. We outline examples of these below.

Physical impacts can include, but are not restricted to, tissue damage, bruising, unwanted pregnancy, sexually transmitted infections (STIs) that can progress to sexually transmitted diseases (STDs), facial damage and chronic pain. There may be long-term or even fatal health damage linked to an undetected STI, for example, with human immunodeficiency virus (HIV) or human papilloma-virus (HPV). Following an attack, a victim-survivor may be reluctant to have a sexual health screening. Victim-survivors also may well commonly avoid physical health preventive measures such as cervical screening. Some strands of HPV are linked to cervical cancer, putting victim-survivors at higher risk for this. In the same vein, we see victim-survivors who were assaulted orally who avoid accessing dental care. Infertility is another possible impact in the event of an undetected STI. This illustrates how the physical, psychological and social impacts can triangulate.

Common psychological impacts for victim-survivors include experiencing depression, anxiety, suicidal ideation, self-harming behaviour, eating disorders and posttraumatic stress disorder. These, of course, are directly linked to the emotional impact of sexual violence, e.g. feelings of guilt and shame, anger and rage, hopelessness, helplessness and low self-esteem.

In terms of potential psychological harms, there is a great deal of preoccupation on mental health needs of students and concerns about the markedly increased levels of reported mental health needs through university counselling services. Some of this will be directly related to students having been subjected to sexual violence either before or at university. The loss of control associated with being subjected to sexual violence can result in poor mental health outcomes for the individual. Some commentators in this area do not advise victim-survivors report to the police because of the potential for re-traumatisation as a function of criminal justice processes. Re-traumatisation as a function of investigative and related legal processes is not just an issue for the broader CJS – it is also an issue at universities – and we need to be mindful of this with the development and enactment of our policies and practices. And herein lies such great potential for university leadership teams to fill this void and offer the services and support that their students subjected to sexual violence need.

Anxiety whether generalised (i.e. in a state of constant anxiety) or specific to a particular situation or in relation to groups (e.g. men) or individuals may markedly restrict and therefore impact upon everyday life. An individual subjected to sexual violence may isolate themselves from others, or there may be other behavioural changes. There may be fears or concerns about existing or future sexual relationships. Another impact may be an avoidance of intimate relationships.

With depression, specialist workers will understand there is a markedly inflated risk of suicide. There can be intervention complications insofar as a victim-survivor may or may not disclose why she is likely to be feeling depressed. There is concern more generally with suicide among student populations. Those subjected to sexual violence may well be at an inflated overall risk of suicide. Self-harm is far more prevalent among women than men. Sexual abuse is linked to an inflated risk of self-harm. The term 'self-harm' is, although relatively narrow in its technical description, the lived experiences of individuals who self-harm and often reveals a much wider spectrum of harmful behaviour to the self, which the physical act of self-harm is simply one manifestation of. Harms to the self can include high levels of alcohol consumption or other drugs, as a means of psychological escape or (mal)adaptation, i.e. coping mechanism.

A loss of confidence and sense of safety and wellbeing can be another common and entirely understandable response to having been subjected to sexual violence. Most of such students will not report, and many may either drop out of university or not do as well as their potential would allow academically. This is an aspect of the aftermath of sexual violence that university communities are especially well positioned to address with all the expertise on student academic progression and support. This is one of the reasons why we are such strong advocates for markedly increasing disclosing rates. If only one message or priority is taken from this chapter for those addressing sexual violence at universities, it would be do all you can to drive up reporting levels. It really is difficult to overstate the need to do this with every new cohort of students. It is only if someone discloses that we are able to provide the specific educational and personal support that they may need.

The argument that it is our civic duty to contribute to prevention, encourage reporting, and provide support and where relevant investigations becomes stronger when we consider the physical, psychological, and social impacts of our inactions. But there are two further arguments that we would wish to make before a brief focus upon the relevant legal frameworks, which require action.

As noted earlier in this chapter, the CJS has not served the interests of victim-survivors well. We have seen how there is very significant under-reporting to the police and of those who do report most do not end up with the resolution being the perpetrator found guilty, sentenced and imprisoned. Despite there being more reports of sexual violence than previously, successful prosecution rates remain stubbornly low, at the low end of single percentage figures. There are also more people imprisoned for sexual offences than ever before. But reporting levels are comprehensively outstripping prosecution levels. Victim-survivors report that the legal processes are traumatic with very little chance of securing a conviction. Given that we know of these failings of the CJS, it is surely incumbent upon us as university communities to do whatever we sensibly can to help prevent perpetration and to support those who come forward and disclose sexual violence.

Universities with plans for a growth in student numbers increase their level of corporate risk if they choose not to invest in student safety and wellbeing. We strongly advise working with, and alongside, Students' Unions (SU). SU activists enjoy a positive history in ensuring that tackling sexual violence at universities remains on the agenda for university communities. Indeed, it is they rather than university leaders who have led the way with tackling our problem with sexual violence at universities. We are firm believers in the disability rights movement mantra, 'Nothing about us without us.' We may sometimes think that we know what is helpful to change to support students more effectively and actively encourage reporting, but we need to listen to what students are saying – social media can be one way into such discourses. We would advise ideally co-creating policy and practice changes, with student communities, particularly in collaboration with survivors.

LEGAL FRAMEWORK

The need to address sexual violence at universities is not new nor is it outside of basic requirements of the sector. The framework for addressing this sits within the need to ensure basic human rights of members of the university community. It is framed as violence against women because women are disproportionately subjected to GBV, i.e. sexual violence, domestic abuse, stalking, trafficking, etc. For the purposes of our book, we balance a discussion of the gendered nature of sexual violence (cause and consequence of gender inequality) with the need to speak to students of all genders as potential victims of sexual violence when considering prevention and response work.

Internationally, we see that the United Nations (UN) requires member states to address men's violence against women. In 1979, the UN issued the UN Convention on the Elimination of All Forms of Discrimination against Women. This was followed by the Declaration on the Elimination of Violence against Women in 1993. The 2015 UN Sustainable Development Goals include Goal 5.2 'to eliminate all forms of violence against all women and girls in public and private spheres, including trafficking and sexual and other types of exploitation.'

The European Union in 2011 developed the Council of Europe Convention on preventing and combating violence against women and domestic violence, known as The Istanbul Convention. This treaty created a legal framework at pan-European level to eliminate violence against women. It recognises that violence against women is a form of discrimination and a violation of fundamental human rights. It is deeply rooted in the structural inequality between women and men in society.

University governing bodies have a responsibility under the Public Sector Equality Duty through the Equality Act 2010 to ensure that all can study safely irrespective of the gender of students. There is a legal requirement to address issues of equality in higher (and further) education (EVAW, 2015). The Equality Act outlines what behaviour counts as unlawful discrimination and who has the right to challenge such discrimination. Sex is a protected characteristic, and thus, if members of a university community are systematically disadvantaged, here in relation to the much higher probability of sexual violence against female than male students, a university not addressing this may be vulnerable to legal action. Women have just as much right as men to education, and sexual violence may impede the ability of women to take full advantage of such educational opportunities. Revealingly some of the submissions to the Australian Human Rights Commission give a flavour of some of the everyday experiences of young women students, 'Catcalling, leering and inappropriate comments just seem like daily and sometimes unavoidable experiences for most young women' (Submission 165 to the Australian Human Rights Commission, University Sexual Assault and Sexual Harassment Project, 2017). It is against this sort of backdrop that the work upon directly addressing sexual violence at universities sits. In short, the current position in the United Kingdom is that we have university environments that are oftentimes not sufficiently proactive for women students in particular to be able to benefit from a university education unimpeded by such hostility.

SECTOR GUIDANCE

In 2021, the Office for Students (OfS) published seven expectations HEIs in England and Wales were expected to meet:

1. Higher education providers should clearly communicate, and embed across the whole organisation, their approach to preventing and responding to all forms of harassment and sexual misconduct affecting students. They should set out clearly the expectations that they have of students, staff and visitors.

2. Governing bodies should ensure that the provider's approach to harassment and sexual misconduct is adequate and effective. They should ensure that risks relating to these issues are identified and effectively mitigated.

3. HE providers should appropriately engage with students to develop and evaluate systems, policies and processes to address harassment and sexual misconduct.

4. HE providers should implement adequate and effective staff and student training with the purpose of raising awareness of, and preventing, harassment and sexual misconduct.

5. HE providers should have adequate and effective policies and processes in place for all students to report and disclose incidents of harassment and sexual misconduct.

6. HE providers should have a fair, clear and accessible approach to taking action in response to reports and disclosures.

7. HE providers should ensure that students involved in an investigatory process have access to appropriate and effective support.

A subsequent and comprehensive evaluation of the implementation of these expectations found unequivocally that as a sector, we were simply not meeting these very basic expectations, thus lending weight to the argument for greater regulation in view of our lack of sector-wide leadership and need to protect and support students (Baird et al., 2022). Our hope is that there will be greater regulation – but regardless, the need for addressing our problem with sexual violence will not simply go away or reduce without active intervention.

Additional sector guidance in England and Wales comes primarily from two sources: Universities UK (UUK) and the Office of Independent Adjudicator for Higher Education in England and Wales (OIA), both of whom have released guidance on addressing sexual violence in universities (OIA, 2018b; UUK, 2016–2023). In Scotland, we see a helpful shift in language where universities are addressing GBV rather than sexual violence only (see the Equally Safe in HE Toolkit). This is useful in that it gets to the heart of the issue and does not separate sexual violence from the structural inequality that is foundational to violence against women. It also is harder for universities to promote the idea of rape as between two students who miscommunicated, when sexual violence issues are appropriately placed within the GBV lens.

For our purposes, we have focused on sexual violence; however, this wider lens should be at the foundation of any action to address any form of GBV. Universities are using sexual violence as an umbrella term to capture a range of behaviours; we encourage universities who feel able to use the term GBV.

RISKS OF NOT ADDRESSING SEXUAL VIOLENCE

Rarely now does a month go by without a high-profile case about how a university has responded poorly to issues of sexual harassment. Of course, this does not mean that they are necessarily worse than anywhere else; rather, their mistakes have simply been made public. Many other universities could swiftly find themselves in a similar position, and many have in the past. It may be a salutary lesson for those universities not yet in the headlines for their difficulties in addressing this area to check with the executive team and governing bodies of those who have experienced such media coverage. It is perhaps easy to underestimate the costs, both financial and human, of such awful publicity. The trust achieved and illustrated in those universities with high reporting levels is hard to gain from the student body but very easy to lose. Cases where things go wrong have tended to take an all-too-familiar pattern. The institution issues a platitudinous statement, such as, 'At X University we take sexual violence very seriously', and social media picks it up and questions the validity of the statement. A qualified statement is then issued usually regretting some aspect of the handling of the case but calmly reiterating how seriously the issue is taken. This approach does not tend to work well. However, much work is done, and however well an institution invests in and prepares to contribute to prevention and student personal and educational support, things can and do go wrong. If governing bodies of universities and Vice-Chancellors are indeed taking sexual violence seriously, then there is no harm in saying so. But this needs to be accompanied by a list of investments made in services and actions taken to prevent sexual violence at the institution. Open, rather than defensive, communication strategies will overall be far more effective. Institutional responses when things go wrong are probably better characterised by a measure of humility and a willingness to learn and should include an apology when necessary.

In a very basic business sense, there is a need to reduce the numbers of students dropping out from their courses. From a corporate perspective, this is linked to League table position and revenue streams. Much of the funding for universities in England and Wales is through student fees funding. If students are helped, they may be more likely to more positively complete National Student Survey (NSS) questions. Interestingly a number of what are widely seen as 'top' universities seem to do very badly in terms of their NSS scores; high reporting levels of sexual violence in combination with policies as outlined in this book and related increased levels of resource could potentially go some way to improving such relatively low scores.

CALL TO ACTION

As managers of communities of people at a formative age, when a disproportionate amount of sexual violence occurs, higher education institutions (HEIs) are uniquely capable of and responsible for addressing sexual violence. HEIs can either sustain the problem through inaction or commit to preventing the problem in our own communities by creating guardians who will go into the world and continue to prevent and respond to sexual violence. In the grand scheme of things, the resource dedicated to this work to have impact on society is very small. This does not require millions of pounds or dollars to research and to create a 'cure'. Scholars researching this area have been offering the sector evidence – informed guidance and tools for several years. However, some would argue that because this has not been required (with any financial consequence) of HEIs, there has thus not been significant change. Even in the United States, where Title IX does have significant financial repercussions for not doing this work, the sector response has been relatively poor. So, it may or may not be the case that linking such work to financial incentives would improve the implementation of such policies. We keep an open mind on that but remain persuaded that some further level of regulation is needed to, at the very least, keep our problem with sexual violence on university leadership agendas.

Doing this work requires commitment, champions, policies and an infrastructure willing to stop the status quo and hold people, staff and students accountable for their actions. It requires universities to have a higher standard than we have seen previously and to change the structural inequality embedded in the sector.

Again, we caution that there is no neutral view on sexual violence in universities. Either the institution is sustaining the problem or addressing it. Starkly put, 'Campuses that are not actively creating an antisexual violence and pro-reporting climate are actively condoning sexual violence' (Griffin, 2017, p. vii).

In the following chapters, we provide guidance on how to begin this work, create policies, implement training, respond to disclosures, investigate reports of misconduct and impose discipline when required. We hope this will help HEIs to focus their work because there is little rationale for not doing so.

The scope of the HE influence is vast. Imagine a map of the world. Picture in your mind a dot on the map for each HEI in each country. For each dot, imagine 5,000 students are taught about sexual violence; they learn how to be active bystanders and graduate entering society with an increased social awareness of this issue and a desire to prevent it. In the United Kingdom, there are around 150 universities. That would mean 750,000 students would graduate with this knowledge. In the United States, where there are about 4,000 universities and colleges, 20,000,000 students would enter the workforce with this knowledge. Doctors, lawyers, physicists, engineers, social workers, teachers, musicians, accountants, dentists, artists, etc. across the globe would be able to take this knowledge forward. Regardless of the legal framework expecting us to do this work and the financial, reputational and legal risks for not doing this work, when we think about the ability to influence society on a macro-level, it begs the key question: why wouldn't we address sexual violence in HE?

📖 Related Resources

- Fenton, R., & Keliher, J. (2023). The legal framework: Limitations and opportunities. In C. J. Humphreys & G. J. Towl (Eds.), *Stopping gender-based violence in higher education: Policy, practice, and partnerships*. Routledge.
- McCarry, M., Jones, C., & Donaldson, A. (2023). The significance of culture in the prevention of gender-based violence in universities. In C. J. Humphreys & G. J. Towl (Eds.), *Stopping gender-based violence in higher education: Policy, practice, and partnerships*. Routledge.
- Office for Students. (2021). *Statement of expectations for preventing and addressing harassment and sexual misconduct affecting students in higher education*. www.officeforstudents.org.uk/for-providers/student-protection-and-support/prevent-and-address-harassment-and-sexual-misconduct/statement-of-expectations

PART 2

HOW

You cannot get through a single day without having an impact on the world around you. What you do makes a difference, and you have to decide what kind of difference you want to make.

~Dr Jane Goodall
Primatologist, Anthropologist, United Nations Messenger
of Peace

5

EMBEDDING A COMPREHENSIVE INSTITUTION-WIDE APPROACH

Universities will not stop sexual violence in their communities with tick-box exercises. Having all students take part in a one-off training on consent will not solve this problem. Saying 'we take sexual violence very seriously' seems little more than a vacuous statement in the absence of a clear statement of financial investment in addressing the problem. In Part 1 of this book, we show that sexual violence is pervasive in higher education (HE). We have laid out our responsibility to ensure students can access their education safely which requires commitment to shifting the culture within our communities which currently permits and thereby for all intents and purposes promotes sexual violence.

Much of the guidance offered thus far in the UK HE sector has focused on the reasons why institutions need to address sexual violence with principles to shape this work (see, e.g. Baird et al., 2019; Office for Students, 2021; UN Women, 2018a; UUK, 2016, 2019a, 2019b, 2022a, 2022b, 2022c, 2022d, 2022e; UUK & Pinsent Masons, 2016; UUK et al., 2024). These recommendations along with case examples have offered information on what should be done; however, there has been less information on *how* to implement these recommendations in practical terms. Therefore, in Part 2, we focus on how to address sexual violence based on sector guidance and good practice. We do not propose that we have all the answers. Nonetheless, we do have a coherent body of knowledge of the literature, policy and practice to be confident that what we suggest, if acted upon, is likely to contribute to prevention, improve support for victim-survivors and offer safer response procedures. We are committed to offering a more sustained and systematic approach by providing practical advice on how to embed prevention and response efforts within institutions. We build on current sector guidance and utilise evidence-informed practice identified in other countries that are relevant to the current UK legislative framework. We also draw upon our considerable joint knowledge and experience of this challenging field.

In this chapter, we focus on building a foundation to sustain this work by using what we refer to as a comprehensive institution-wide approach. We will consider what this approach is, how institutions can implement this approach and how institutions can resource their efforts and feel confident that senior leadership is supportive and engaged.

COMPREHENSIVE INSTITUTION-WIDE APPROACH

To address sexual violence safely and effectively, there are key principles which create the foundation of this work which we present in our model of the comprehensive institution-wide approach. We define the comprehensive institution-wide approach (shown in Fig. 1) as an ethical framework to sexual violence prevention and response that is trauma-informed, survivor-centred, human rights–based and social justice–based while being intersectional and requiring perpetrator accountability. It is not focused exclusively upon one perpetrator and one victim-survivor, but rather, it is aimed chiefly at addressing the structural issues that tolerate, minimise or otherwise perpetuate sexual violence in a community. The term *comprehensive* requires consideration of all forms of sexual violence and related violence affecting university communities (e.g. sexual harassment, rape, technology-facilitated sexual violence, stalking and domestic abuse), within all forms of university business (e.g. conferences, field trips, laboratories and sporting events) and affecting all community members (e.g. students, employees and marginalised groups) (Humphreys & Towl, 2023a). As proposed by UN Women (2018a), building from the

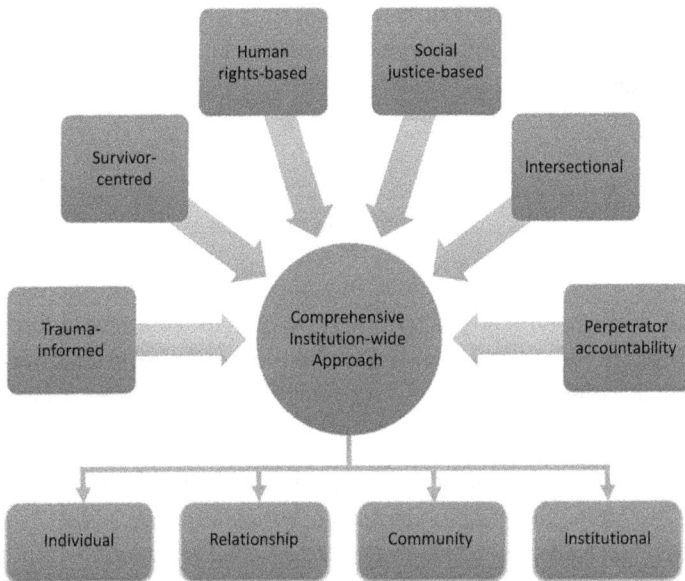

Fig. 1. Model of a Comprehensive Institution-wide Approach.

social-ecological model by the Centers for Disease Control and Prevention (2024) on sexual violence prevention, this approach is applied at each level of the community including:

- **Individual:** by building skills and awareness through training individual students and staff.

- **Relationship:** by offering education on consent, bystander intervention and healthy relationships to support students in developing respectful relationships and by having clear policies and codes of conduct that outline acceptable professional boundaries and conduct between students and staff.

- **Community:** by promoting that all members of the community, students and staff, work together to create a safer environment and demonstrate that perpetrators will be held accountable for their actions.

- **Institutional:** by creating policies and strategies aimed at preventing sexual violence and responding appropriately if this is not achieved and by demonstrating strategic leadership through a strategic plan for the prevention of sexual violence within the community.

Trauma-Informed Approach

There are multiple definitions of trauma depending on the field which it is used. For our purposes, we refer to the definition provided by the Substance Abuse and Mental Health Services Administration (SAMHSA), an agency within the US Department of Health and Human Services:

> *Individual trauma results from an event, series of events, or set of circumstances that is experienced by an individual as physically or emotionally harmful or life threatening and that has lasting adverse effects on the individual's functioning and mental, physical, social, emotional, or spiritual well-being. (2014, p. 7)*

An experience of trauma is subjective in that each of us experiences the same events uniquely. Thus, the same event may be experienced as traumatic for one person and not the other based on other life stressors, current (mal)adaptive or coping strategies, cultural beliefs and related protective factors. An individual does not consciously choose if an event is experienced as traumatic. Individuals who are subjected to trauma respond in a variety of ways and can experience short-term and long-term physical, emotional, psychological, practical and social effects. Individuals present with a wide range of trauma responses, and the varied responses to trauma are considered normal responses to an abnormal experience.

A trauma-informed approach to preventing and responding to sexual violence is considered best practice across many sectors internationally including criminal justice, health, social care and education (Donaldson et al., 2018; SAMHSA, 2014). Whereas it has become fashionable to refer to the need for trauma-informed approaches to a range of mental health–related problems, we think that it is important to specify precisely what we mean by such an approach. In 2014, SAMHSA identified six key principles of a trauma-informed approach which have now been adopted by the UK government to guide trauma-informed practice (Office for Health Improvement & Disparities, 2022). The following summarises these principles and builds on the American College Health Association's (2018) recommendations of how to apply these principles in HE:

1. **Safety:** Trauma-informed institutions promote physical and emotional safety for victim-survivors, train staff to respond to disclosures appropriately and create trust in the institution by demonstrating sexual violence is not tolerated by communicating actions taken to hold perpetrators accountable for sexual violence within the community.

2. **Trustworthiness and Transparency:** Policies and procedures are transparent so that victim-survivors can predict what will happen after making a disclosure and/or report with an understanding of the limitations available within the institution's response, e.g. possible interim measures, precautionary measures and sanctions for different forms of sexual violence. Investigations are conducted transparently, keeping both parties informed of the status of the investigation and sharing the outcome.

3. **Peer Support:** Peer supporters are available to aid in recovery, which helps establish hope for victim-survivors. Peer support groups, student activist groups and protected spaces for victim-survivors are accessible on campus.

4. **Collaboration and Mutuality:** Partnerships are unbiased by power differences. There are opportunities for students and staff to work together and have shared decision-making in the development and review of prevention and response efforts.

5. **Empowerment, Voice and Choice:** The strengths and agency of individuals who have experienced trauma are recognised, and victim-survivors are enabled to make their own choices and are offered opportunities to input into prevention efforts, e.g. through participation in focus groups, university committees and/or climate surveys.

6. **Cultural, Historical and Gender Issues:** The institution acknowledges the stereotypes, myths and biases associated with sexual violence. Policies are intersectional. Historical trauma is recognised and addressed, including, for example, institutional abuse or cultural historic trauma, i.e. institutional racism.

We argue that if all six principles are not part of the approach, it is not truly trauma-informed. Recognition of trauma may make an organisation trauma-aware or sensitive, but meeting the six principles lead to a trauma-informed organisation. Outcomes for a trauma-informed higher education institution (HEI) would include leaders demonstrating an awareness of the impact of trauma, decisions made to promote safety, actions taken to avoid re-traumatisation of victim-survivors and efforts made to empower victim-survivors to make their own choices on choosing to report and/or access support (Donaldson et al., 2018; Henry et al., 2016; SAMHSA, 2014). Two practical examples of demonstrating a trauma-informed approach are: (1) to minimise the number of times a victim-survivor recites their experience and (2) to ensure those receiving disclosures or investigating sexual misconduct have been trained appropriately (Tillapaugh, 2017).

The comprehensive institution-wide approach must be trauma-informed to effectively understand and address the harm caused through sexual violence for the victim-survivor and wider community and mitigate the risk of re-traumatising victim-survivors which would cause more harm. More information on why we must use a trauma-informed approach, particularly in investigations, is covered in Chapter 11.

Survivor-Centred

In law in the State of Illinois in the United States under the *Preventing Sexual Violence in Higher Education Act*, survivor-centred is defined as:

> ... *a systematic focus on the needs and concerns of a survivor of sexual violence, domestic violence, dating violence, or stalking that (i) ensures the compassionate*

and sensitive delivery of services in a nonjudgmental manner; (ii) ensures an understanding of how trauma affects survivor behavior; (iii) maintains survivor safety, privacy, and, if possible, confidentiality; and (iv) recognizes that a survivor is not responsible for the sexual violence, domestic violence, dating violence, or stalking. (110 ILCS 155/5)

To be survivor-centred is to place the victim-survivor at the centre of the process with the aim of promoting recovery, reducing the risk of further harm, treating them with dignity and respect and reinforcing their agency and self-determination (Bull et al., 2019; UN Women, 2018a, 2018b). Supporting victim-survivor agency means empowering them and respecting their choice to make their own decisions about accessing support and/or choosing to report sexual violence to the police and/or university (in the case of adult survivors). Survivors should be included in the development and review of prevention and response initiatives (see e.g. Blake & Dickinson, 2023 on how to include students in work on gender-based violence [GBV]). A practical example of being survivor-centred when focusing on the Reporting Party's safety would be to inform the Reporting Party of precautionary measures placed on the Responding Party during an investigation and to inform them of the outcome and sanctions (if issued) following a complaint and/or discipline process.

Human Rights–Based

Embedded in the comprehensive institution-wide approach is the recognition that sexual violence violates human rights (Griffin, 2017, p. viii; UN Women, 2018a, 2018b).

There is no 'ish' or 'in between' when it comes to the violation of human rights and acts of sexual violence – ranging from sexual harassment to relational abuse to rape to street harassment to cyberstalking – violate bodily integrity and human rights. (Griffin, 2017, p. viii)

Not only is sexual violence a violation of human rights, but under the Human Rights Act 1998, individuals have a right to an education; the fear of being subjected to or being subjected to sexual violence impacts students' access to education. Therefore, HEIs must prioritise the prevention of sexual violence for the protection of human rights and respond appropriately when these rights are violated. According to UN Women (2018a, 2018b), a human rights–based approach needs to address the needs of all victim-survivors, recognising the many discriminations an individual may face based on the intersection of aspects of their identity.

Social Justice–Based Approach

Sexual violence is a community issue as current culture and structures support perpetration. Within the HE setting, having a social justice–based approach includes (1) focusing on the individual and structural interrelationship by understanding intersections of identity, power and privilege; (2) naming the agency of a perpetrator and the system which supports their actions; (3) representing a range of narratives to represent the broad experiences of victim-survivors; (4) embedding prevention efforts across the institution and (5) changing the culture and core values of the institution rather than overlaying efforts on existing practices (Hong, 2017; Hong & Marine, 2018). In embedding social justice within the comprehensive institution-wide approach, the HEI can disrupt and challenge culture that supports sexual violence rather than approaching sexual violence as an issue between individuals, which is common practice particularly in complaint and disciplinary processes.

Intersectional

'Intersectionality' is a term coined by Kimberlé Crenshaw, who highlighted that race and gender are not experienced as separate identities but rather are overlapping, impacting on experiences of oppression and privilege (1989, 1991). This idea of multiple forms of identity intersecting to frame experiences of oppression and privilege applies beyond race and gender. Intersectionality allows us to understand power dynamics based on age, (dis)ability, sex, gender identity, race or ethnicity, nationality, religion or belief, sexual orientation and socio-economic status. A valid critique of traditional sexual violence prevention and response programmes is that they are centred on white heterosexual women who are subjected to violence by heterosexual men (Garvey et al., 2017; Griffin, 2017; Harris, 2017; Linder & Myers, 2017). Prevention and response efforts that fail to be intersectional create added barriers to victim-survivors seeking support and minimise, tolerate or otherwise ignore sexual violence perpetrated by individuals who do not 'fit' within the expected idea of a perpetrator. In Chapter 9, we discuss specific barriers to disclosing sexual violence. We will take a moment here to consider just one example of how intersectionality can develop our understanding of someone's choice to disclose. Consider how difficult it may be for a woman to tell someone they were sexually assaulted. Consider what other barriers a Black woman may face. How many more barriers will a Black woman who has a disability experience? What if she is also bisexual and from another country at the institution on a student visa? All these aspects of her identity are not felt one at a time but rather as a whole. These are not different hats she wears in different points of the day but rather aspects of who she is that creates her unique experience of oppression and privilege. An intersectional approach is another reason why we need to get better at collecting data at universities. For example, if we record details of protected characteristics plus social class of who is reporting sexual violence, it will reveal at an institutional level which groups are not reporting sexual violence. This may shine a light on who we are and are not including within our reporting procedures. Of course, it may also reflect different rates of being subjected to sexual violence – but the first port of call must surely be an assumption that we are more likely to have some institutional and/or cultural barriers to reporting among some groups.

Policies and procedures must address the needs of students of all groups; otherwise, they will be ineffective (Baird et al., 2019; Garvey et al., 2017; Harris, 2017). Institutions can and should review their materials, websites and trainings to ensure an intersectional approach (Sundaram et al., 2019; Tillapaugh, 2017). Victim-survivors who are women of colour, non-binary, men or have disabilities need to be centred as well rather than marginalised in services offered. Adopting an intersectional approach allows students (and staff) of all identities better access to services and ensures delivery of a more comprehensive institution-wide approach.

Perpetrator Accountability

In the comprehensive institution-wide approach, perpetrators are held accountable through due process that is fair and transparent. Institutions must have clear conduct standards that outline the potential consequences for not meeting these standards. Furthermore, these must be enforced; if an individual is found not to have met these standards, then appropriate and proportionate consequences must be imposed. Failure to hold perpetrators accountable following the finding of a breach of policy undermines the work to address sexual violence and impacts the integrity and credibility of a university that claims to 'take sexual violence seriously.' Worse still, it offers no remedy to the Reporting Party who the Responding Party harmed.

Many organisations including UN Women (2018a; Sen, 2019) and the National Union of Students (NUS, 2011) call for a zero-tolerance approach. This is described as, 'the certainty that the organisation will never do nothing in response to knowledge of sexual harassment, will always support those who report, sanction perpetrators and will proactively ensure that equality and non-discrimination inform its work' (Sen, 2019, p. 28). While we fully support the description and principle of zero tolerance, we offer a word of caution on language. The language of 'zero tolerance' is used often in university settings; however, from a practitioner's perspective, in practice, it can become problematic as it can mislead the community, and more importantly victim-survivors, on what the university can and will do if it is not communicated appropriately. Students may have a vastly different expectation of what 'zero tolerance' looks like. The language itself may be taken to imply that any form of sexual violence may result in expulsion. The reality is that any breach of policy may receive a sanction that is proportionate to the misconduct that occurred and any mitigating, aggravating and compounding factors that were present. That sanction can only be imposed following due process and a finding of a breach based on a balance of probabilities. An institution may expel a student for a sexual act with another person without their consent but may simply issue a reprimand for an individual who makes multiple inappropriate sexual remarks to another student. From the HEI's perspective, they will have enacted a zero-tolerance approach by imposing sanctions in both cases. However, from a victim-survivor's perspective or even from the wider student community, the HEI may be tolerating sexual harassment by only using a reprimand which is not a visible sanction. Worse still, if institutions use this language and then fail to enact a zero-tolerance approach, this will undermine the work the institution does in this area. In short, if a university chooses to use the language of zero tolerance in their strategy, they need to clearly define this to manage expectations of their community and then show how and communicate when they take action. The language of perpetrator accountability may be more representative of practice and may help manage expectations of the community, especially linked to clear sanctioning guidance.

We, along with others, recommend making public the anonymised outcomes of reports made against Responding Parties to increase trust in the institution (e.g. Bull et al., 2019). Statistical data and anonymised case summaries of disciplinary outcomes linked to sexual violence can, and should, be made public. This conveys to all in and beyond the university community that the problem of sexual violence at universities is actively being addressed. And this is important for those subjected to sexual violence informing their decision-making as to whether they will make a report to the university. For example, an institution could release that during an academic year, 50 reports were made to the institution under the relevant policy that deals with sexual violence, of those 40 were investigated, 30 were founded, 15 students were expelled during that year, 10 were excluded from the university for one year and 5 were issued No Contact Orders and letters of reprimand on their student record. This has the advantage of demonstrating to the wider university community that action is being taken and perpetrators are being held accountable without naming individual perpetrators or identifying victim-survivors. There is no right to anonymity for victim-survivors in HEI internal proceedings beyond the protections afforded under the General Data Protection Regulations.

EMBEDDING THE APPROACH

The comprehensive institution-wide approach is the foundation for addressing sexual violence. It should underpin the implementation of all initiatives from prevention to response and recovery. From here, we consider specific areas of implementation which build from the foundation.

Assessing the Local Problem

For Vice-Chancellors and governing bodies of HEIs who do not believe they have a problem, because of low reporting rates, the most likely explanation is that victim-survivors are not reporting their experiences to the institution due to a multitude of barriers, and/or staff who do receive information regarding incidents of sexual violence are not reporting this centrally, leaving the administration unaware of the issue. It is not merely a matter of students having the confidence to report when subjected to sexual violence; staff need to feel confident in their institution to do the appropriate follow-up work with such reports and not act as gatekeepers to conceal this information. However, recognising that there is a problem is different from understanding the problem. Therefore, it is important to formally assess the situation. Another reason why such university leaders may not believe that they have a problem may come simply from a place of ignorance. A lack of awareness and understanding of this challenging field may contribute to such complacency.

The evidence is overwhelming that we would expect the spectre of sexual violence to affect all HEIs; however, it is helpful to assess local prevalence data to provide foundational information regarding the gap between incidents of sexual violence and reporting rates and equally important, to allow for evaluation of prevention initiatives in the future. This can also help support business cases for resourcing support. Most of the data an HEI will hold will be 'reported' data that are not representative of the prevalence of sexual violence occurring at the institution. Reported data only capture when students/staff have disclosed incidents, and this has been recorded. Therefore, Vice-Chancellors and their senior executive teams may choose to run campus climate surveys locally to access prevalence data. This prevalence data will act as a starting point to measure cultural norms, attitudes and beliefs and can be useful when designing prevention and response measures tailored to the institution. Very importantly, these data will provide a baseline for measuring progress in cultural change and, potentially, the prevalence of sexual violence across a multi-year period. Therefore, not only does this help assess the situation, but it also provides a tool to monitor and evaluate progress.

In a campus climate survey, students (and staff) are asked directly and anonymously about their experiences. These surveys can be conducted within one institution as a one-off although that is not very useful. We recommend conducting them on an annual or biennial basis to make the data more useful in identifying change. Campus climate surveys conducted within one institution can be tailored to the institution. Alternatively, institutions may wish to run climate surveys across multiple institutions. This may produce more generalised data compared to the tailored survey; however, having the ability to compare across the sector may be preferred.

There are examples of large-scale multi-institution campus climate surveys from the United States where the surveys and methodology have been made available for HEIs to view as an example (see, e.g. Cantor et al., 2015; Krebs et al., 2016). As of 2019, 31 universities in the United Kingdom had completed campus climate surveys, but the data remain unpublished (Bull et al., 2023). In 2023, the Office for Students (OfS) conducted a pilot multi-institution campus climate survey to better understand sexual misconduct in HE. At the time of writing, the pilot survey results have also not been published.

Good Practice Example: Cultivating Learning and Safe Environments, the University of Texas System

The Cultivating Learning and Safe Environments (CLASE) study is a comprehensive, proactive and scientific effort to combat and reduce intimate and interpersonal violence at all University of Texas (UT) System institutions. The project is unprecedented in its scope, duration and depth of understanding on the issues of sexual assault, sexual harassment, dating violence/domestic violence and stalking that UT System students may face. The primary deliverable was a system-wide prevalence and perception survey completed in March 2017. The research included:

- Benchmarking the prevalence and perceptions of students about their experiences with and concerns about sexual assault, sexual harassment, dating violence/domestic violence and stalking through a comprehensive online survey.
- The impact of students' personal experiences with sexual assault, sexual harassment, dating violence/domestic violence and stalking in their lives, including understanding the use of alcohol and other drugs, addictions, post-traumatic stress disorder (PTSD), depression, time off from school or work, and other variables.
- A four-year longitudinal study of 1,200 first-year students.
- In-depth qualitative interviews with members of the entire HEI ecosystem.
- Ongoing engagement of institutional working groups with the aim that the CLASE project was the 'means to the beginning'.

These findings inform institution-specific efforts that address victimisation and perpetration risks across the UT System, including the impact of victimisation, health and wellbeing and addiction among college students. The 'means to the beginning' objective acknowledges that the CLASE research team must hand over the findings to campus working groups comprised of thought leaders, researchers and representatives from multiple disciplines around their campuses to implement the research findings into programmes to increase student safety. Implementation/evaluation is ongoing.

For more information, see:
Busch-Armendariz et al. (2017)
sites.utexas.edu/idvsa/research/campus-initiatives/clase-project

With special thanks to Noël Busch-Armendariz, PhD, LMSW, MPA (University Presidential Professor and Director of IDVSA) and Caitlin Sulley, LMSW (Director of Research & Operations) from the Institute on Domestic Violence & Sexual Assault, Steve Hicks School of Social Work of the University of Texas at Austin for reviewing and approving this summary.

Building From the Foundation

In 2019, consultants through Advance HE (commissioned by the OfS) evaluated the spending of catalyst funding that was dedicated to supporting universities in advancing work to address sexual harassment and produced suggested minimum safeguarding practice recommendations (Baird et al., 2019). With permission, we have captured the recommendations here as a starting place for practitioners and senior leaders to consider as a minimum check on the progress within their own institution (Table 1).

Building from Chapter 4, there are many 'business risks' associated with not preventing and responding to sexual violence, including the legal, financial and reputational risks which may most often be considered first. However, there are also significant risks to the health and wellbeing of students and staff and their ability to study and work in environments free from harassment and discrimination.

Table 1. Advance HE: Possible 'Minimum' Safeguarding Practice.

Action	Summary
1) **Annual reports to the institutional governing body which are publicly available covering reports, disclosures and outcomes**	The format of such reports needs to preserve the anonymity of reporting parties of sexual misconduct and hate crimes/incidents. Under each such rubric, the date of the report and date of the incident should be recorded. The date of the safeguarding multidisciplinary team meeting should be included too. Providers' responses may be codified under four headings:

    i. Personal and health support;
    ii. Educational support;
    iii. Internal investigations; and
    iv. Police investigations.

For each of these categories there needs to be a clear narrative statement of the inputs and outcomes. Inputs are actions taken by the institution. Outcomes are just that. In terms of 'inputs' we would anticipate that in every case there should be an input in terms of i) and ii) subject to the agreement of the Reporting Party.

Inputs in terms of iii) and iv) are likely to be less common but offered and discussed as option for the decision of reporting parties as to whether or not to go ahead with either iii) or iv) both or neither.

In terms of 'outcomes', personal and health support could, for example, include specialist counselling and educational support could be educational adjustments made

Table 1. *(Continued)*

Action	Summary
	mindful of the particular 'mitigating circumstances'.
2) **Integration into communications for prospective students so they are aware of the behaviour expectations and student safety support in place, and which will remain in place throughout their student journey**	It is potentially reassuring for prospective students to hear of arrangements in place to ensure their wellbeing and safety, and which will remain in place throughout their student journey. Open discussion of matters such as addressing sexual misconduct and hate crime sends a message of reassurance out to potential victims/survivors and a message of an intolerance of such behaviours to potential perpetrators. For those students who are uncertain of the precise requirements of establishing consent and capacity, or what constitutes a hate crime/incident or online harassment, such communications may give them the opportunity to reflect upon such matters before they need such decision making.
3) **There need to be active communications campaigns urging victims/survivors to come forward and report their experiences**	In short, very high reporting levels need to be actively encouraged along with disclosure levels too, to inform the development of services to ensure that victim/survivor support is optimised. This may very well deter some would be perpetrators too. Campaigns will need continued support, coordination and reinforcement at sector level to protect individual providers against reputational damage and ensure take-up.

(Continued)

Table 1. *(Continued)*

Action	Summary
4) **Staff and student training programmes need to be in place.**	Disclosure training is key for staff and students enacting representational roles. Sessions on consent for undergraduate and postgraduate students are important early in their time at the provider along with the option to engage with bystander intervention training to contribute to prevention. This should be co-created and designed with students.
5) **A member of the senior executive team needs to hold accountability for work on addressing sexual misconduct and hate crime/incidents**	Executive level responsibility and accountability for decision- making and driving and monitoring the work is effective in ensuring that a whole-institution approach is taken to addressing sexual misconduct and hate incidents.
6) **Good policy and practice**	Communications and policy documents need to make it explicit that internal investigations rely on a civil, in other words balance of probability level of evidence, rather than beyond reasonable doubt as per criminal justice levels of evidence. This may help encourage more students to come forward to report.
7) **Resources**	It is especially important for HE providers to plan for the rise in reporting levels to ensure that support and investigations may be put in place in a timely fashion. One FTE (Full Time Equivalent) per 10,000 students who specialises solely in this area would seem to be a basic requirement to support staff

Table 1. *(Continued)*

Action	Summary
	training and coordinate investigations and organise awareness campaigns working with student leaders.
8) **Partnership working**	Local and regional collaborative working and liaison with local Sexual Violence Referral Centres (SARCs), local police, other HE providers, schools and expert specialist voluntary and community organisations should be in place.

Source: Reproduced with permission (Baird et al., 2019).

Vice-Chancellors and governing bodies can own this problem at the highest level by understanding the nature of the risk, ensuring that it is documented and identifying and mitigating contingent actions to manage the risk. In addition to the recommendations in Table 1, the Advance HE review confirmed that HEIs would be wise to include sexual violence on their strategic risk registers. They explicitly noted the benefits of this would include 'awareness raising; embedding safeguarding work across the institution; providing clarity for governing bodies; challenging the executive to act; increasing visibility; and requiring active mitigation and management (controls)' (Baird et al., 2019, p. 12).

Committing Resource to Change

At universities, what gets funded tends to get done. And what does not get funded is much less likely to happen, especially upon a sustained basis. UN Women's seventh essential action as noted in Chapter 2 is to have a dedicated budget (2018a). Without a budget, this work will fail. If institutions are serious about addressing this issue and creating sustained culture change, it is necessary to invest time, personnel and money into this area. To create an appropriate budget, a costing exercise may be performed. UN Women recommend the following to be considered when developing a budget:

- Information-gathering costs.

- Infrastructure costs.

- Awareness efforts.

- Sensitisation and capacity building of those providing support and service in university.

- Monitoring and evaluation.

Some have observed that many campuses resource funding into compliance efforts leaving prevention efforts second (e.g. Hong, 2017). Interestingly in England and Wales, with funding from the OfS (originally HEFCE Catalyst Funding), more funding was initially used towards prevention efforts with less resource spent on responding to sexual violence (Baird et al., 2019; UUK, 2019a). In this section, we outline different resources that need to be considered in a budget including the above suggestions.

Staffing

Progressing in this area works best when there are key staff and student (peer) champions advocating for this work with senior leader support. Consideration for where this work will be placed within the structure of the institution is important. We suggest that there be a member of the HEI executive team with responsibility for the management of the institutional strategy, tactics and operations in relation to reducing sexual violence and supporting those students subjected to it, a strategic lead (Baird et al., 2019; UUK, 2019a, 2019b). There needs to be explicit links between the strategic, tactical and operational implementation. The strategic framework is derived from the overarching strategy of the institution. The tactical involves a political reading of the culture and a clear focus upon what changes will have the maximal impact, supporting the effective design and delivery of a detailed and integrated programme to reduce sexual violence while ensuring appropriate support for anyone subjected to it.

A dedicated specialist manager is needed to supervise prevention and response initiatives for students and staff. Therefore, this manager should be able to liaise with Human Resources, student discipline offices and senior leaders; they should be independent of those departments. In June 2019, HEIs in England and Wales saw the first published guidance on resource with the expectation that one full-time specialist would be employed for every 10,000 students; institutions with between 10,000 and 19,999 students may view it as prudent to have two full-time specialist staff (Baird et al., 2019). This is congruent with recommendations by UN Women (2018a) who stress the importance of the assignment of a dedicated university coordinator to address violence against women. Again, the specialist member of staff should coordinate and manage the implementation of the strategic response. This person should have a senior level of authority on the issues and should regularly address senior leadership on the work in this area (UN Women, 2018a).

Specialist case managers with relevant expertise around sexual violence and related GBV to coordinate responses to reports made to the institution and/or police is required. We discuss the case manager role in detail in Chapter 10. Additional student support staff is required to offer support to the Reporting Party and Responding Party separately. In some HEIs, we are seeing the use of Sexual Violence Liaison Officers (SVLOs) or Independent Sexual Violence Advisors (ISVAs) who are trained to provide support to victim-survivors within the institution (UUK, 2019b). Any support provided to the Reporting and Responding Parties would need to be separate and delivered by different members of staff, preferably in distinct locations on campus. Staff to investigate reports of sexual violence and to adjudicate on sexual misconduct discipline cases are also needed.

It is important to note that one person cannot do all the work because inherent in a one-person approach are embedded conflicts of interest (e.g. the person providing education then manages an investigation into a report of sexual violence with the same students). Also one person even for the smallest of institutions is simply not going to be able to deal with the sheer volume of such cases if reporting rates reflect even a significant fraction of prevalence rates. In addition, without proper resourcing, there is a considerable risk of burnout and failure to deliver a comprehensive institution-wide approach. Skilled facilitators are required for delivering effective training; training options will be discussed further in Chapter 8. Finally, staff need to be offered appropriate support to do this work including clinical supervision (if appropriate), networking across institutions with others in the role and appropriate physical space to do the role. Case managers and investigators should have a confidential workspace so they can respond to cases and meet with students and staff as needed. Finally, it is important also to ensure that all such staff involved in cases which for any of us involve an emotional labour need the opportunity to have appropriate clinical supervision or reflective practice and support. This is not an optional extra for any institution that is truly 'serious about addressing sexual violence'.

Resources for Investigations

Internal investigations into sexual violence can be time- and resource-intensive. At minimum, a case manager and investigator are required. Accepted practice in the sector involves hiring internal investigators or using a pool of investigators who do this as part of their role or as a volunteer position outside of their role. In some cases, universities will outsource investigations to experienced investigating firms. This is particularly true for cases that may be more complex, high-risk or high-profile. In Table 2, we outline the various options for ways institutions may wish to source investigators noting the pros and cons of each.

Institutions will need to weigh the pros and cons of each option to find an option that fits the institution's needs best. 'Needs' used here means fitting within the ethos of the institution, supporting the desire to prevent sexual violence in the community and providing fair and transparent investigations to all parties involved while providing the best value for money. The aim of resourcing investigators well is to ensure the integrity of the policy for all concerned and so that it acts as a deterrent to perpetration and offers safety for students and staff alike.

Table 2. Comparing Internal and External Investigator Resourcing Options.

	Internal	External	Internal/External
Options	• Appointing full-time or part-time internal investigator/s • Adding investigations to job descriptions of certain roles or grades • Using a pool of internal volunteer investigators	• Buying in investigators from a third party either on an ad hoc basis or by retainer	• Using an internal or external investigator depending on the complexity of the case and/or capacity of internal investigators and/or high-profile nature of the case
Pros	• Trained in internal policies and procedures • Parity in investigating all types of misconduct by internal investigators • For an FT/PT-hired investigator, the investigator can prioritise an investigation to complete within set timescales. • When using a pool of volunteer investigators, there may be more variety in investigator skill sets; thus, there is the potential for matching skills sets to individuals' cases.	• Experienced investigators with relevant backgrounds, e.g. law, criminology or policing • Can prioritise an investigation to complete within set timescales • May be seen as independent • May work across institutions and be able to benchmark outcomes	• Allows flexibility based on the needs of individual cases • Provides access to larger pool of investigators if caseload increases • Provides access to potential development options for internal investigators

(Continued)

Table 2. *(Continued)*

	Internal	External	Internal/External
Cons	• When investigating is not the individual's main role, the ability to begin and/ or complete an investigation may be dependent on other responsibilities causing delays in investigations. • When using a pool of internal volunteer investigators, there will likely be varied expertise and experience which may cause inconsistency in investigation quality and reliable outcomes. • Perceived bias that investigators are internal and therefore part of the system trying to protect one of the parties or the institution itself • When using a pool of internal volunteer investigators and/ or investigating is added to another role, there may be concerns about the competence of such 'amateur' investigators.	• Likely require a payment to retain the firm's services plus a fee per case per hour causing the institution to incur a significant cost depending on the number and complexity of individual cases • May be difficult to budget for an external service without knowing how many cases per year are likely to be reported and how complex individual cases may be • May not fully understand the internal policy and procedure or university ethos. Greater chance for appeal due to procedural error • Using an external investigator may not be sustainable for institutions as their reporting rates increase and the cost of investigations increase	• Potential concern that cases are not being treated equally. This may happen within sexual violence cases or across other forms of misconduct. Either the Reporting Party or Responding Party may argue that they should have been investigated by an internal/external investigator if they see their peers' investigations being handled by the opposite. • Requires training internal staff and paying for external retainer for investigation firm's services, requiring double the resource

Table 2. *(Continued)*

Internal	External	Internal/External
• Relying on internal volunteer investigators may not be sustainable as reporting rates increase and the need for volunteers' time increases. • There is a lack of training available across the sector to train investigators to the recommended level of expertise, and no oversight of the training that is available. • There is a history of relying on senior staff of a certain grade to conduct investigations confusing seniority with skill competency.	• External providers may be seen to provide the answer wanted by the institution, as the institution is the customer, rather than providing a truly independent view. • This is an unregulated area of service provision, with anyone being able to claim expertise, so there may be little control over the quality of such work.	

If the institution chooses to use an external investigating firm, we encourage institutions to share feedback on the success or failures of this option. Any such appointed service would need to demonstrate the detail of their competence rather than simply be reliant upon generalisations, especially as this is not a regulated service so in that sense, there is more corporate risk to going outside the institution in terms of assurance around quality and professionalism. If using volunteer investigators, we recommend that this be added to an individual's workload model to allow time in the workday to conduct investigations when needed or as agreed, e.g. two per academic year. Investigators should not be expected to work outside their contracted hours to complete the investigation. If using internal volunteer investigators, we recommend that two investigators be assigned per case. We would typically advise one woman and one man for undertaking such investigations. In our experience, using two investigators offers the potential to run a more thorough investigation and provides increased confidence in the outcomes. This also allows for shared responsibility, complementary skills and mutual support in an often-difficult area. Volunteers need training, and this needs to be on a 'pass-fail' basis – if the competencies for the role are not met even after training, then individuals who do not demonstrate the competencies should not be deployed in the investigatory role. Such decisions need to be independent of rank or status. When using internal professional investigators, one investigator per case is likely sufficient.

Investigators must be supported to conduct a reasonable and reliable investigation. They may require administrative support to schedule meetings, book rooms, communicate with parties/witnesses, and take notes of meetings. Investigators may need access to emotional support during or after an investigation. Crucially, all such investigators (internal and external) need training to a high standard to cover both specific content and procedures (which we cover in Chapters 8 and 11).

Multiple Doors for Reporting

Institutions that do this work well should expect to see an increase in reports of sexual violence. This most likely demonstrates that victim-survivors have trust in the institution, know how to report, and believe something will be done in response. This is a key message of this book that we wish to emphasise - high rates of reporting need to be actively encouraged. Therefore, it is important that how this is done is methodical in timing and resource.

The term 'doors' is used to convey the different opportunities that students and staff have to disclose sexual violence, access support, seek help and/or make formal reports to the institution for further action.

Institutions should offer multiple doors, or ways in, to these services for students as there are many barriers victim-survivors already face. By offering multiple options, students are more likely to access support. Example options may include dedicated teams or specialist staff (e.g. SVLOs/ISVAs) that students can disclose to in person, online reporting platforms or anonymous reporting tools.

However, if institutions create doors for disclosing or reporting and no one answers the door, students will quickly lose trust in the institutional response. This is one of the reasons why resourcing in this area is important. Institutions need to ensure qualified staff are available to respond to disclosures. If institutions encourage reporting but are not prepared to respond to an increase in disclosures and reports, victim-survivors will stop reporting and perpetrators will see no action taken which may increase risk of perpetration. If the institution uses an online reporting tool, students and staff need to know it is there and how to access and use it. Otherwise, it is useless. It is not good enough to say, we have a tool. Reporting tools, policies, services, etc. need to be accessible and responsive.

Governance

Finally, there needs to be embedded mechanisms for monitoring, evaluation and quality assurance. Institutions can collect reported data (disclosures and reports) centrally to better understand trends to inform prevention and response efforts and to allow senior leadership at the highest level to better understand the trends occurring across the institution. If universities across the sector recorded this information in a unified way, it would be easier to consider data and observe trends on a macro level. This is related to a campus climate survey; comparing the prevalence data with the reported data would, for example, be especially useful to understand rates of reporting. Capturing the trends shown in Resource 2 allows the HEI to quality assess its own performance at responding to reported sexual violence as well. Furthermore, this information can be made public, as it will not reveal identities of involved parties.

This chapter has considered how to embed a comprehensive institution-wide approach. Culture change is not instant. Unfortunately, there are no quick fixes, and this work cannot be treated as a tick-box exercise; it requires an investment in years of work. The aim of embedding prevention and response initiatives is that they are effective and become business as usual. These are not one-off activities. This is why there is a staffing requirement for a permanent member of staff to lead in this area. Part-time or fixed-term staff may be appropriate for the development of special projects, administrating campus climate surveys or evaluating programmes. It should not be expected that someone will add this to their workload, but rather this should be a dedicated specialist resource. In the remaining chapters, we build on this approach and discuss specific areas including tackling resistance to prevention and response initiatives, policy development, training, responding to disclosures of sexual violence, case management, investigating reports of sexual violence, adjudicating and sanctioning in cases of sexual violence and how leadership and partnerships sustain this work.

📖 Related Resources

- Humphreys, C. J., & Towl, G. J. (2023). Comprehensive institution-wide approach: What it means to be comprehensive. In C. J. Humphreys & G. J. Towl (Eds.), *Stopping gender-based violence in higher education: Policy, practice, and partnerships*. Routledge.
- Baird, H., Towl, G., Renfrew, K., & Buckingham, R. (2022). Evaluation of the initial impact of the statement of expectations – Final report. *SUMS consulting*. https://www.officeforstudents.org.uk/publications/evaluation-of-statement-of-expectations-final-report/
- UN Women. (2018). *Guidance note on campus violence prevention and response*. https://www.unwomen.org/en/digital-library/publications/2019/02/guidance-note-on-campus-violence-prevention-and-response

6

TACKLING RESISTANCE TO CHANGE

'This work is not easy' seems to be a common refrain. Working to prevent sexual violence in HE communities *is* challenging. Responding to incidents of sexual violence can be difficult. Attempting to change culture, educate communities, holding survivors' trauma and keeping students and employees safe is a huge undertaking. Staff must practise self-care, have good boundaries, protect themselves from the effects of exposure to vicarious or secondary trauma and keep professional relationships with those with whom they work and help.

What may feel the most difficult in this work though is trying to do this work without support or willingness for positive change to occur. Resistance. Hitting brick walls. Hearing 'no' repeatedly. Feeling like we are not helping survivors, like we are not keeping students and staff safe, or worse, like we are working for organisations that perpetuate sexual violence and/or harm victim-survivors.

We know there is resistance to this work. We know resourcing this work is not readily available or always supported. We know that sexual violence can be placed in a large bag full of other priorities and may not be chosen to be resourced. There are many reasons given not to progress prevention and response work, e.g. fear of 'reputational damage', lack of resource through budget, staffing or time, lack of in-house expertise, lack of support from senior leaders or other stakeholders, other initiatives take priority or refusing to make meaningful change when tick box measures are already in place.

Positive change is not easy. Individually and collectively, change is often met with challenge and resistance. However, to truly address sexual violence in higher education (HE), individually and collectively change must occur. In this chapter, we walk you – the changemakers – step-by-step through identifying resistance to your change initiatives and developing strategies to tackle the resistance you face. The aim of this chapter is to support you to be better prepared and skilled to identify and overcome resistance to progress positive change initiatives focused on addressing sexual violence.

STEP 1: RECOGNISE THAT YOU WILL FACE RESISTANCE

If you are an effective changemaker, you will face resistance. Change is not easily received or welcomed. As we will see later in this chapter, there are various motivations for resisting change. It is natural for social change to be met with resistance (Agócs, 1997; Warrick, 2023). Therefore, if you are facing resistance – congratulations! Resistance tactics are being used because there is potential for your change initiative to work. Resistance is a sign that you have the potential to successfully make the change (Colpitts, 2020; Flood et al., 2021; VicHealth, 2018).

STEP 2: DETERMINE IF THE RESISTANCE YOU FACE IS INSTITUTIONAL OR INDIVIDUAL RESISTANCE

Resistance tactics can be used at various levels. In the next section, we will discuss the diverse types of resistance tactics that may be used. However, first, it is helpful to understand where the resistance sits, i.e. is the organisation setting its position on the matter or is an individual within the organisation giving a view. If it is an individual providing their position, but not an agreed decision by the organisation, this would be considered *Individual Resistance*. Whereas

Institutional Resistance is the 'pattern of organizational behaviour that decision makers in organizations employ to actively deny, reject, refuse to implement, repress or even dismantle change proposals and initiatives' (Agócs, 1997, p. 46). If it appears that leadership does not support the change initiative, this gives individuals permission not to support it too as 'institutional resistance intensifies and licenses individual resistance', (Flood et al., 2021, p. 397).

It is important to note that all the resistance tactics that we will present in the next section can be used at the institutional and individual levels. We also must highlight that all the tactics can be used directly against victim-survivors. When victim-survivors are targeted directly using these forms of resistance tactics, this is often experienced as *Institutional Betrayal* (Humphreys & Towl, 2023b). We provide examples of how these tactics can be used against victim-survivors directly in Chapter 13 and in Humphreys and Towl (2023b). However, for the purpose of this chapter, we will focus the discussion on when this resistance is used at the institutional or individual levels against culture change initiatives.

STEP 3: IDENTIFY WHAT RESISTANCE YOU ARE FACING OR WHAT YOU PREDICT YOU WILL FACE

In Humphreys and Towl (2023b), we present eight types of resistance that can be used to block, stall or reverse positive culture change initiatives to address gender-based violence (GBV) in HE. These are presented from passive to active forms of resistance. The model we use was developed by VicHealth (2018) in response to resistance tactics used to stop gender equality work. In this section, we will show how this model helpfully articulates resistance tactics used against sexual violence prevention and response initiatives.

Denial

Denial is a passive form of resistance where the problem or the credibility for the case for change is denied. This is where the institution or an individual within the institution does not accept that sexual violence is an issue or does not accept that it is a large-enough issue within the organisation or department to support the need for the change initiative. Although it may seem illogical for universities to deny sexual violence is a problem given the wealth of evidence to the contrary, denial continues to be a used resistance tactic (Baird et al., 2022). But even for the higher education institutions (HEIs) that do recognise that sexual violence is an issue, denial can be used to stall progress on change initiatives. For example, an HEI might resource consent education for first-year undergraduates agreeing that sexual violence is a concern in this cohort while at the same time denying that sexual violence is an issue for postgraduate students and not resourcing prevention education for that cohort. If universities do not conduct campus climate surveys to seek prevalence data on sexual violence within the community and/or do not centrally record anonymised information on disclosures and reports of sexual violence, then they could argue that there is 'no evidence' of sexual violence affecting their student community. Other examples of denial include denying that diverse types of sexual violence occur within the community, e.g. technology-facilitated sexual violence, domestic abuse and stalking. The evidence is clear that students are also subjected to domestic abuse, stalking and other forms of GBV in person and online.

Disavowal

Disavowal is the refusal to recognise responsibility. This passive resistance tactic is where the institution or an individual within the institution rejects the obligation to address the issue of sexual violence, stating that it is another organisation's (e.g. the police) or employee's role to deal with the situation. This is a passive form of resistance that in short can be summarised as 'it's not my job.' Disavowal can still be seen across the sector by institutions who have such narrow scopes of their policies that they refuse to investigate sexual violence just because it has not occurred on university property or university business specifically. Individuals easily use disavowal when sexual violence prevention and response work is not part of their job description, so literally 'not their job'. Disavowal can also be seen when universities purport that sexual violence is not a university problem but a societal problem. This is an attempt to lessen the responsibility universities hold to prevent and respond to sexual violence by trying to demonstrate the issue is not unique to universities.

There is a compelling argument that sexual violence prevention and response sits soundly under safeguarding, equality/equity, diversity and inclusion and health and safety. In most universities, elements of each of these areas are embedded in all job descriptions. Therefore, including prevention and response to an appropriate level for all jobs is possible and supports mitigating for this form of resistance. In other words, all employees can be responsible for supporting a safe work and learning environment for staff and students.

Inaction

Inaction is not implementing the change initiative. This is a passive form of resistance as no action is taken. Inaction can be simply refusing to put the change initiative on the agenda for consideration, refusing to attend meetings related to the change initiative, or not attending training. A survey conducted in 2018 of how HEIs were tackling GBV, harassment and hate crime, found that 19% had 'not yet started' to implement the 2016 Universities UK (UUK) and Pinsent Mason guidance and 5% did not even provide a response to the question (Universities UK, 2019a). An evaluation conducted in 2022 of how HEIs responded to the OfS *Statement of Expectations* found that 20% of responding HEI providers still had 'not yet started' to implement the 2016 UUK and Pinsent Masons guidance (Baird et al., 2022).

Inaction is an easy form of resistance when there is no accountability or consequence for failing to implement a change initiative. If regulators are not holding providers accountable, if governing bodies do not hold senior leaders accountable, if senior leaders do not hold management accountable and so on…, no action will be taken. Highlighting the business case for action is imperative, so that HEI decision-makers can see the legal, financial and reputational risks for not addressing sexual violence.

Appeasement

Appeasement is moving into a more active form of resistance as it is placating or pacifying those advocating for change to limit its impact. In other words, this is saying 'yes' to appease, without taking action or demonstrating a meaningful commitment to enacting the change. Examples of appeasement could be agreeing to training but not approving the training budget, stalling the implementation of a new campaign that has been approved or offering resource but not following through with delivery. In a study which considered challenges to implementing the 2016 UUK and Pinsent Masons' guidance, 24% of respondents said they had received verbal support but not sufficient investment of resources to implement the guidance (Donovan et al., 2020). Other examples of appeasement could include agreeing to adopt a new policy, but not implementing it or agreeing that discipline decision-makers will receive training, but not providing training. It is common to see appeasement used when student activists or Students' Union representatives are pushing for change due to their time-limited presence in the organisation. For example, student activists raise concerns to an institution about the amount of sexual violence that is occurring within the student community and the lack of university action to prevent this. The university offers the student activists a meeting where university leaders listen to their concerns, take note of these and say that they will consider this feedback. The university leaders tell the students they have been heard and that their concerns will be taken seriously. Following this, no action is taken. The action to hear their concerns and tell them they would be taken seriously in this example is used to placate upset students. However, without any meaningful action following this, this is only an example of appeasement, and it belies a contempt for the safety of students despite periodic vacuous statements of 'taking sexual violence very seriously'.

Appeasement is best mitigated by confirming timeframes for action, clarifying who is responsible for ensuring action is taken, and who needs to be informed if this does not occur or if action is delayed. If there is resistance to answering these questions, it is likely any 'yes' is appeasement. Keeping email trails is key so that, for example, any periodic reminders serve to highlight the lengths of delay in action despite verbal support for any such policies and practices.

Appropriation

In the model we use adapted from VicHealth (2018), appropriation is simulating change while covertly undermining it, making it an active form of resistance. An example of appropriation could be having a sexual violence policy but actively discouraging victim-survivors from making reports or making the process so convoluted and lengthy that victim-survivors choose not to report. On the surface, the organisation looks like it has taken an important step by implementing a policy; however, if the policy is not accessible or is not used, it is not preventing or responding to sexual violence, undermining its purpose. Another example of appropriation could be appointing a committee to be responsible for implementing the change initiative; however, failing to empower the committee to fulfil this responsibility or appointing those who are most likely to accept the status quo (Agócs, 1997). A common example of appropriation shared among practitioner networks in the United Kingdom is when universities employ specialists from the Violence Against Women and Girls (VAWG) sector who hold expert knowledge, skills and experience, but then the HEI leadership dismisses their advice because they are not high enough in the organisation (by grade) or do not hold the credentials (PhD/Professorship) seen as valuable in HE. On the other hand, a study in the United States found that universities favoured hiring inexperienced and non-specialist candidates when recruiting for posts to lead on sexual violence response in case management and discipline (Bedera, 2023), thus undermining the specialist nature of this work and leading to unsafe practices and outcomes.

Appropriation can be difficult to identify as on the surface, it may look like the individual or institution is supporting the change initiative in the first instance. Close monitoring and evaluation of action taken can help identify this form of resistance.

Co-option

Co-option, an active form of resistance, is using the language of progressive frameworks and goals for reactionary ends or to maintain the status quo. In sexual violence prevention and response in universities, it is commonly used to shift the focus from victim-survivors to alleged perpetrators, and given the gendered nature of sexual violence, this is often a gendered discussion. Sexual violence is disproportionately men's violence against women; therefore, discussions on prevention and response initiatives often can focus on the impact on women, given this is the highest risk group within the university community to be targeted. A common form of co-option is to respond to any discussion that focuses on women with 'What about men?' thus diverting from and silencing discussions related to women. This deflection is sometimes to ask about men who have been subjected to sexual violence; however, often, it is to ask about men who have allegedly been falsely accused. The focus is shifted to consider how to protect these 'young men with great futures.' This protects the status quo and ignores the impact and detriment to the futures of young women subjected to sexual violence. This choice to deflect from discussing women and change the focus to men is best explained through the concept of what has been referred to as **'himpathy'** which is advantaging men at the expense of women (Bedera, 2023; Manne, 2021). In a study conducted in a university in the United States, Bedera (2023) considered how men accused of sexual violence were treated compared to women who reported they were subjected to sexual violence. This study found that although overt victim-blaming may not be used as this is now seen as taboo, himpathy was used to justify maintaining the status quo in GBV cases, even when men had been found to have committed misconduct. In cases of academic misconduct, substance use misconduct and violent assault on other men, himpathy was not used (Bedera, 2023). Likewise, co-option can be seen in any attempt to create equal rights for Reporting Parties in discipline procedures. This can be met with the rejection that Reporting Parties are disadvantaged and Responding Parties are privileged in the process despite clear evidence to the contrary where sector guidance from organisations such as the Office of Independent Adjudicator for England and Wales (OIA, 2018a) attributes all rights to Responding Parties, making Reporting Parties witnesses only, in a case with no rights to test evidence and appeal outcomes. Indeed, the OIA's guidance to date seems to specialise in protecting Responding Parties at the expense of those students who have been subjected to sexual violence.

Co-option is an easily identifiable form of resistance as it takes away from the focus of the change initiative to maintain the status quo. In relation to the gendered dynamics described, one way to mitigate for co-option is to highlight the benefits men will experience when women's safety is prioritised and individuals of all genders are held accountable if they perpetrate sexual violence.

Repression

Repression is reversing or dismantling a change initiative. It is an active form of resistance where the institution agrees to or an individual within the institution chooses to actively reverse the already implemented change initiative. Carol Agócs (1997) effectively summarises repression highlighting how demoralising this form of resistance is for changemakers, particularly as they will have already overcome resistance to make the change in the first place:

> *Perhaps the most severe and demoralizing form of institutionalized resistance experienced by advocates of fundamental change is to see hard won accomplishments dismantled by organizational decision makers. This occurs when a policy or program that has been initiated is rescinded, shut down, deprived of resources or otherwise rendered ineffective. At times repression also results in the termination of a change advocate's role or position in the organization. (p. 56)*

Additional examples of repression could include removing bespoke sexual violence procedures and returning to generalised misconduct procedures, reducing or removing funding for specialist counselling despite the service maintaining a waiting list and successful outcomes or reducing or removing funding for training for students or staff.

Repression is easy to identify once it has occurred; however, it may be difficult to anticipate or notice until it has happened. Changemakers attempting to prevent and respond to sexual violence are not implementing one change. To effectively change the culture that perpetuates sexual violence, multiple changes across varying levels of the organisation must occur. Therefore, once a change is made, the changemaker is focused on the next goal. One way to mitigate for repression is to closely monitor changes that have been implemented and to utilise a network of allies and champions to continue to support the changes made.

Backlash

Backlash is an active form of resistance that is attacking or aggressive in manner. Examples of backlash may include bullying, harassing and/or creating a hostile work environment for those working on the change initiative (Bedera, 2023). It may be blocking promotion opportunities for changemakers or even pressuring them to resign (Agócs, 1997; Colpitts, 2020), which could be considered *constructive unfair dismissal* (ACAS, 2021). Backlash can include attacking the credibility of the changemakers by questioning their motives (Flood et al., 2021). Due to the gendered nature of this work, anti-feminist backlash is common. Feminist academics may be automatically discredited in participating in the change initiative as seen as biased – rather than in comparison, seen as resources to lead on change initiatives related to gender equality (Colpitts, 2020). Changemakers and activists who identify as victim-survivors may be discredited and seen as biased or sidelined as a special interest group – despite having lived experience that can help create survivor-centred policies. An overt and violent example of backlash occurred in 2016 when the editor of the student newspaper for a

Canadian university reported on a naked pub crawl that was organised by a student society. She discussed rape culture on campus and spoke about witnessing students 'eating pubic hair, eating a donut off another team member's penis, piercing a clitoris and encouraging team members to have sex with the judges of the Vet's Tour' (Schnurr, 2016). In response to her report, she received sexist, racist and Islamophobic harassment and threats to rape and murder her. At the time of reporting on the event itself and the subsequent violent backlash towards this student editor, the university provided no comment (Schnurr, 2016). Clearly, providing no comment is a far from neutral act.

Backlash can be formal or informal and is hugely damaging to the cause, the changemaker and victim-survivors. Without leadership and accountability, backlash can occur, and the culture which perpetuates sexual violence is strengthened.

STEP 4: IDENTIFY THE POTENTIAL MOTIVATION FOR THE RESISTANCE

There are many motivations for why institutions and individuals resist change to prevent and respond to sexual violence in universities. Some motivations stem from ignorance, some stem from individual experiences, some stem from competing priorities. Some motivations are malicious; some are benign in motivation – although not in impact. In this section, we will highlight four potential categories for types of motivation which may lead to resistance. These are not exhaustive but may provide examples of the motivation that we can more easily recognise and work with as changemakers.

The Tired

This is not everyone's cause. There are many people who care deeply about something they want to fix in the world. Climate change, racism, ableism, homophobia, transphobia, child abuse, animal cruelty, gun laws (for our American colleagues), poverty, hunger, access to clean water and the list goes on. This creates fatigue.

Whether that is compassion fatigue or just general fatigue – humans only have so much energy to give. Between working, having a personal life and caring about their cause, not everyone has energy to give to another issue. It can be emotionally draining to take on caring about another negative problem in our community. For those of us who care passionately about this issue, it is important that we recognise that in the same way we may not have the capacity to offer energy to another cause at the same level, the individual we approach may be in a similar position. Therefore, we can offer empathy and understanding to those who may not be as ready to give their full attention to this issue. We do not have to convince everyone to make this their cause. It is also important to note that for primary and secondary survivors with personal lived experiences connected to sexual violence, they too may be tired and asking them to take this on may be too much at that point in time. It is not necessary for you to know if someone is a survivor as it is their choice whether they share that. Some survivors may actively engage to support the work, and others may not be in a position to do so.

The Tired can still support the initiative. However, as change-makers, we need to have a variety of options for how people can support this work, so that people can engage in a way that keeps them safe and supports work–life balance. For example, one person may have the capacity to attend monthly meetings focused on the institution's strategic work to address sexual violence, while another person has capacity to ensure leaflets and posters for the local rape crisis service are available in the communal areas of the department. Both are supporting the work, but at quite different levels based on what is appropriate for them. Both are equally needed.

Change fatigue can occur in organisations that are frequently altering direction, making large structural change, e.g. following voluntary severance schemes or redundancies to reduce business costs or implementing new technology. Just because the organisation has change fatigue does not mean that change cannot be successful. It simply means that careful consideration needs to be made to implement change in the right way at the right time working with staff and students empathically recognising the demands of such contributions especially perhaps in terms of the emotional labour of working on such changes.

The Benign

We see this category of The Benign as those who are not actually against the change initiative in principle, like The Tired, yet due to competing priorities and limited resource, they do not see how the change initiative could be implemented; therefore, they resist the change altogether. The Benign individual may be spinning too many plates and may not have the capacity to take on something new. They may have a set budget that cannot be changed until the following budget planning process which significantly stalls the change initiative. Their diary may be full, and even getting time to discuss the initiative with them may be a barrier.

The Benign can still support the initiative. Similar to working with The Tired, it is useful to find what capacity or resource they do have and help demonstrate how their engagement at that level can support the project. It can also be useful to seek commitment for when additional capacity or resource becomes available that this is allocated to the project if they are supportive.

The Benign institution, where we use the word benign very lightly, has finite resource and may allow competing priorities to take precedence over sexual violence prevention and response. Key here is developing a strong business case for why this needs to be priority and is in the best interest of the university as a business, specifically.

The Ignorant

Ignorance, meaning lacking knowledge or awareness, is a reality when discussing issues of sexual violence. Many people's under-standings of sexual violence – how it works, who is a victim, who is a perpetrator, what reports are true or false – are based on societal rape myths. Even those who have been subjected to sexual violence can have a narrowed view of how sexual violence works based on their own experience and/or internalised rape myths. These myths are pervasive and hugely damaging. Unlike other subjects, people often have very emotive opinions on the issue of sexual violence. These, often, incorrect views or unrepresentative views of how sexual violence works mean that decision-making on change initiatives can be impacted. The Ignorant can lack understanding of sexual violence or have internalised rape myth acceptance which causes resistance.

The Ignorant institution can also lack an awareness of how sexual violence impacts universities; however, given the shift in sector guidance in 2016 (UUK, 2016; UUK & Pinsent Masons, 2016) and the OfS (2021) *Statement of Expectations*, it is hard to justify university leadership feigning ignorance to these issues.

Finally, both individuals and the institution can resist the change if they do not have enough information about the change initiative, if there is uncertainty about what change will occur or if there is conflicting information (Warrick, 2023). The helpful way to deal with ignorance is to educate through clear communication which sets out arguments for the change and explains what the change will be. In the next step, we provide useful tips on how to raise awareness, dispel rape myths and build the case for change.

The Malicious

The Malicious are actively against the change initiative as they do not support preventing or responding to sexual violence, and they want to maintain the status quo. Sometimes, such individuals may have personal histories of subjecting others to sexual violence of one kind or another. Thus, addressing the issue puts them in a state of dissonance. For those in positions of power, shifting the status quo can be seen as a threat to their position. Even if they may agree with the change on some level, politically, they may fear repercussions for supporting the change. This can be seen when HEIs choose not to engage in sexual violence prevention work for fear of the purported 'reputational damage' that is predicated upon the argument that the exposure of sexual violence is worse than not doing something about it. We think that ultimately, the latter is far worse than the former. Best to be transparent. A failure of transparency can contribute to underestimating the extent of the problem. It can also lead to subsequent exposes, and in addition to any exposed case of sexual violence, the story also becomes linked to the lack of integrity in the organisation associated with a culture of 'cover up'.

Flood et al. (2018) offer examples of sources of resistance including (1) sexist and violence-supportive attitudes and norms, (2) the defence of privilege where dominant groups feel threatened by change which supports minority groups, and (3) the denial of privilege which is the rejection of the claim that women are disadvantaged by sexual violence and men are privileged. Some individuals sympathise with perpetrators believing rape myths that are victim-blaming absolving, or at least providing mitigation for, the perpetrator of guilt for their actions. Others are led by *himpathy* (mentioned earlier), which is a concept coined by Kate Manne (2021). In terms of sexual violence, it is best defined as 'the disproportionate or inappropriate sympathy extended to a male perpetrator over his similarly, or less privileged, female targets in cases of sexual assault, harassment, and other misogynistic behaviour', (p. 36). These internalised views can result in resistance to any prevention and response work. We also must note that there are employees who perpetrate sexual violence themselves (Bull & Rye, 2018; NUS, 2018). Ultimately, if someone believes their self-interest is threatened or that the change will cause adverse effects to them, they may well respond with resistance (Warrick, 2023).

Key to working with The Malicious is highlighting how preventing and responding to sexual violence is in the best interest of all students and employees and for the university as a business. And this is exemplified in cases which are subsequently 'exposed'.

STEP 5: STRATEGISE

Yes, there are people who do not support this work because the status quo supports their position of power. Yes, there are people who do not support this work because their view of sexual violence is based upon rape myths. But not everyone is malicious. Not everyone is ignorant. Some are simply tired and protecting themselves. So how do we push through resistance with such varied reasons for resistance to begin with? Identifying motivations of resistance will not always be easy or possible. So having a range of potential solutions and strategies to push though different forms of resistance is key.

It is likely you will face multiple forms of resistance to the change initiative; therefore, you will need to use a combination of strategies to push through the resistance you face. We offer 10 strategies for consideration. These are not exhaustive but provide key strategies we and others (Agócs, 1997; Colpitts, 2020; VicHealth, 2018) have found useful and effective in overcoming resistance tactics.

Strategy 1: Build a Network of Allies and Champions

You cannot and should not do this work alone. When developing your change initiative, it is incredibly important to create a network of allies and champions from internal and external stakeholders and partners. Internal stakeholders may include student groups, survivor groups, staff networks, academics with expertise in the area and even local branches of Trade Unions. External partners who can support internal change can include the local rape crisis centre, sexual assault referral centre, public health and the police. Changemakers can also benefit from joining national HE networks aimed at sharing good practice and acting as a sounding board for problem-solving.

When building your internal network of allies, strategic placement of these individuals is key – aim to build a network that connects to the various levels of the institution where peer change agents can be useful. The most effective allies and champions will be internally motivated to progress the change and have informal influence, respect, social power and credibility among their peers (Li et al., 2023).

Building this network can be a hybrid of formal and informal champions and allies. You may have an operational or working group dedicated to addressing sexual violence, where members are formally agreeing to champion this work through their membership on the group. However, beware of those who were 'volun-told' rather than volunteered to join. You may also have informal champions who support the work, but not through formal channels. For example, someone who has a large network at the university also forwards advertisements for sexual violence prevention training to the various networks they are part of within the organisation. This is not formally part of their role, and it is not time-consuming action, but as your ally in this work, you know you can rely on them to help get the word out about training outside of the formal communication channels you may use.

The student voice is immensely powerful and partnering with them is key. Dickinson and Blake (2023) present the work of the National Union of Students (NUS) Women's Officers from 2009 to 2018 that put sexual violence in HE on the agenda in the United Kingdom and was a catalyst for the sector to consider this work. The Students' Union, student representatives, student groups and individual students are some of the strongest allies you can work with on your change initiative. Simply put 'the work of student representatives is vital to the success of change within the Higher Education sector,' (Dickinson & Blake, 2023, p. 43). To support strategies on working with students to champion this work, Blake and Dickinson (2023) outline types of support and risk mitigation steps that should be considered to ensure that student and peer-led work is impactful and safe. Indeed, the whole area of getting university leadership teams to acknowledge that we have a problem of sexual violence at universities has been led by student activists in particular. Without the work and personal sacrifice of student activists, it is highly unlikely that university leaders would be even purporting to take 'sexual violence very seriously'. Given the sizeable proportion of university finances that come through university tuition fees despite its problems, it does potentially result in more influence for the student voice – a voice that has been very vocal on sexual violence as indicated in the work of Dickinson and Blake.

Finally, allies can also include those working on other social change initiatives or training programmes. Building a network of allies with other changemakers means you can support each other and seek joint action where possible (VicHealth, 2018).

Strategy 2: Create Short-Term and Long-Term Goals

When developing your change initiative, it is helpful to identify the short-term and long-term goals of the project. Culture change takes time. However, there are tangible small goals that can be met immediately which will bring you closer to achieving the long-term goal. Identify the best strategy to reach each short-term goal. Remember, not every step in your change initiative must be made by committee decision. Take action to progress the change initiative to the point that it needs the committee decision. For example, one short-term goal may be to get buy-in with the Students' Union (SU) where you already know the student representatives and staff are likely to be receptive. This may be a short-term goal because you do not expect resistance and their buy-in does not require university committee agreement. So, formalising their support for the project can be done before wider work begins. Alternatively, if you anticipate resistance from the SU, then a short-term goal might be to set up series of meetings where you can speak to key individuals within the SU to present your arguments for why the change initiative is needed and how the SU can support this.

Breaking up the work into small achievable goals can help sustain energy for the work and allow you to demonstrate progress on the change initiative. Some universities will use 'busyness' as a form of resistance whereby they take on tick box or soft actions to be seen to be doing something, without making meaningful change (Hodgins & O'Connor, 2021). Therefore, it is important to confirm how each small goal leads to the larger piece of work which ultimately will be aimed at changing the culture to prevent and respond to sexual violence.

Strategy 3: Develop a Business Case Noting Potential Resistance Tactics

Writing a business case for the change initiative is key. The business case should outline the key arguments for why this change is needed, the risks of not implementing the change and the benefits of doing so, the required budget or resource and how the change initiative supports the HEI's strategic vision. The business case can also highlight anticipated forms of resistance and how the changemaker hopes to mitigate for this seeking senior leadership support to challenge any resistance met. It should also include estimated timeframes and planned milestones for the project.

When outlining the arguments for why this change is needed, focus on the moral, ethical and legal reasons why the change is required highlighting existing legislation and regulation if relevant. Consider constructive criticism of the change initiative and ensure the evidence and arguments for change are as effective as possible (Agócs, 1997). Where appropriate, you can use victim-survivor stories with permission as case studies to help connect your audience with these reasons. Some have already made stories public for the use of building the case for change and training purposes, see, e.g. Drouet and Gerrard-Abbott (2023). Present the arguments from internal and external stakeholders to demonstrate support for the change.

When highlighting the risks of not implementing the change, it is useful to outline the legal, financial and reputational risks connecting to the strategic risk register where possible. When presenting anticipated resistance to the change, use the language of the resistance tactics explaining how these could present during the project. For example, if you anticipate appeasement, note this in the business case and request clear timeframes for action, resource and where to escalate concerns if these are not met. In the business case, highlight the long-term goal is meaningful cultural change which requires commitment beyond tick box exercises – outlining how this can be achieved.

Strategy 4: Monitor, Assess and Report on Progress and Resistance

A key strategy to overcoming resistance is monitoring and reporting on progress and resistance. Feedback loops at all stages of the change initiative can help monitor progress and identify emerging issues quickly (VicHealth, 2018). Through the business case, you will likely have a timeline set for meeting your short-term and long-term goals. You can track progress using a Blue, Red, Amber, Green (BRAG) traffic light system (Harrin, 2023):

- Blue – Project/action completed.

- Red – Project/action is delayed or over budget, or there is an issue that needs escalating as the changemaker cannot resolve it.

- Amber – Project/action has missed some targets/milestones, or there is notable resistance from stakeholders, but the target date/budget is not impacted.

- Green – Project/action on track, no issues identified.

By using a BRAG tracker, you can clearly monitor progress on the project and report on successes and barriers, including resistance tactics. You can keep management or senior leadership updated on the progress and note when and what type of resistance is impacting advancement.

Implementing change is difficult, but that is not where it ends. Work is required to sustain the change otherwise repression can be used. It is important to have a plan for evaluation of the change initiative too. This can be particularly useful in maintaining the business case for the initiative if it is showing successful results or for making changes if the results are not positive. This can be particularly useful in mitigating for repression. Collect and share data, e.g. the numbers of cases that are needed in support of the business case for more financial investment in this area.

Strategy 5: Challenge Rape Myth Acceptance and Himpathy

In training, in formal committee papers, in key messages of communication plans – every opportunity to discuss the change initiative is an opportunity to educate the audience and advance the cause. Communicate the importance of recognising unconscious bias and the impact this has on the change initiative (VicHealth, 2018). Recognising the various motivations for resistance include ignorance and opposition, it is important to directly address rape myth acceptance and himpathy which may be motivating the resistance tactics used. All rape myths seek to shift blame to the victims and absolve perpetrators of guilt. Himpathy seeks to privilege men to the detriment of women (Manne, 2021). Therefore, when presenting arguments for the change initiative, it is useful to highlight these attitudes and the impact of these before encountering them. It is important to model the use of neutral and factual language using Reporting and Responding Party rather than accuser, alleged victim, complainant, alleged perpetrator and accused. Some of these terms when derived from criminal justice-based systems can beget a criminal justice–based approach in terms of e.g. the levels of evidence needed; this is to be avoided in view of the civil context. However, when educating and speaking of those who have been subjected to sexual violence, it is important to use clear terminology like victim-survivor or of those who have committed sexual violence, perpetrator.

Strategy 6: Create Opportunities for Discussion and Debate in Moderated Spaces

Creating a culture that encourages safe and open dialogue to discuss concerns is crucial in supporting change initiatives (Warrick, 2023). People can have strong opinions about sexual violence which may be influenced by whether they have any lived experience related to this. As highlighted in the motivations section, there will be many reasons why someone resists this change. Therefore, it is helpful to create opportunities for safe discussion and debate where individuals can make comments, voice concerns or ask questions and be heard without judgement (VicHealth, 2018; Wiggins-Romesburg & Githens, 2018). In this type of setting, attitudes and beliefs which support rape myth acceptance and himpathy can be challenged safely using facts and stories in a facilitated conversation. The way this is facilitated is crucial as confronting negative attitudes in a negative way can increase resistance and deepen bias (Wiggins-Romesburg & Githens, 2018). 'When people can have their say and talk about their own beliefs (and biases and fears) without being shut down, they are more likely to be open to other messages,' (VicHealth, 2018, p. 14). Therefore, facilitated conversations should have established ground rules to support safe discussion, changemakers should demonstrate a willingness to listen and be open to constructive criticism, and offer calm responses acknowledging the comment, concerns and questions and responding with facts and evidence where appropriate.

Strategy 7: Accountability

If you have Senior Leader buy-in and the institution has taken the position to support the change initiative, then it is helpful for senior leaders to help mitigate for individual resistance, by communicating expectations and the institution's position. For example, during the COVID-19 pandemic, by necessity organisations permitted working from home. When it was safe to do so, policies changed to allow for hybrid working, and yet some organisations took a view that working from home was no longer permitted. Likewise, if an HEI chooses to implement, for example, a policy that bans relationships between staff and students, whether the employee agrees or not is not up to them. The organisation has set the professional and behavioural standards for their employees. Some elements of addressing individual resistance will be helping someone move through the change process on the journey of building awareness and knowledge; however, some change will be required and exected for employees regardless of personal agreement with the change. Therefore, it is important that this is clearly communicated, and management is given tools to support queries and concerns when these changes are made.

Strategy 8: Create Tailored Communication Plans Based on Audience

We recommend working with your communications team within the organisation to develop a communication plan for communicating the proposed change initiative and progress on the change initiative to different audiences. The communications team will have knowledge of formal and informal communication channels available and be able to offer advice on how to use them. The communication plan should be developed with careful consideration of what, how and how much information is shared with each audience as information overload can dilute the communication effectiveness (Warrick, 2023). For each audience, you will likely need to clarify the reasons for the change, what the change will be, how the change will impact the audience (student or employee) and how the student or employee can contact the changemaker to provide feedback or ask questions (Warrick, 2023). The communications team may help develop assets or materials which can help spread the message about the project. You may wish to develop specific messages for groups expected to resist the sexual violence prevention and response work (VicHealth, 2018). Finally, it is helpful to keep the community informed of the progress of the change initiative and invite feedback throughout the process (Warrick, 2023). By keeping students and employees informed of the change progress, this creates a culture of transparency and openness in line with trauma-informed principles as part of a comprehensive institution-wide approach.

Strategy 9: Practise and Support Self-care for Changemakers

Exposure to resistance can increase the changemaker's risk for burnout and have a significant impact on their wellbeing (Colpitts, 2020; Flood et al., 2021). The 11th Revision of the International Classification of Diseases defines burnout as:

> ... a syndrome conceptualized as resulting from chronic workplace stress that has not been successfully managed. It is characterised by three dimensions: 1) feelings of energy depletion or exhaustion; 2) increased mental distance from one's job, or feelings of negativism or cynicism related to one's job; and 3) a sense of ineffectiveness and lack of accomplishment. Burn-out refers specifically to phenomena in the occupational context and should not be applied to describe experiences in other areas of life. (World Health Organization, 2019)

It is important to note that burnout is not directly linked to exposure to trauma but more often connected to experiences of structural oppression and social injustice at work. Separately, we discuss the risks of exposure to vicarious or secondary trauma in Chapter 10.

As regularly facing resistance is expected for changemakers, it is crucial that changemakers are supported. One strategy to mitigate for the risk of burnout and deal with resistance is to practise self-care (VicHealth, 2018). Self-care can include maintaining clear professional and personal boundaries, practising healthy coping skills, seeking support, taking time for mental health days and maintaining a healthy work–life balance. We discuss additional self-care tips in Chapter 10.

Strategy 10: Celebrate Success

One manifestation of human nature can commonly be to notice and focus on negatives and failure. However, when working on pre-vention and response of sexual violence, it is imperative to the health of those working on this and to the health of the project itself, to notice, focus on and celebrate success. When you meet your short-term goal, when you get the 'yes' to a policy change or access to funding from someone unexpected, when your allies and champions progress the cause, when your budget gets approved, when a training receives positive feedback, when a victim-survivor says 'thank you' – celebrate. As you now know you will face resistance, give yourself and your team permission to be proud when things work. Regularly take time to reflect on progress made to date. Remember, two steps forward and one step back is still one step forward. Hold on to that momentum by celebrating it and working to the next short-term goal as you build and progress.

Ultimately, dealing with resistance to initiatives aimed at pre-venting and responding to sexual violence may be one of the most common and difficult aspects of a changemaker's job. We hope through this chapter we have provided tools to identify types and motivations for resistance. Hopefully, you can more clearly identify potential motivations for the lack of support and have practical strategies for tackling the resistance likely to be encountered as an effective changemaker.

📖 Related Resources

- Humphreys, C. J., & Towl, G. J. (2023). We should do something (someday): Identifying and working through resistance to gender-based violence prevention. In C. J. Humphreys & G. J. Towl (Eds.), *Stopping gender-based violence in higher education: Policy, practice, and partnerships*. Routledge.
- Our Watch. (2021). *Change the story: A shared framework for the primary prevention of violence against women in Australia* (2nd ed.). Our Watch.
- VicHealth. (2018). *(En)countering resistance: Strategies to respond to resistance to gender equality initiatives*. Victorian Health Promotion Foundation.

7

DEVELOPING A SEXUAL VIOLENCE POLICY AND PROCEDURE

Universities are expected to have policies that actively address sexual violence (Office for Students, 2021). The policy sets out the comprehensive institution-wide approach establishing the elements of that approach throughout all prevention and response efforts. It defines the expected behaviour for all members of the Higher Education Institution (HEI) community and provides the framework for response to potential policy breaches. The policy becomes part of the contract between the university and its employees and forms part of the terms and conditions of the contract it has with its students as 'consumers'.

One of the risk factors for the perpetration of sexual violence within Higher Education (HE) is a lack of deterrents. Implementing a robust policy that specifically names and defines sexual violence can act as a potential deterrent for those perpetrators who fear being caught and facing consequences. This is important because if it is widely commu nicated that reporting is the new norm and that investigations make a judgement based upon the balance of probabilities, this may powerfully contribute to prevention. It is not enough to craft such policies. What is needed are ongoing communications with the university community. Much of this can be targeted, e.g. around induction week, events organised which are likely to involve much alcohol consumption and fieldwork.

So, a policy alone is not enough. A clear and robust policy needs a clear and transparent procedure that explains to all parties what will occur if a potential breach of policy is reported. 'A complaint procedure is how you learn what to do, where to go, in order to make a complaint. If policies lay out principles, procedures offer paths' (Ahmed, 2021, p. 31). A well-written procedure can reduce barriers to disclosure by communicating in detail each step of the process, so that Reporting Parties can make informed choices, e.g. details on how to make a disclosure and report, what will happen if a Reporting Party makes a disclosure and/or report, what support is available, what interim and precautionary measures may be used, what will happen during an investigation and disciplinary process, and information on the potential outcomes and timeframes.

In this chapter, we discuss the elements of a sexual violence policy and procedure. We offer example definitions to outline forms of misconduct and to define consent. We also consider how to frame the scope of the policy based on sector guidance. In the latter part of this chapter, we describe different parts of a procedure to operationalise the principles outlined in the policy.

POLICY OUTLINE

In this section, we present a sample outline of a policy that includes a procedure with a discussion of the contents of each section. The outline provided are key elements HEIs may wish to include in their policy and procedure but are not an exhaustive list. For example, HEIs may wish to also include statements around the expectations of behaviours of students, staff, contractors and visitors. During the development of a new policy and any substantial changes to an existing policy, we recommend these changes go through a consultation process involving staff, students, any student groups that focus on sexual violence or supporting victim-survivors and relevant external partners (e.g. local rape crisis, sexual assault referral centres and police) prior to implementation. Policies normally require approval at the highest level of HEI governance since they form part of the contracts for students and employees. Procedures which operationalise policies may not require amendments at the same level allowing updates to practice, based on lessons learned, to be implemented more efficiently.

Sample Policy and Procedure Outline

1. Policy Statement and Principles
2. Scope of the Policy
3. Definitions

    3.1. Types of Misconduct

    3.2. Consent

    3.3. Key Terms

4. Support Options

    4.1. Optional Interim Measures

5. Reporting Options
6. Confidentiality and Information Sharing
7. Governance of Policy and Procedure
8. Procedure

    8.1. Disclosure and Reporting

       8.1.1. Risk Assessment

       8.1.2. Optional Precautionary Measures

    8.2. Investigation

    8.3. Adjudication

    8.4. Discipline

    8.5. Review/Appeal

Policy Statement and Principles

At the beginning of the policy, the HEI can provide a policy statement which explains the purpose and reasons for the policy along with outlining key principles that create the foundation for the policy and procedure. The principles should represent the comprehensive institution-wide approach that is trauma-informed, survivor-centred, human rights-based and social justice-based while being intersectional and requiring perpetrator accountability. This is an opportunity to ensure that the policy speaks to all students and staff regardless of identity, so that all members of the community recognise the policy is for them (Donovan & Roberts, 2023). There may be principles that need to be emphasised to connect the policy to any related regulations or disciplinary processes that sit above or outside the policy. In addition, the principles may reflect expectations of an external body that reviews student complaints (e.g. the Office of Independent Adjudicator for Higher Education in England and Wales or 'OIA'). The following are examples of principles that may be considered:

- Acknowledge that anyone can be subjected to sexual violence regardless of their identity and/or protected characteristic, e.g. age, (dis)ability, gender identity, marriage or civil partnership, pregnancy or maternity, race/ethnicity, religion/belief, sex, sexual orientation and/or socioeconomic status or class.

- Acknowledge that sexual violence is gender-based and can be a cause and consequence of gender inequality; victim-survivors are overwhelmingly women, and perpetrators are overwhelmingly men.

- Explicitly state that although women are subjected to sexual violence at disproportionately higher rates, note that individuals of all genders and sexualities can be subjected to sexual violence, and that any victim-survivor of any identity will be offered support.

- Identify that support is available for all victim-survivors regardless of when an incident occurred and their choice to make a formal report.

- Highlight that adult Reporting Parties will be empowered to choose how to take forward a disclosure of sexual violence and that their choice will be respected.

- Explain that sexual violence may be addressed through criminal and/or internal disciplinary processes.

- Note the burden of proof is on the university to determine the outcome of any investigation and disciplinary process.

- Note the civil standard of proof will be used to determine a potential breach of policy.

- Include an amnesty clause that ensures that a Reporting Party will not be disciplined for consuming illicit substances in relation to an incident of sexual violence, and this information will not be used to discredit them during an investigation into sexual violence. This approach is supported by UN Women (2018a) who add, 'Under no circumstances should substance abuse be used as an excuse to blame the victims for the abuse experienced' (p. 15).

Rights of Involved Parties

This section may also highlight the rights of the Reporting and Responding Party, or this may be explained at the start of the procedure section. Procedures should be equitable for all parties (UN Women, 2018b). Both parties should have access to any evidence submitted to the investigation and have a right to respond to any new relevant evidence submitted. Both parties should be permitted to be accompanied to any meetings with university staff/investigators. This may include a peer, staff member or students' union representative. Some institutions may allow a family member to attend or an external support person such as an Independent Sexual Violence Advisor. Few institutions will allow a legal representative to attend with either party as the institution is conducting an internal investigation into a potential breach of policy and not a legal or criminal proceeding. We do not recommend the involvement of legal representatives. There is no legal obligation to allow legal representatives into proceedings. Individuals who accompany either party are expected to provide support, not present evidence. Both parties should receive the outcome of the investigation and any further disciplinary process on the same day where possible in separate meetings. In Chapter 12, we argue that they should have equal rights in having the option to appeal the final decision, and that they should both receive information on the outcome and any sanctions applied at the end of the process.

Scope of the Policy

The scope of the policy needs to be clearly outlined, as it will determine when the HEI can take action. Sexual violence and related forms of gender-based violence (GBV) can occur in person, online or through other means of communication. A comprehensive institution-wide policy will apply to all students and staff while individuals are members of or affiliated with the university regardless of the location of the incident. It can also apply to visitors while they are on campus or attending the HEI's events. The institution can respond to potential breaches of policy that have happened since the Responding Party joined the university if the Responding Party is still a member of the institution. The OIA is clear that an HEI can take action in the following:

> … *where the behaviour has affected: The provider itself; A student or employee of the provider; Others visiting, working or studying at the provider; or A member of the public [and] in response to misconduct which: Happens during off-campus activities such as placements and field trips; Happens whilst studying at partner organisations, such as associate schools; Affects the provider's reputation in the local community or more widely; or Happens on social media. (OIA, 2018a, p. 22)*

Policies that only respond to incidents that occur on campus will fail to create safe learning environments for students as it is already confirmed that most incidents of sexual violence and GBV will take place in someone's home. Therefore, a policy that is limited to campus locations will be disproportionately applied to students who live on campus, which will be a small portion of the student population. Perpetrators who are aware of the limits of any such campus-only policy will more likely perpetrate sexual violence off campus. Elsewhere in this book, we make the case for addressing student sexual violence independently of the geographical location of the incident. From a trauma-informed approach, it will be expected that disclosures and reports of sexual violence will be delayed considerably, and therefore, a comprehensive institution-wide policy will not have a time limit after any such incidents on when Reporting Parties can report.

Should HEIs Cover Domestic Abuse and Stalking in Policy as Forms of Misconduct?

Yes, and many HEIs in the United Kingdom already do (Khan et al., 2023). Research conducted by the Honour Abuse Research Matrix (HARM) network found that in UK universities, 185,833 people (23,760 staff and 163,073 students) were subjected to domestic abuse annually (Khan, 2021). The Domestic Abuse Act 2021 statutory guidance applies to HEIs meaning universities have a duty of care to safeguard victim-survivors. Nicole Jacobs, Domestic Abuse Commissioner for England and Wales, said:

> Universities have a duty of care to safeguard victims of domestic abuse, but often, the appropriate safeguarding procedures have not been in place to support and protect victims. I am pleased to see that the evaluation of the 'Domestic Abuse Policy Guidance for UK Universities' has shown that as a result of the guidance, more universities are proactively strengthening support for staff and students by creating new or updating existing policy, creating new training, and issuing domestic abuse communications to staff and students. (2023, p. 3)

(*Continued*)

Domestic abuse, stalking and sexual violence are intrinsically linked as forms of GBV which are often perpetrated by a current or former partner of the victim-survivor. These may be arguably the two highest risk (i.e. homicide and suicide risk) forms of GBV present within university communities. The Office of National Statistics highlights these as forms of 'Intimate violence' defined as:

> ... *a collective term used to refer to a number of different forms of physical and non-physical abuse consisting of partner abuse, family abuse, sexual assault and stalking. The term reflects the intimate nature either of the victim-perpetrator relationship or of the abuse itself. (p. 95)*

Whether domestic abuse and stalking are included within a sexual violence policy, a separate domestic abuse policy (as modelled by Khan, 2021) or captured within a GBV policy (as modelled for Scottish universities in the *Equally Safe in Higher Education Tool Kit*), domestic abuse and stalking should be included as forms of misconduct, i.e. behaviour not tolerated within the university community.

Definitions

The language used in the policy will shape how sexual violence is discussed in the institution. Language is a powerful tool in impacting culture change and can affect how the policy is received. Gender-nonspecific language in a policy is recommended so that students and staff of all genders recognise the policy is available and applicable to them; however, this should not diminish efforts to identify sexual violence as GBV and using this lens for prevention work. As noted previously, institutions may wish to use the language of sexual violence or GBV to frame their policy work depending on their context and sector guidance.

Should We Use Criminal Language?

At the time of writing, the Office for Students (OfS) has not yet provided their response to the consultation on the *New Approach to Regulating Harassment and Sexual Misconduct in English Higher Education*. As part of the consultation, the OfS has suggested requiring the use of criminal justice terms and definitions for rape and sexual assault (2023). Within prevention work such as campaigning and training, we fully support the use of criminal language. However, within a policy describing misconduct, we caution the use of criminal justice terms as it has significant ramifications. If the university is investigating a breach described as 'sexually touching another person without their consent' compared to 'sexual assault', the focus on misconduct or a breach of policy is easier to maintain. Universities do not have the authority to determine if someone has committed a criminal offence of sexual assault, so to use the same language within a policy breach may cause backlash. For example, the use of the civil standard of proof may be challenged and procedures may be forced to become more adversarial moving into 'criminal justice drift' as defined by Cowan and Munro (2021). Responding Parties may be advised by legal representatives to 'no comment' internal disciplinary proceedings as to not incriminate themselves. There may be more willingness to allow legal representation in disciplinary hearings as finding sexual assault as a form of misconduct may be seen as having potential impact on a Responding Party's future career, and outcomes may face increased legal challenges. Finally, there may be even more resistance to sharing the outcomes and sanctions of disciplinary processes with Reporting Parties when using criminal justice language. That being said, we do strongly recommend the use of the legal definition of consent as the foundation of discussing consent in all prevention and response initiatives.

Types of Misconduct

This section of the policy should clearly outline and define types of behaviour that would be considered misconduct or a breach of the policy. This will provide clarity to members of the HEI community on conduct standards. It will enable investigators to clarify the scope of their investigation by providing clear definitions of types of misconduct that may be considered.

We recommend refraining from using criminal justice terms *where possible*, as the institution is unable to find against a criminal offence. The following definition examples build from Durham University (2017–2024) and Goldsmiths, University of London (2019–2024), publicly available sexual violence policies. Where appropriate, we include explanations of why specific definitions are suggested.

1. **Sexual violence and misconduct**: any non-consensual act of a sexual nature. This can be used as an umbrella term to capture a range of behaviours; however, additional examples of forms of sexual violence should be outlined in the policy itself to aid in clarifying behaviours to all members of the community and to support investigations. Information can be added here to explain that the sexual violence and misconduct could happen in person or through other forms of communication, e.g. online, and could occur on or off campus.

   - **Non-consensual sexual contact**: sexually touching another person without their consent, as experienced by the recipient.

   - **Non-consensual sexual act**: engaging or attempting to engage in a sexual act with another individual without consent or making someone engage in a sexual act on another without their consent.

   - **Sexual harassment**: unwanted and unwelcome words, conduct or behaviour of a sexual nature that has the purpose or effect of creating (or that could create) an intimidating, embarrassing, hostile, degrading, humiliating or offensive environment for the recipient. This may include one incident or a pattern of behaviours. The behaviour itself does not have to be sexual in nature for the recipient to experience this as sexual harassment, e.g. threatening or coercive behaviour following rejection of romantic advances. The behaviour does not have to be directed to the Reporting Party; the Responding Party does not have to intend to cause harassment (OIA, 2018b). The impact on the Reporting Party is the focus and whether a reasonable person in the position of the Reporting Party would find the behaviour harassing.

2. **Technology-facilitated sexual violence (TFSV):** The following examples of TFSV use definitions offered by Universities UK (2019a) and Humphreys (2021).

- **Online sexual harassment:** offensive, degrading, intimidating and/or humiliating unwanted conduct of a sexual nature through social media, email or group/private online messages. This can include gender-based hate speech, 'slut-shaming', denigration, threats and cyberbullying. Gender-based hate speech can intersect with other forms of hate speech targeting the individual's race or other protected characteristics.

- **Cyberstalking:** repeated and deliberate use of the internet and other electronic communication tools to engage in persistent, unwanted communication intending to frighten, intimidate, harass someone or to spy on someone.

- **Image-based sexual abuse:** recording or sharing sexual or intimate photos or videos without the consent of the person pictured or threatening to share private sexual images without consent.

- **Upskirting:** filming or photographing under a person's clothes without their consent to capture images of their body or underwear.

- **Fakeporn:** digitally altering images/videos of an individual to represent them in a sexual way without their consent.

- **Cyberflashing:** Sending an unsolicited genital image to another person.

3. **Indecent exposure:** inappropriately showing one's genitalia to another person. This can include directing this behaviour to a specific person and/or more generally with no targeted person, but where individuals are subjected to this without their consent.

4. **Stalking:** unwanted, repeated, fixated, obsessive and/or controlling behaviours that are intrusive and make the recipient distressed or scared.

5. **Domestic/dating abuse and/or coercive or controlling behaviour:** any incident or pattern of incidents of controlling, coercive, threatening behaviour, violence or abuse between those who are, or have been, intimate partners regardless of gender or sexuality. This can include, but is not limited to, psychological, physical, sexual, economic, emotional, identity and/or spiritual abuse.

6. **Promoting rape culture:** Arranging or participating in events which may reasonably be assumed to cause degradation and humiliation to those who have been subjected to sexual violence, for example, social events or initiations themed to promote or are underpinned by rape myths. It is important to acknowledge that groups of individuals or organised groups such as teams or societies can also perpetrate sexual violence. Examples of group misconduct may be planning or attending inappropriately themed events aimed at degrading individuals subjected to sexual violence or initiations that involve non-consensual (often coerced) sexual acts. Examples seen across the UK sector in recent years include a rugby team planning a party where directions were given on how to spike women's drinks (Sherriff, 2013b) or a rugby team playing 'It's not rape if...' (Sherriff, 2013a). Other examples that may come under this type of misconduct would be Jimmy Saville parties and themed socials such as Vicars and Tarts, CEOs and Corporate Hoes, Golf Pros and Tennis Hoes, Pimps and Hoes, and Geeks and Sluts.

7. **Abuse of power:** Abuse of power enacted by any employee in their relations with students or abuse of power between

students who have unequal institutional power. Examples include grooming/boundary blurring, sexual invitations, comments and non-verbal communication with sexual content or overtones, creation of inappropriate sexual atmosphere and promised resources in exchange for sexual interaction.

8. **Acts of force:** physical force, threats, intimidation or coercion that takes away an individual's freedom to consent to sexual activity. Physical force may include the intentional physical impact upon another, strangulation/choking/suffocation, physical restraint and/or the use of a weapon or an object as a weapon. A threat is when there is a negative consequence if the individual said no. Intimidation is the use of power or authority to influence someone's decision and/or physically being larger or stronger than someone where they fear physical violence if they say no. Coercion is when someone is pressured unreasonably for sex, which can include manipulation.

9. **Acts to incapacitate:** spiking drinks or forcing someone to drink and/or use substances (legal or illegal drugs) to take away an individual's capacity to consent to sexual activity.

10. **Complicity:** any act that knowingly helps, promotes or encourages any form of sexual violence by another individual. Complicity may not be reported at high rates as individuals may not realise that another person was complicit in the sexual violence. However, this should be included in policies and may be particularly apparent in group sexual misconduct. Examples of complicity include:

   • Student A is a first-year student who joined the football team. They are holding their first party of the year, and Student A and the other first years have been tasked with ensuring that all the women that attend the party have drinks when they walk in the door and that their cups are never empty. Student A is pouring quadruples and has been told to make sure he gets as 'many girls as drunk as possible' and to escort the prettiest ones upstairs to the bedrooms of teammates. Student A agrees because he wants to be part of the team.

- Student B is bartending tonight, and his housemate Student C asked him to slip a pill into Student C's girlfriend's drink when they come in later that evening. Student C explains that his girlfriend has been nervous about having sex, but he knows she wants it and just needs a little something extra to relax. Student B agrees to do this.

11. **Retaliation:** any adverse actions against another person, including, but not limited to, harassment, threats, intimidation or coercion, made in response to someone disclosing or reporting any form of sexual violence. It is necessary to include this as a type of misconduct, and this should be clearly communicated to Responding Parties and witnesses involved in investigations at the start of their involvement in a case. Ensuring Reporting Parties that retaliation is a form of misconduct that will be addressed with further disciplinary action can reduce barriers to reporting and create a safer environment.

Consent

1. **Consent:** the agreement by choice where the individual has both the freedom and capacity to make that choice. Consent can be withdrawn at any time before or during a sexual act. Consent is specific to the type of sexual act at the time of the act. Consent cannot be assumed even in an intimate relationship. The first line of this definition represents the definition of consent in law (CPS, n.d.). Although we argue that in general we should steer away from using criminal offence terms, the consent definition is thorough and clear; therefore, we argue using this especially because it will help students understand consent in the wider community as well and assists with investigations as explained in Chapter 11.

    - **Freedom:** For consent to be able to be given, the individual, along with having the capacity to give consent, must also be able to freely choose to participate in the specific sexual act. A person is not free to choose if they are threatened, intimidated, forced, coerced and/or if there is an abuse of power present.

    - **Capacity:** For consent to be able to be given, the individual, along with being free to give consent, must have the capacity to give consent. Capacity means an individual is physically and/or mentally able to make a choice without their judgement being impaired, and they understand the consequences of that choice. An individual is incapacitated when asleep, unconscious or in a state of intermittent consciousness, or any other state of unawareness that a sexual act may be occurring or state where their judgement is impaired due to substance – including alcohol, medication and/or illicit drugs. In England and Wales, the age of consent for sexual activity is 16 years old and to take/have taken and/or send/receive intimate images is 18 years old.

- **Agreement:** For consent to be able to be given, the individual, along with being free to give consent and having the capacity to give consent, must then agree to the choice by providing words and/or non-verbal actions that demonstrate consent. Examples of consent may be saying 'yes' and actively participating. Examples of when consent is not given may include not moving/being frozen, not actively participating, saying 'no', silence, saying 'maybe?'.

Key Terms

As noted in the introduction, language within policy should be neutral. Terms like complainant, alleged perpetrator and complaint are inherently biased and will invite criticism into proceedings. We recommend using the following terms that, currently, remain neutral.

- **Reporting Party:** individual disclosing or reporting to the institution that they have been subjected to any form of sexual violence.

- **Responding Party:** individual who has been reported to have committed any form of sexual violence.

- **Disclosure:** telling a member of staff about an incident of sexual violence.

- **Report:** telling the University and/or Police about an incident of sexual violence for the purposes of further action being taken through investigation procedures.

- **Burden of proof:** The burden of proof is on the university. This means that it is not the responsibility of the Reporting Party to prove they were subjected to sexual violence, nor is it the responsibility of the Responding Party to prove they did not commit sexual violence. It is the responsibility of the university to evidence the outcome that is determined (OIA, 2018a).

- **Standard of proof:** The civil standard of proof is used to determine a breach of policy, meaning the evidence will need to show that it is more likely than not that the behaviour occurred for a breach of policy to be determined.

Standard of proof means the level of proof required to make a decision (OIA, 2018a). When considering whether there is a breach of policy, we, along with UN Women (2018a), Universities UK (2016), Pinsent Masons and Universities UK (2016), Advance HE (Baird et al., 2019) and the White House Task Force to Protect Students from Sexual Assault (2017), recommend that investigations, adjudication and disciplinary decisions are made only using the civil standard of proof also referred to as the 'balance of probabilities', 'more likely than not' or the 'the preponderance of evidence'. This is a finding that there is a preponderance of evidence by 51% that what was reported and investigated happened. A clear statement that the civil standard of proof is used to determine a breach of policy can be included in the principles section of a policy.

The Health and Social Care Act 2008 requires that the civil standard of proof be used in fitness to practise procedures. The OIA (2018a) expects that the civil standard be used in disciplinary cases which may lead to fitness to practise proceedings against a student. Therefore, if this is the standard used for students studying to enter regulated professions, it seems appropriate that all students be treated to the same standard.

The CJS uses beyond reasonable doubt as the criminal standard of proof to determine whether a criminal offence has occurred. The university is separate from the CJS. It can never determine whether a criminal offence has occurred. The only remit is to determine whether there is a breach of policy and therefore a breach of contract. Therefore, the only standard of proof that is available is the civil standard. This same standard of proof should be used throughout the institution for all types of complaints, discipline and grievances for students and staff.

Individuals may argue that the criminal standard of proof should be used in sexual violence cases. It must be emphasised that the institution only has authority to determine a breach of internal policy. We cannot send students to prison if they are found to be 'guilty' of a policy breach, and rightly so – such matters are for the courts. This reflects how sexual violence at all levels is dealt with in other sectors outside of the CJS. The institution does not have the necessary capabilities to determine an outcome that is beyond reasonable doubt (e.g. no ability to process forensic medical or electronic evidence), and as such, the application of this standard of proof would inherently lead to an unsafe outcome. In the same way that a case can end in criminal court and be taken to civil court using the balance of probabilities, HEIs can use the balance of probabilities to determine a breach of an internal policy.

Support Options

It is important that the policy clearly outlines options for support available to Reporting Parties who disclose and/or report sexual violence. Explaining in the policy how support is accessed, where Reporting Parties will be referred to (e.g. Sexual Assault Referral Centre) and key timelines for accessing support, is necessary. Demonstrating these options in the policy will help reduce barriers to reporting, as Reporting Parties will recognise that they can receive support.

Interim measures are temporary measures used to support Reporting and Responding Parties and should be decided in collaboration with the individual who requires them. Interim measures may cover support in the areas of housing, academic progress, finance, welfare, specialist support, access to facilities and more. Examples of interim measures are provided in Chapter 10.

These are separate from precautionary measures that are used to mitigate risk. Throughout this book, we highlight the impact that sexual violence has on victim-survivors. It is necessary to recognise that an allegation of sexual violence can have a significant emotional impact on the Responding Party causing feelings of desperation, anger and even suicidal ideation (Murphy & Van Brunt, 2017). Support measures should be offered to Responding Parties during an investigation and disciplinary process (if applicable).

Reporting Options

Individuals subjected to any form of sexual violence should be provided with options to report their experiences. The policy should outline what the reporting options are and cross reference to any reporting procedure. Normally, HEIs reporting options will include:

- reporting to the police;

- reporting to the university;

- reporting anonymously;

- reporting to the police and university;

- seeking support only.

CONFIDENTIALITY AND INFORMATION SHARING

The policy should clearly explain confidentiality and information sharing and any limits on this based on the Data Protection Act 2018 and General Data Protection Regulation (GDPR) legislation and internal privacy statements. The threshold for when confidentiality may be breached should be noted, e.g. for legal obligations, safeguarding purposes in cases involving those under 18 years old or if someone is in imminent risk of serious harm (Khan, 2021; UUK, 2019a).

GOVERNANCE OF POLICY AND PROCEDURE

Finally, the policy should note who is responsible for the policy and procedure and who is accountable for safeguarding students and staff (Khan, 2021). This may include discussion of different roles and responsibilities as well as when the policy and procedure are reviewed.

PROCEDURE

An HEI may have multiple procedures under their sexual violence policy related to the status of the Responding Party, i.e. student, employee or visitor. As an HEI has different obligations under employment law, it is likely that a separate, but very similar, procedure will be used if a student or employee makes a report against a member of staff then when a student or an employee makes a report against a student. Therefore, an HEI may have a student procedure, staff procedure and even a visitor procedure if required. The procedure should explain in detail what will happen at each stage of the procedure, so that Reporting and Responding Parties know what to expect. A procedure cannot include enough detail to cover every eventuality; therefore, to allow for some flexibility in actions, using words like 'may' and 'normally' can assist the HEI in outlining what would normally be expected, but allowing for some flexibility to adjust to case needs. The flexibility will still be led by the principles of the policy but may mean that, e.g. action can be taken in a different order if a case requires this.

Depending on how the HEI approaches sexual violence, the procedure can be set up to be one full procedure which covers disclosure to appeal incorporating the complaints procedure and discipline process into one bespoke procedure. Alternatively, an HEI may use the sexual violence procedure as a complaint process first, and then if a complaint is upheld, move the case into the discipline procedure. In Fig. 2, we outline this option as it is most commonly used within UK HE.

We do not recommend that the case only be addressed in a discipline process though, as current sector guidance does not permit the Reporting Party to appeal the outcome of a discipline process but does allow the Reporting Party to request a review of a complaint process (OIA, 2018a, b). Inherently problematic in using the option where a complaint is upheld and then moved to a discipline process is the repetition of adjudication. This means that one part of the HEI will view the case on a balance of probabilities to determine if a complaint is upheld or dismissed, and then another part of the HEI will view the case to determine on the balance of probabilities if the behaviour that occurred in the upheld complaint amounts to misconduct. If a complaint of sexual violence is upheld, then a finding of misconduct should be automatic, and the discipline stage should only be considering sanctioning at that stage. However, due to current sector guidance, this is not how many universities operate, allowing for a complaint to be upheld (where the Reporting Party has an option to review the outcome) and then the same case to be dismissed at the discipline stage (where the Reporting Party has no right to appeal). We represent this problem here to provoke discussion and to encourage sector guidance to actively address this issue. Our recommendation is to take out the second adjudication from Fig. 2, which allows both parties to request a review at the end of the complaint process but then moves the case into a sanctioning stage only in the discipline process. Should adjudication be done twice or for those organisations that only take the case through a discipline process, we recommend that the Reporting and Responding Parties have the right to appeal the outcome of the discipline process.

Disclosure

The policy will have already explained some information about disclosing and reporting. The procedure provides the extra detail about how to do this and what exactly will happen. The procedure should tell Reporting Parties how they can disclose, e.g. online reporting platform or in person. Information on who is trained and available to receive disclosures should be outlined in the procedure. Information on how disclosures will be received and how the recipient should respond can be included, e.g. the recipient will Believe, Listen, Offer Options and Resources to the Reporting Party. The recipient will not tell the Reporting Party what to do but

DISCLOSURE

- Support Offered
- Reporting Options
  Provided

COMPLAINT PROCESS

- Report
- Precautionary Measures
- Investigation
- Adjudication
- Review

DISCIPLINE PROCESS

- Adjudication
- Sanctioning
- Appeal

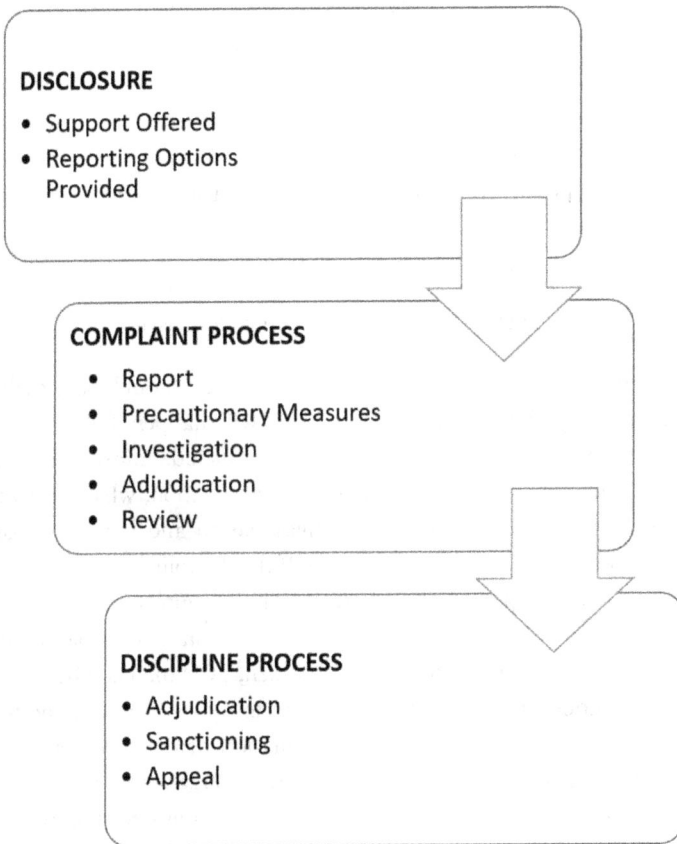

Fig. 2. Example Procedure Stages.

will provide information in a non-directive, supportive way. It should outline what interim measures can be offered while a Reporting Party considers their reporting options, e.g. temporary change in accommodation.

Report

As with explaining how to make a disclosure, the procedure should explain in clear detail how to make a report, e.g. online reporting platform or through a written form. The procedure should explain in detail what will happen when a report is received. It should explain who will manage the case and how a risk assessment will occur. It should outline what precautionary measures (temporary, non-judgemental measures that are used to mitigate identified risk presented by the Responding Party) may be used to allow for an investigation to proceed. Examples of precautionary measures are provided in Chapter 10. It should outline timelines for a response.

Investigation and Discipline Processes

The investigation and disciplinary procedures should be clearly outlined explaining step by step what will happen following a report made to the institution. This should include information on what evidence can be submitted to the investigation, what types of witnesses may be included in the investigation and how evidence will be tested during the investigation. If the disciplinary process sits outside of this policy, then how this policy intersects with the disciplinary process needs to be explained. It should include clear timeframes that are followed (UN Women, 2018b). The OIA considers it good practice for the institution to inform the Responding Party as soon as possible after confirmation of the report and to complete the initial investigation and formal stage within 90 days of informing the Responding Party (2018b). Consideration of an appeal should be completed within 30 days. This is similar to good practice in the United States where it is expected that investigations and disciplinary processes occur within 60 days of a report to the university (Office for Civil Rights, 2007). It is noted in both countries that there may be reasonable delays in meeting that timeframe for more complex cases. However, any delays should be clearly and promptly communicated to both parties explaining the reason for the delay and indicating new timescales. In England and Wales, Reporting Parties are now able to submit complaints to the OIA prior to completing the institution's internal process if there has been undue delay. The OIA will consider accepting the complaint for review if the complaint is not progressed, is being obstructed or remains unresolved after an unreasonable length of time (OIA, 2018b).

Review/Appeal

Any option to review and/or appeal at the appropriate stage of the procedure should be clearly noted setting out the grounds for a review/appeal, timeline for requesting a review/appeal, timeline for the HEI to conduct the review/appeal, potential outcomes of a review/appeal and who will conduct this.

COMMUNICATION OF POLICY

Finally, we must note that once the policy and procedure(s) are in place, the institution must very actively communicate this to all its members and educate students and staff on what behaviours are acceptable and what is considered misconduct. It is not enough to send a mass email to inform the university community that a new policy is in place. This is akin to communications box ticking and is not good enough or effective. HEIs may wish to work with experts in their corporate communication teams and with student leaders to access a variety of communication channels to ensure this is communicated well. The policy may be implemented alongside the launch of a related campaign to increase visibility and begin building awareness around these issues. Likewise, students and staff must be made aware of the policy when they first join the institution (UN Women, 2018a). For students, this can best be communicated pre-arrival through online and written communications and at arrival during induction or orientation sessions followed up by email communications. For staff, this may be included in orientation sessions as well as policy briefings based in departments. Although it is not expected that students (or employees) will read each policy the institution has, the institution should be able to reasonably show they communicated to the student about the policy and that the student was made aware of its existence, as well as their responsibilities and where to access the full policy at the time of registration. The student enters into a contract with the institution and by breaching the policy may be breaching their contract with the institution. Therefore, it is important the institution can demonstrate these efforts. Senior managers may wish to include questions around the level of familiarity that students and staff have with such policies – again this affords us with the opportunity to check whether what we are doing is making a difference.

In this chapter, we have provided example elements of a bespoke sexual violence policy and procedure. This is very much an overview of a policy, hopefully offering reasons for more specific parts of the policy that may be met with resistance during a consultation process. We recommend that policy and procedures be reviewed regularly and revised to implement lessons learned and changes in legislation, and to keep updated with other internal changes. HEIs may wish to seek feedback on the policy and procedures formally and informally from students and staff through focus groups, online surveys or anonymous feedback surveys. It is also important that HEIs practise routine case audits to prepare for policy reviews along with remaining up to date with new sector guidance and changes in legislation.

Related Resources

- Khan, R. (2021). *Domestic abuse policy guidance for UK universities. Honour abuse research matrix (HARM)*. University of Central Lancashire.
- Donaldson, A., McCarry, M., & McGoldrick, R. (2018). *Equally safe in higher education toolkit*. University of Strathclyde. www.strath.ac.uk/humanities/social-worksocialpolicy/equallysafeinhighereducation/eshetoolkit
- Anyadike-Danes, N. (2023). Perceptions of consent in UK higher education: Implications for policy and training. In C. J. Humphreys & G. J. Towl (Eds.), *Stopping gender-based violence in higher education: Policy, practice, and partnerships*. Routledge.

8

COMPREHENSIVE
INSTITUTION-WIDE EDUCATION

The ultimate purpose of a comprehensive institution-wide approach is twofold: (1) to make a significant impact upon reducing perpetration and (2) to ensure those who are subjected to sexual violence receive an appropriate and safe response to access support. Students and staff join the institution with their own beliefs and experiences related to sexual violence. Much of the focus of any course is to help participants consider new ways of thinking and attitudes about sexual violence to generate culture change rather than just disseminate information. Equally important is the opportunity to teach skills too. Campaigning, education and training aimed at students and staff are at the heart of any prevention efforts.

In this chapter, we discuss different types of education and training universities may consider embedding into their students' academic careers and their employees' annual training programmes. As discussed in Chapter 2, there are known risk factors where individuals may be at more risk to perpetrate sexual violence in a higher education institution (HEI) (i.e. high rape myth acceptance [RMA], a lack of empathy for rape victim-survivors, the personal use of alcohol, hostility towards women and hyper-masculinity), and there are clear community risk factors which increase perpetration (i.e. 'lad culture', rape culture and lack of effective deterrents and guardians) (DeKeseredy, 2017; McPhail, 2017; Murphy & Van Brunt, 2017;

Powers & Leili, 2017). As we discuss the various training options, we will highlight how these connect to mitigating these risks. As perpetrators are likely to represent a heterogeneous group, we cannot use a one-size-fits-all approach to prevention (Swartout et al., 2015). What will become evident is the need to offer comprehensive prevention programmes to address known risks, rather than one-off courses. We endeavour to present a range of evidence-informed prevention and response education options, highlighting examples of good practice. We note that this is an ever-evolving area of development.

Our Watch (2021) sets our four levels of prevention drawing from a public health–based approach, to address violence against women visualised in a pyramid which we will use to consider prevention of sexual violence in higher education (HE) described as follows in order from the base to the top of the pyramid:

1. **Primary Prevention**: initiatives used to prevent the drivers of sexual violence applied to the whole population of the university community– all students and staff – former students and visitors/ contractors may be included in this broader category too.

2. **Secondary Prevention or Early Intervention**: initiatives targeted at those who may be at higher-than-average risk of perpetrating or being subjected to sexual violence.

3. **Tertiary Prevention or Response**: initiatives used to support those subjected to sexual violence and to hold perpetrators accountable for their behaviour to prevent recurrence.

4. **Recovery**: initiatives used to support victim-survivors to recover, access their education/workplace safely and to thrive in all areas of their life.

In this chapter, we focus on primary prevention and secondary prevention options referring to these as prevention and response courses or comprehensive prevention education. Developing a comprehensive prevention programme requires resource, planning and expertise. HEIs can purchase or access (sometimes for free) off-the-shelf courses or create their own that are bespoke to their community. We recommend using evidence-informed courses and practices where available. Whether it is purchased or designed in-house, we recommend any education delivered is always assessed and evaluated to test whether it is having positive impact on cultural change.

CORE ELEMENTS OF TRAINING

When it comes to training in sexual violence prevention, there are key areas that we suggest always be covered in training as foundational: understanding consent, understanding the sexual violence continuum and debunking rape myths. These are crucial in raising awareness and changing social norms that may promote RMA.

We discuss consent education later in the chapter, so here we consider the sexual violence continuum. It is necessary to highlight the sexual violence continuum in training to raise awareness about sexual violence and perpetration. For expository purposes, the continuum is sometimes shown in a pyramid or circular visual. In the pyramid visual (See, e.g. *Pyramid of Discrimination and Violence*, Intervention Initiative), the base of the pyramid represents attitudes and beliefs of oppressions (e.g. sexism, racism, disablism). Above this cultural, microaggressions are listed followed by verbal expressions of sexual violence such as sexual harassment. At the top of the pyramid, the physical expressions of sexual violence are shown (e.g. rape and sexual assault). The pyramid highlights the structures that perpetuate sexual violence. If communities did not support the base, the top would fall. Perpetrators do not typically start with physical expressions of sexual violence but often work up to this, offering opportunities in prevention by addressing the lower behaviours first. Visually, it can also demonstrate the prevalence rates in that sexist beliefs are likely much more prevalent than those that express them through verbal and physical forms of sexual violence. In the circular visual (See, e.g. Guy, 2006), the intersections of different forms of oppression are interconnected in the middle of a circle demonstrating the intersectionality of sexual violence experiences and perpetration. Different forms of sexual violence, from sexist jokes to indecent exposure to rape, surround the inner circles making a middle ring. The outer ring represents the norms that perpetuate these behaviours. Teaching the sexual violence continuum helps raise awareness of the range of behaviours victim-survivors may be subjected to while also highlighting the need to not address sexual violence as an issue between two individuals, but a wider societal concern.

When training students and staff, it is necessary to address misperceptions of sexual violence often referred to as 'rape myths'. Rape myths blame victims and absolve perpetrators of guilt. We provide a list of common rape myths from the Crown Prosecution Service (CPS) in Resource 5. These are gendered and by no means exhaustive. The examples represent common myths that we aim to debunk through comprehensive education. The recommended strategy for addressing rape myths in training is to use the *Fact → Myth → Fallacy* approach where the facts are presented first then the myths are addressed by explaining the fallacy the myth uses to distort the facts (VicHealth, 2018). From experience, this part of any course can be the most challenging for participants regardless of how it is presented, through group activity, lecture, video or self-assessment. There are many reasons why individuals and society so easily believe rape myths. As rape myths blame victims, to believe these myths gives a sense of control to individuals that they can protect themselves from being targeted. For example, we know that stranger rape is very rare, and most rapes are committed by men who are known to the victim-survivor. The myth that rape is committed by strangers in dark alleys implies that homes and people we know are safe and that if people avoid dark alleys and speaking to strangers, then they will remain safe. After all, from a young age, many people are taught 'stranger danger'. Similarly, because rape myths blame victims and the idea that someone would choose to harm another person in this way is so difficult to hold, rape myths are a way to minimise or excuse behaviour, absolving perpetrators from guilt. When we discredit myths, we are asking participants to shift their beliefs: to stop blaming victims, to hold perpetrators accountable for their behaviour and to recognise the actual risk of sexual violence in our community, which in turn can make many people very uncomfortable. Hence, sometimes this can be met with resistance. Looking at the facts while highlighting the implications for believing myths, such as absolving perpetrators from any guilt, restricting women's movement, excluding entire groups of victim-survivors (e.g. men, individuals with disabilities, etc.) and victim-blaming, can help participants to reframe these issues.

Risk Reduction Courses: Whose Risk?

When developing a comprehensive prevention programme, one might consider whether prevention education should focus on teaching individuals to reduce their risk of being victimised or if education should focus on reducing the risk of potential perpetrators committing sexual violence. Starkly, the question posed is, 'Do we teach "don't get raped" or "don't rape"?' The reality is in a comprehensive prevention programme, we do both. In the following discussion on consent and active bystander education, we focus on the impact that those courses have on reducing risks of perpetration, but they also educate and empower students as well.

Previously, risk reduction in HE meant offering self-defence courses to women. These courses were considered a radical intervention as a part of the feminist antirape movement in the 1970s (Hollander, 2016; Kelly & Sharp-Jeffs, 2016). However, over time, self-defence classes changed from being empowering to focusing on safety tips and restricting women's movement leading to critiques that self-defence courses were victim-blaming, ignored acquaintance rape and coercive sexual violence and taught women to fend off strangers (Hollander, 2016; Kelly & Sharp-Jeffs, 2016; Linder & Myers, 2017). We strongly argue that prevention (and response!) should never be victim-blaming, leaving victim-survivors feeling like they did something wrong or could have prevented an assault (Murphy & Van Brunt, 2017). In active bystander courses, we take much care to ensure that students do not feel at fault if they did not intervene in a situation that led to harm. After all, there are many reasons why bystanders may not be able to intervene, such as safety risks. Sexual violence is only ever the perpetrator's fault (CPS, 2021).

In recent years, there has been a shift of some feminist thought arguing that feminist self-defence also called 'empowerment-based self-defence', or 'women's self-defence' still has a place and is effective in preventing sexual violence too (see, e.g. Hollander, 2016;

Kelly & Sharp-Jeffs, 2016; Senn et al., 2008). Some have been able to demonstrate the efficacy of self-defence courses that are not victim-blaming as part of a wider programme of interventions, e.g. Senn et al. (2008) in Canada. Advocates for empowerment-based self-defence emphasise the importance of such classes being part of an integrated programme rather than a standalone course. This is not a one-off martial arts course, which would be anticipated to be largely ineffectual, but evidence-informed curriculums with on average 30 hours of instruction depending on the course. The minimum standards for evidence-informed women's self-defence include:

> ... *accurate information on VAW; the opportunity to explore and challenge constructions of femininity; trusting intuition and setting boundaries; learning to use voice; practicing simple techniques adapted to women's bodies and capacities; witnessing other women/girls in a group grow in confidence and competence; that the decision which technique, if any, to use is personal and contextual. (Kelly & Sharp-Jeffs, 2016, p. 20)*

Ultimately, we do not think the question is one or the other and as blunt as presented previously. Evidence shows there is a place for education aimed at reducing risk of victimisation and reducing risks of perpetration in a comprehensive education programme. The following discussion of student education, staff training and campaign work will focus on doing both. We regard it as ideologically indulgent to ignore any evidence which may indicate that we can reduce the number of cases of individuals being subjected to sexual violence. We think that an approach which follows the evidence and its applications has the most to offer the sector.

STUDENT EDUCATION

A comprehensive prevention education programme for students will cover expectations of students' behaviour under policy (i.e. identify what is expected and what is considered misconduct), sexual consent, the sexual violence continuum, root causes of sexual violence, debunking rape myths, active bystander skills, healthy relationships and how to access support (Edwards et al., 2018).

Consent Education

Consent education is necessary. In England in 2020, Relationships and Sex Education (RSHE) was made compulsory for all secondary school students. In 2023, the Prime Minister and Education Secretary began the first review of the curriculum following reports of pupils being taught inappropriate content; at the time of writing, the curriculum remains under consultation with further guidance to be published (Department of Education, 2024). Therefore, consent education is developing for students in England. Arguably, consent education in schools is not consistent within one country, let alone when we consider students entering HE from other countries. For example, in the United States, which has similar laws to the United Kingdom, only eight states require the importance of consent to sexual activity be covered during sex education (Guttmacher Institute, 2023). International students may have different understandings of consent based on their home countries' laws and varied school education. Consequently, it is essential to offer consent education to students.

Consent education typically includes: (1) legal (criminal) and internal university definition of consent, (2) sexual offences and misconduct defined, (3) debunking rape myths, (4) rape culture vs consent culture, (5) respecting sexuality, (6) addressing sexism and (7) a call to action to create consent culture. In relation to how consent education addresses risks of perpetration, it typically addresses individual risk factors of RMA, hostility towards women and hypermasculinity and addresses community risk factors by acting as a deterrent and challenging rape culture (McPhail, 2017; Murphy & Van Brunt, 2017). It raises awareness of what consent is and how to communicate consent. It empowers individuals to speak out against rape culture while promoting consent culture.

In consent education, it is important to present the material in an inclusive way. Students that come to university may already be sexually active, some will not be sexually active, others may be waiting to become sexually active until after marriage, some may be asexual and others still may be exploring their sexuality. Unlike in policy, where we encourage shying away from using criminal justice terms to label misconduct, in education, it is necessary to cover the relevant laws in relation to sexual offences. Criminal language may make it easier to discuss because the language may more accessible than misconduct policy definitions. Consent education can be delivered in multiple ways and is often delivered in peer-facilitated workshops that allow students to engage in the material through more informal but guided discussions and activities.

It is also important to include consent education when training staff. Discussing consent is not normalised, and therefore, it is unlikely that staff will be able to accurately define consent too. In a later section of this chapter, we discuss how to add consent education into staff training.

Good Practice Example: Active* Consent, University of Galway

The Active* Consent programme has pioneered sexual consent education and research with young people in Ireland since 2013, developing into a socio-ecological approach that engages professionals, staff members and institutional leadership. Supported by philanthropy, the University of Galway and the Irish government, the programme includes subject areas such as psychology, health promotion, theatre and drama, psychotherapy and social media. The programme initiated HE student campus climate surveys in Ireland in 2020, later expanding to staff surveys. The programme's research and practice approach has helped shape the national sectoral framework, while also working with the post-primary and Further Education (FE) sectors.

Grounded in research with students, Active* Consent has developed tiered awareness raising, education and training resources, including:

For Students and Staff:

- Social media campaigns, e.g. *Start Here, Consent is for Everyone.*
- Campus initiatives, e.g. *Consent Week, Green Flag Stall.*
- eLearning module on consent, sexual violence and harassment.
- ConsentHub national website.
- Consent workshop facilitator training.
- Campus climate survey tools.

For Students:

- Consent educational resource for orientations.
- Discussion and scenario–based consent workshop.
- Theatrical drama, e.g. *The Kinds of Sex You Might Have at College*, study guide and video.

For Staff:

- Staff awareness-raising information video.
- Management briefing session.
- 10-European Credit Transfer and Accumulation System (ECTS) continuous professional development module.
- 4-session First Point of Contact in disclosure management skills (with Galway Rape Crisis Centre).

For more information:
www.consenthub.ie
Active* Consent. (2023). *The Active* Consent programme 2019–2022: Actions, outreach, partnership & impact.* University of Galway.

With special thanks to Pádraig MacNeela, Head of the School of Psychology and Co-Lead of Active Consent at the University of Galway for reviewing and approving this summary.*

Active Bystander Education

Active bystander, also called positive bystander intervention or upstander intervention education, can address all the individual risks of perpetration noted previously. It can create guardians in the community and challenge rape and lad culture by identifying and challenging social norms, building empathy and a sense of responsibility and identifying participants as part of the solution (Bows et al., 2015; McPhail, 2017; Murphy & Van Brunt, 2017). Active bystander education teaches students to risk assess intervention options to intervene safely. Skills learned during an active bystander course are applicable across problem behaviours (e.g. intervening in racist, transphobic, homophobic, classist behaviour or other forms of discriminatory behaviour). This type of upskilling course also builds leaderships skills.

During an active bystander course, participants learn that a person needs to (1) notice an event, (2) interpret it as a problem, (3) feel responsibility to intervene and (4) have the skills to intervene in a safe way (Fenton et al., 2014; Latane & Darley, 1969; Sundaram et al., 2019). The participants learn that they can prevent incidents occurring by intervening before they occur or to stop them as they happen (Fenton et al., 2014). Active bystander courses are often interactive courses utilising role-plays, scenario-based group work, videos, storytelling and lecture teaching methods. Participants are taught different ways to intervene and are encouraged to be creative in considering their options. The aim of an active bystander course is not to provide a formula for students to take away but to encourage them to consider a range of different ways to intervene and find methods that they will do. A common way to teach intervention methods are to use the '4 Ds' of intervention:

1. **Direct:** where the bystander directly calls out the behaviour.

2. **Distract:** where the bystander distracts the perpetrator changing the focus and ending the behaviour.

3. **Delegate:** where they bystander asks someone else, such as a person in a position of authority, to intervene.

4. **Delay**: where the bystander checks in with the victim-survivor to offer support or with the perpetrator to call out the behaviour later when it is safe to do so.

All options are helpful forms of intervention; a group of four students might choose four different options based on their own identity, the identity of the individuals involved and their confidence, experience and personality. The helpful point to make in active bystander courses is that all four options, if safe for the bystander, are valid.

Good Practice Example: The Intervention Initiative, University of the West of England, University of Exeter and Public Health England

The Intervention Initiative is a free active bystander programme for HE and FE settings, developed in 2014 by the University of the West of England on receipt of a grant from Public Health England. It is an evidence-based educational programme for the prevention of sexual coercion and domestic abuse, through empowering students to act as pro-social citizens. The programme is designed to be delivered by experienced facilitators across 8 separate sessions, each of two hours in length. The programme has been developed to ensure the length of time and purpose of each session accords with the theory of change. Research shows this length and duration should be viewed as a minimum for effective behaviour change. The curriculum and tools for each of the sessions is provided in the form of facilitator notes, PowerPoint slides and handouts. A full theoretical rationale for the programme is available. Uniquely and helpfully, evaluation is built into the programme. Evaluation results show significant changes across a range of measures.

For more information:
www.exeter.ac.uk/research/groups/law/interventioninitiative

(Continued)

Fenton, R. A., Mott, H. L., McCartan, K., & Rumney, P. (2014). *The intervention initiative.* UWE and Public Health England.

Fenton, R., & Mott, H. (2018). Evaluation of the intervention initiative, a bystander intervention programme to prevent violence against women in universities. *Violence and Victims, 33*(4), 645–662.

The Intervention Initiative continues to be developed and refined by Fenton for different contexts under the auspices of the University of Exeter spin-out company Kindling Transformative Interventions www.kindling-interventions.com

Special thanks to Rachel Fenton, Associate Professor of Law at the University of Exter, for reviewing and approving this summary.

Training for Postgraduates

Postgraduate students can benefit from consent and active bystander education but may find that these courses are commonly aimed at undergraduate students. Training particularly aimed at postgraduate students can ensure a comprehensive approach. This may include delivering consent and active bystander sessions that are specifically modified to target postgraduate student needs. Postgraduates may have higher representation of mature students, students with families and international students. Full-time students studying for a Master's degree may only be at the university one to two years, whereas students studying for a PhD may remain for three to four years, if not longer. Training to prevent sexual violence for postgraduate students may benefit from focusing on specific areas of HE experiences where sexual violence risk is higher, e.g. fieldwork or attending conferences. Uniquely, postgraduate women are at higher risk of being subjected to sexual violence perpetrated by staff. This book does not directly address staff sexual misconduct. However, we note this here as training for postgraduate students must identify and deal with staff sexual misconduct directly. To support this, we recommend the work of The 1752 Group.

Good Practice Example: Professional Boundaries and Awareness of Sexual Harassment Workshops for Postgraduate Researchers (PGRs), Supervisors and Staff, The 1752 Group

The 1752 Group is a UK-based research, consultancy and campaign organisation dedicated to addressing staff sexual misconduct in HE. Due to their expertise, they are well-placed to offer training for postgraduate students and staff, two of which we highlight here.

Recognising professional boundaries and sexual harassment as a PGR

This workshop supports PGRs to recognise sexual harassment and other boundary-blurring behaviours, introduces the concept of professional boundaries, enables PGRs to better recognise and respond to inappropriate behaviours in different academic contexts and helps them understand how to raise concerns or report these issues.

Professional boundaries and sexual harassment experienced by PGRs: A workshop for supervisors and staff.

This session helps supervisors and staff reflect on shared understandings of professional boundaries within the school/department and ensures staff can recognise sexual harassment and know how to support PGRs and colleagues to recognise/report this.

At the time of writing, a formal evaluation was underway to assess whether and how participants' attitudes changed as

(Continued)

a result of the training. Challenges in devising an evaluation process for this training were a lack of available data at institutional-level and a dearth of appropriate tools to assess attitudes in this area. As a result, existing survey tools on workplace sexual harassment were adopted to create an appropriate measure to evaluate these sessions.

For more information:
www.1752group.com/consultancy

Special thanks to Anna Bull, Senior Lecturer in Education and Social Justice at the University of York and co-founder and Director of Research at The 1752 Group, for reviewing and approving this summary.

STAFF TRAINING

Staff training can focus on many areas of prevention and response related to both student and staff-perpetrated sexual misconduct. Key topics often covered in staff training include awareness raising, the institution's policy and procedure, the prevention of sexual harassment in the workplace, responding to disclosures of sexual violence, supporting Reporting Parties and Responding Parties during investigation and disciplinary procedures and conducting trauma-informed investigation and disciplinary procedures. Staff training can be focused on generating culture change addressing the risk factors of RMA, lack of empathy and rape culture while creating guardians in the community. All faculty and staff should be trained (UN Women, 2018a). Awareness raising and disclosure training may be offered to all staff, whereas more specialist training may be offered to staff dependent on their role.

Awareness Raising and Responding to Disclosures

We recommend that all staff engage in awareness and disclosure response training. This can be considered a foundational course for staff to understand the policy (i.e. identify what is expected and what is considered misconduct), their responsibilities as employees under the policy and procedures to follow, as well as learning a basic but appropriate disclosure response to signpost students (and colleagues) to the appropriate support and reporting options (see Chapter 9), i.e. first aid for sexual violence. USVreact has developed courses like this available for HEIs to access for free. In addition, universities may wish to use their internal (e.g. academic experts) and/or external partnerships to create a course specific to the institution. Often organisations such as local rape crisis centres offer training to organisations and can create bespoke courses based on an institution's needs.

Investigation Training

The Office of the Independent Adjudicator for Higher Education in England and Wales requires investigators of misconduct allegations to be properly trained, resourced and supported (2018a). We recommend that investigators into reports of sexual violence should be experienced, trained in trauma-informed investigation techniques and understand sexual violence. It is imperative that investigators are well trained in understanding consent and the policy definitions of different types of misconduct. In Chapter 11, we discuss a consent analytic that will guide investigators responding to a consent defence. To apply this analytic, investigators need to be able to deconstruct the definition of consent, 'a person agrees by choice, only if they have the freedom and capacity to make that choice' (CPS, n.d.). Investigators need training in identifying signs of force, threat, intimidation and coercion which would mean consent could not be freely given. Investigators need to be able to identify signs of incapacity and understand factors that lead to substance-induced incapacity. Training should cover alcohol-facilitated and drug-facilitated sexual violence.

In addition, we would expect investigators to have training on the sexual violence continuum and the prevalence of sexual violence at universities, including information on prevalence in marginalised groups. The training should cover individual and community risk factors for perpetration. And of course, we would expect this training to cover debunking rape myths and how rape myths can impact an investigation. Fundamentally to conduct a trauma-informed investigation, training must cover the neurobiology of trauma including traumatic memory production and retrieval, trauma response and presentation and trauma-informed interviewing techniques. Investigation skills require a working understanding of the policy and protocol which investigations are being conducted, types of defences, analysing evidence, assessing credibility, weighing evidence, applying the appropriate standard of evidence and writing an investigation report.

Adjudication and Sanctioning Training

We recommend that discipline decision-makers (including student members of disciplinary panels) also be trained in understanding trauma, debunking rape myths, how to ask questions that are not victim-blaming and how to adjudicate and apply sanctions based on the institution's policies and procedures (Loschiavo, 2017). The Association for Student Conduct Administration has a long list of expected areas of training for adjudicators and included in this they recommend that adjudicators need to be trained in the institution's policies, procedures and appeal process, applying the civil standard of proof, how to facilitate a disciplinary hearing, how to evaluate credibility, how to determine sanctions, how to ask appropriate questions, and how to deliberate, to name a few (Bennett et al., 2014).

Good Practice Example: Sexual Misconduct Case Toolkit, the University of Surrey

The Sexual Misconduct Case Toolkit provides a framework for both academics and professional services staff to work to when cases of sexual misconduct involving students and staff are reported. It offers training for frontline staff and bespoke training for sexual misconduct investigations and Panel hearings which can ensure the investigation process and outcome is clearer and more transparent, building confidence in the system. The toolkit covers:

- Major forms of sexual abuse.
- Trauma-informed approaches.
- Interviewing skills.
- Navigating consent issues.
- Weighing evidence and decision-making.
- Identifying and confronting biases and myths.
- Principles of case management and investigation.
- Perpetrator strategies.
- Memory.

For more information, see:
www.surrey.ac.uk/sexual-misconduct-case-toolkit

Special thanks to Melissa Hamilton, JD, PhD, Professor of Law and Criminal Justice at the University of Surrey for reviewing and approving this summary.

FACILITATING PREVENTION AND RESPONSE TRAINING

Training Delivery Methods

Institutions will likely consider whether to deliver training face-to-face or through self-paced online (eLearning) packages. Face-to-face training can be delivered in person or online using interactive video conferencing platforms, e.g. Zoom. Self-paced online or eLearning courses are often hosted on the HEI's virtual learning platform (VLE), e.g. Blackboard. Depending on a learner's preferred way of learning and personal experience related to sexual violence, they may prefer learning online in their own time away from interacting with others. Others may find training where they can interact with other participants and an instructor more conducive to learning. Some participants may prefer to engage in this type of education on a more anonymous basis either by taking an online course or taking an in-person course with individuals they do not know. Others may find self-paced online courses difficult to engage with, which may fuel thoughts that the training is only a tick-box exercise. We offer the advantages and disadvantages of these options for consideration through a pros and cons list in Table 3.

Table 3. Comparing Training Delivery Options.

Training	Face-to-face	Self-paced Online
Pros	• Participants are more likely to engage in the course fully and may be less likely to ignore large portions of content. • The facilitator can challenge negative beliefs (e.g. if someone argues that most reports of rape are false, the facilitator can work through that comment, challenge it for the group and present facts. In a self-paced online course, that same participant may skip over that content and continue to the next slide.) • The course can be more interactive allowing participants to ask questions, work in groups and challenge ideas. • Participants may experience a sense of community building and shared responsibility. • Facilitators can be flexible and adaptive to the needs of participants in the group delivering material using a variety of training methods. • Face-to-face courses can be run in person or online with the use of online video conferencing platforms without losing opportunities for interaction.	• The course can be made available to all students and/or staff as required. • Participants can take the course in their own time, taking breaks as needed. • There may be additional tools to make the course even more accessible to participants with a range of disabilities if designed well that may not be as easily used in an in-person course (e.g. voice-over, large print, captions, transcriptions, high contrast colour combinations and use of screen readers), • The course may be more cost-effective for reaching all members of the university community. • The course quality remains the same for each participant. • The course does not require the instructor to have specialist knowledge as courses can be purchased from external organisations. • There is no staff time required to deliver the course to participants.

Table 3. *(Continued)*

Training	Face-to-face	Self-paced Online
Cons	• The quality and effectiveness of the course can be impacted by the facilitator's competence, ability to build rapport with participants and energy level. • It may be more resource intensive in cost, time and materials. • Participation in the course is scheduled which may limit engagement. • It is more difficult to reach large groups of students and/or staff. • Participants who attend are likely to already be interested in the material, possibly missing individuals who need the training more. • When running face-to-face training online, participants may not engage as readily if they have the option to keep their cameras turned off and may experience 'Zoom fatigue', i.e. burnout from the overuse of online platforms.	• The quality of engagement will vary with some participants fully engaged while others may click through slides or skip to an end-of-course quiz. • If participants disagree with the content, there is no ability for the course instructor to challenge negative beliefs and provoke thoughtful discussion. • There may be no or limited options for participants to ask questions. • There may be no or limited options for group work. • There may be limited ability to use multiple training methods.

Here, we highlight examples of self-paced online learning that can be used in this way or, with use of the optional workshop materials, can be combined for blended learning.

It is important to incorporate varied training techniques into in-person and online training options to fully engage individuals. In-person courses may include lecture, group discussion, small

Good Practice Example: Support and Wellbeing Programmes, Epigeum: A Sage Resource

Consent Matters: Boundaries, Respect, and Positive Intervention 2.1, 2023

This is an evidence-based, self-paced online course for HE students covering consent education, communication, healthy relationships and bystander intervention. The curriculum includes in-person workshop materials for optional blended learning.

https://learningresources.sagepub.com/epigeum/support-and-wellbeing/consent-matters

Responding to Disclosures of Sexual Violence 2.0, 2022

This is a research-based, self-paced online training for HE staff and student leaders to upskill them to respond to disclosures of sexual violence in line with best practice. The curriculum includes in-person workshop materials for optional blended learning.

https://learningresources.sagepub.com/epigeum/support-and-wellbeing/responding-to-disclosures

For more information:

https://learningresources.sagepub.com/epigeum/support-and-wellbeing

With special thanks to Naomi Wilkinson, Associate Director of Publishing at Epigeum for reviewing and approving this summary.

group work, individual work, movement, video and space for reflection. Online courses may also include individual work, video, audio, small group work through a moderated online discussion board and space for reflection. All training should be designed to be accessible for individuals with different types of disabilities. Ultimately, a range of training delivery options can be made available for students and staff.

Choosing the Best Facilitator

When considering student training, a common question is whether staff or students should facilitate the sessions. Staff facilitators may have more expert knowledge in the course content area and more experience facilitating in general. Student facilitators, referred to as peer educators, leaders or mentors, have the power to influence norms and beliefs when interacting with their friends outside of the course. Research shows that peer education can impact on peer group norms thus affecting individual behaviour (Powell, 2011). We recommend when using student facilitators that they are paid, trained and supervised. Peer facilitators should be trained in the content of the course and have more knowledge regarding the content than is required to deliver in the course. They need to be trained in the continuum of sexual violence and facilitation skills, including how to create safe and inclusive learning environments, active listening, how to answer difficult questions and manage difficult participants (Thomas-Card & Eichele, 2017). They should receive opportunities to practise facilitation with active feedback provided. They should be supported and offered supervision following trainings if required. Peer facilitators should be trained in how to respond to disclosures of sexual violence as facilitating courses on consent or active bystander education can lead students to see the facilitators as a trusted individual who they may wish to disclose to outside of the course.

Facilitation Skills and Techniques

Facilitating courses that discuss sexual violence require thoughtful preparation. Facilitators should be experienced and be able to manage the room to keep track of how participants are responding. For interactive courses, we recommend no more than 25 people per course per 1 staff facilitator or 2 peer facilitators, so the facilitator(s) can monitor and check in with participants.

We recommend always setting ground rules at the start of any training with students and staff. The following are examples of helpful rules to run a safe interactive course:

- **Challenge the idea and not the person.** This means that we encourage questions, and debate differences of opinion, but that we ask everyone to express these respectfully.

- **Take care of yourself.** This rule is to recognise that any course discussing sexual violence will be emotive for all involved regardless of personal experiences of sexual violence. We recommend setting training spaces up so that the door to exit is in the back or the side of the room. Participants can move freely around the room or 'zone out' in their seats if needed.

- **No self-disclosure during the session.** This is important as facilitators cannot respond appropriately to disclosures in a public setting, but more importantly for primary survivors and secondary survivors, it can be triggering to hear someone's personal story in a training session when it is unexpected.

- **Be present.** This is the rule where we ask (staff especially) to refrain from doing other things during the course, such as working on emails or spending time on social media.

Regardless of the type of training, when delivering a course related to sexual violence, people can respond in varied ways. Sometimes, these can be disruptive to running a safe and effective course. It is important that participants who are disrupting a course are not ignored, minimised or escalated. The most common types of difficult participants may be thought of as **keen monopolisers** (those who know about this topic and want you to know they know), **apathetic attenders** (those who were forced to attend and would rather be doing anything else) and **aggressive arguers** (those who like to argue for arguments' sake).[1] We have found one method that tends to help respond to a range of difficult participants that keeps them, and everyone else, engaged in the course and allows the facilitator to continue with the course as planned. We recommend *acknowledging and signposting*. This means that the facilitator acknowledges the contribution of the participant and then signposts to facts, the

---

[1] These terms were coined be C. J. DiSantis for the purposes of 'train the trainer' courses.

course, or further resources. Done well, this re-engages the participant into the course material and helps the facilitator move to the next point/activity in the training without isolating the participant. For example, if the aggressive arguer says, 'I think all women cry rape, and the MeToo movement is a hoax.' The facilitator might respond by calmly saying, 'Thank you. I appreciate that you feel that way, and maybe others in the room are thinking something similar. Many people think false allegations are common, but the Crown Prosecution Service has confirmed this is a societal myth. According to the CPS, between January 2011 and May 2012, the Director of Public Prosecutions required the Crown Prosecution Service areas to refer to him all cases involving an allegedly false allegation of rape and/or domestic violence. During that time, there were 5,651 prosecutions for rape but only 35 for making false allegations of rape' (Starmer, 2013). This acknowledges the participant's contribution but quickly signposts to facts. The facilitator does not engage in an argument or express frustration. If the apathetic attender says, 'This is a waste of time.' The facilitator might say, 'Thanks for speaking up. I acknowledge you feel that way, especially if you are here because you were instructed to come on this course. We are going to be together for the next two hours, so I hope you might find at least one part of today's course interesting or useful. Either way, I look forward to your contribution.' Again, this is an authentic response acknowledging how the participant feels, signposting to the course and encouraging participation. Finally, for our keen monopoliser who fills each offered space or tries to answer each question, the facilitator might say, 'Thank you so much. It sounds like you know a lot about this topic and might be a resource for your peers. We are going to first offer the space to anyone who has not had a chance to answer but may come back to you.' This is acknowledging their contribution and knowledge but signposting to the group.

Ultimately, to be an effective facilitator, the way the facilitator engages with participants needs to be authentic, credible and empathetic (VicHealth, 2018). If reading the examples above sounded insincere, then we recommend coming up with answers that sound more genuine to the individual facilitator based on their personality. When participants are treated with respect and acknowledged, they are more likely to engage in the course.

CAMPAIGNING

Many forms of education can be linked directly to larger campaign work, see e.g. *Active* Consent*. Training that can link into campaigning is more likely to have a lasting impact on students and staff as this will connect their learning to involvement in the campaign. It reinforces messages learned on a course and helps move from a one-off dose to seeing a recurring message. It also creates a built-in 'call to action' for any course that allows participants to make a commitment to making their time in the course mean something more. For example, towards the end of the NUS's *I Heart Consent* workshop (see, https://www.nusconnect.org.uk/liberation/women-students/lad-culture/i-heart-consent), there is a Take Action section where participants can create ideas to challenge misperceptions of consent and promote consent culture. If the course is delivered in November and there is already a campaign week planned for the first week in February (See, e.g. Sexual Abuse and Sexual Violence Awareness Week, sexualabuseandsexualviolenceawarenessweek.org), this could be an opportunity to link students into the campaign or to promote the campaign early, especially if it is more than a print campaign (posters and social media images).

Campaigns need to have a target audience with one message/aim. Campaigns that attempt to send multiple messages to a varied audience risk losing impact and diluting or confusing the message. This is another area where student involvement and expert academics already within the institution are great resources to the institution. Even experience in a communications and marketing team, although more corporate, can help identify communication channels and challenges including potential backlash. Student focus groups can be used to test out messages. Campaigns, like poorly designed training, risk backlash; therefore, it is important to test messages first with a group of diverse students.

It is important that all training and campaigns work is evaluated to measure impact. There should be methods in place to ensure quality delivery, but also that the training and campaigns are affecting positive culture change. We recommend practitioners/facilitators work with academic staff who are well equipped to

Good Practice Example: #erasethegrey Campaign, Glasgow Caledonian University (GCU)

In 2018, Glasgow Caledonian University launched a gender-based violence (GBV) awareness raising campaign, challenging common myths and signposting to support. The campaign uses a series of banners, posters and motion graphics displayed on campus and social media to challenge stereotypical views and reiterate the university's zero-tolerance approach. The campaign originally had 14 messages with nine new messages addressing forms of GBV that were exacerbated by the lockdowns associated with COVID-19, for example, domestic abuse and technology-facilitated abuse, added in 2020. The campaign now has 23 messages covering a range of forms GBV can take.

In 2019, the campaign was Highly Commended by Edurank the education sector's leading social media benchmarking awards, was a finalist in the Times Higher Education Awards for Outstanding Student Support, and in 2020 #erasethegrey was the winner of the Purpose Awards Best Equality and Inclusion Campaign. The visually striking campaign runs regularly on the GCU campus and has been shared under licence with a wide range of education and public sector organisations. The campaign has the 'take home' message in black and the myth in grey, calling on people to 'erase the grey'.

#erasethegrey messaging examples include:

- 'They came on to me, so I don't **need consent**' with 'They came on to me, so … don't' in grey, leaving '**I need consent**' in black.
- 'It's not **rape** if she's sleeping' with 'not… if she's sleeping' in grey, leaving '**It's rape**' in black.

(Continued)

For more information:
www.gcu.ac.uk/theuniversity/commongood/erasethegrey

Special thanks to Lou Clave, GBV Prevention and Response Coordinator at GTU for reviewing and approving this summary.

design course evaluations. One example of an evaluation method for training is to offer a pre-test at the start of the course, a post-test at the end and a follow-up post-test six months later. These tests or surveys might measure the participant's knowledge, skills and attitudes against the objectives of the course.

As we conclude, we note a word of caution. Education pro- grammes can easily become a tick-box exercise to attempt to demonstrate that the institution is doing something in this area. However, education programmes must be run well to truly effect culture change and prevent sexual violence. It is not enough to ask students to take a one-off consent workshop or a 45-minute online course. That will not prevent perpetration, and senior leadership should recognise that is not effectively addressing sexual violence.

> *Prevention education that intends to have an impact must be sustained over time and be multifaceted, leaning into the complexity of how and why sexual violence occurs. Simple or single-message, onetime, narrowly focused programs will not generate behaviour change. (Hong, 2017, p. 36)*

Education and training must be resourced and thoughtfully embedded. If senior leadership is committed to addressing sexual violence in their institution, embedding effective education will be one of the more straightforward changes because academic insti- tutions are in the business of educating, and therefore should have the necessary skills and resources to add this to the curricula.

Related Resources

- USVreact. (2024). *Training resources.* https://usvreact.eu/resources/training-resources/
- Survivors' Network. (2024). *Training & consultancy.* https://survivorsnetwork.org.uk/training-and-consultancy/
- Sundaram, V., Shannon, E., Page, T., & Phipps, A. (2019). *Developing an intersectional approach to training on sexual harassment, violence and hate crimes: Guide for training facilitators.* University of York.

9

RESPONDING TO DISCLOSURES OF SEXUAL VIOLENCE

There is compelling evidence that sexual violence is significantly underreported in society with estimates that 80% of people raped or sexually assaulted at universities in the United States do not report the incident to the police (Bureau of Justice Statistics, 2014), and estimates that 94% of students in the United Kingdom do not report the incident to the police or to their university (Revolt Sexual Assault and The Student Room, 2018). When we consider sexual violence as a continuum of behaviours, the behaviours at the far end of the spectrum which may be considered 'serious sexual offences' by the criminal justice system (CJS) may be disclosed at higher rates (although still underreported) than those behaviours towards the opposite end of the spectrum that are more pervasive in everyday life for many women in HE (and further education) in particular, e.g., unwanted sexual comments or street harassment (NUS, 2011, 2019). Regardless of the type of sexual violence a perpetrator subjects a survivor to, the principles that underpin a supportive and appropriate disclosure response remain fundamentally the same.

In this chapter, we consider barriers to disclosing incidents of sexual violence and offer practical ways to reduce or remove identified barriers with the aim to increase disclosures rates. Increasing disclosure rates, and markedly so, is key if we are to effectively address our problem with sexual violence. In Chapter 5, we discussed creating multiple pathways or doorways in for students to access appropriate support. We considered who might be best placed to receive disclosures and reports. In this chapter, we take a broader view, recognising that anyone can receive a disclosure as survivors often tell someone they trust. We present principles that underpin a supportive disclosure response followed by guidance on how to respond and signpost to key areas of support. We consider how receiving a disclosure may impact on a police investigation and provide guidance on how to record first disclosures. We conclude this chapter with considerations on the important, but often overlooked, area of self-care for the recipient of the disclosure.

BARRIERS TO DISCLOSURE

Part of a good disclosure response is creating ways for victim-survivors to disclose in the first place. There are many reasons why individuals choose not to tell anyone about what they have been subjected to, which may be linked to internal and/or external factors at the individual or institutional level. Often there is not just one reason, but a combination of multiple factors that impact on a survivor's decision to delay or not disclose at all. It is important that survivors feel that they have the option to disclose, so that they can access support, gain back some level of control following an incident (as this is linked to better mental health outcomes) and decide what they want to do next. However, no one should be forced to share their experience. This is always an individual choice. From a trauma-informed perspective, a delay in disclosing an incident is to be expected and common. We discuss this further in Chapter 11.

Senior leadership teams may be hesitant to encourage disclosures out of the (misplaced) fear that increased disclosure rates will negatively impact the institution's reputation. Some have persuasively argued that the opposite is true and that there is now more reputational risk not to actively encourage disclosures of sexual violence among students (see, e.g., Towl, 2016). Receiving disclosures helps the leaders of an institution understand what is occurring and aids prevention efforts. An increase in disclosures is considered a measure of success (UUK, 2017). It is indicative of an increased awareness of an institution's support pathways and an improved level of trust from students and staff in the institution's ability to respond and support survivors. Likewise, it demonstrates that barriers to disclosing are being reduced and survivors are not being silenced. With this aim in mind, Table 4 provides a non-exhaustive list of common examples of barriers to disclosure and offers practical solutions for how to remove or minimise them.

Table 4. Addressing Barriers to Disclosure.

	Barriers	Solutions
1	**Fear of not being believed** Perpetrators often tell survivors, 'No one will believe you. It's your word against mine.' Media coverage of sexual violence can promote myths of high levels of false allegations including the myth that women 'cry rape' when they regret sex. Survivors may have not been believed in the past and/or worry that the reputation or position of the perpetrator means that no one will believe them.	• Tell survivors they will be believed. Run a 'Start by Believing' or 'We believe you' campaign (See e.g., startbybelieving.org). • Train responders to believe disclosures. • Include information on how to disclose in staff and student induction and wellbeing materials, e.g., dedicated webpage. • Include rape myth-busting activities in staff and student training.
2	**Relationship with the perpetrator** Most rapes and sexual assaults are committed by a perpetrator known to the survivor (CPS, n.d.; NUS, 2011). Survivors may minimise sexual violence by an acquaintance more than by a stranger. They may be concerned about 'ruining' the perpetrator's life by impacting on their studies,	• Offer anonymous reporting options and/or explain that survivors do not have to identify perpetrator/s when disclosing. • Make sanctioning guidelines accessible so survivors can see potential outcomes for misconduct. • Include a statement that explains survivors' wishes will be considered, but the

(Continued)

Table 4. *(Continued)*

	Barriers	Solutions
	career, or reputation or feel responsible for the punishment the perpetrator may face, e.g., expulsion or prison. The perpetrator may have threatened suicide if the survivor were to report them. The survivor may also fear impacting relationships with shared social groups.	institution will make the disciplinary decision that is proportional, relational and consistent to the misconduct and any mitigating or aggravating factors identified. This alleviates some sense of responsibility for survivors whilst still being survivor-led. • Explain that Responding Parties will be offered support if a report is made against them, just as Reporting Parties will be offered support if they disclose or make a report.
3	**Family** Survivors may be concerned that their family will learn about the incident, blame them for what happened, or learn about their behaviour surrounding the incident, e.g., substance use. They may not want to cause their family distress if the family is already dealing with other stressors, e.g., divorce or illness. They may be estranged from their family or have experienced abuse from a family member.	• Include a clear confidentiality statement/privacy notice in the policy that information would not be shared with the family or anyone else without the adult survivor's explicit consent. Consider including a note that the institution's relationship is with the adult student regardless of who pays for their education. • Include information about confidentiality on the website, online reporting tool and on signs/leaflets. • Include information on how support officers or case managers can help the survivor inform family if this is what they want and signpost to support available for family through specialist services.

Table 4. *(Continued)*

Barriers	Solutions
4 **Cultural background** Survivors may not want to disclose due to their cultural background or religious beliefs. Survivors may be concerned of being seen as 'unclean' or may be worried about disclosing other behaviours involved in the incident, e.g., drinking alcohol or being alone with a man. Survivors may not want to bring negative attention on their community by exposing that such issues exist in their community (e.g., Deaf community) or they may be concerned that there is a danger that it may reinforce negative stereotypes about the community (e.g., Black, Asian and Minority Ethnic community) (Crenshaw, 1991).	• Listen to experiences of students in minoritised communities (Harris, 2017) by building relationships with diverse student groups. • Provide information that is accessible for individuals of multiple backgrounds. • Include information about confidentiality on the website, online reporting tool and on signs/leaflets. • Reinforce that there is nothing a survivor did to deserve sexual violence; only the perpetrator is responsible. • Signpost to community-specific support services where possible. • Include discussions of intersectionality and cultural competence in staff training.
5 **'Everyone will know.'** Small communities in the institution may include residence halls, international student groups, Deaf/hard-of-hearing community, postgraduate community, or groups based around extracurricular activities, e.g., sport, music and theatre. There may be witnesses to the incident or it may be captured or discussed on social media. If the incident occurred on site, the police may attend the scene of the crime, which may bring further attention to the survivor.	• Raise awareness of the prevalence of sexual violence, especially as this relates to smaller communities who are disproportionately affected, e.g., LGBT+ community and women with disabilities. • Include information about confidentiality on the website, online reporting tool and on signs/leaflets available for students. • Request that police attend the campus in plain clothes when possible.

(Continued)

Table 4. *(Continued)*

Barriers	Solutions
6 **Language barriers** If English is not their first language, survivors may not have the language skills to explain what has happened in English, especially if in crisis. Note: this may include survivors in the Deaf community as sign language is not universal and British and American Sign Language (BSL and ASL) differ from English.	• Ensure the institution has access to interpreters; build a relationship with the interpreter service specifically around this issue; offer training to interpreters; advertise the availability of interpreters. • Provide messages/materials in multiple languages capturing the most common first languages spoken by international students. • Provide information that is accessible and understandable using plain English rather than jargon or complicated terminology.
7 **Guilt/Shame/Self-blame** Survivors may feel they are at fault for the incident occurring and may internalise feelings of guilt, shame and self-blame. This can be exacerbated when a perpetrator used coercion or grooming. This is reinforced through common societal rape myths which perpetrators and survivors' friends and family may voice and survivors may internalise.	• Raise awareness through rape myth-busting activities during staff and student training and campaign work. • Reinforce that only a perpetrator is to blame for sexual violence. • Teach responders not to ask victim-blaming questions when responding to disclosures.
8 **Gender identity** Trans survivors may be reluctant to disclose (especially to an often cisgender responder) as they not only have to disclose their traumatic experience, but they may also have to disclose their trans status or history and be willing to	• Where at all possible, have diversity in those members of staff trained to respond to disclosures, i.e., age, gender, race, sexual orientation, etc. • Provide online disclosing and reporting options.

Table 4. *(Continued)*

Barriers	Solutions
discuss aspects of their body such as their genital configuration (Marine, 2017). Men may be reluctant to disclose for fear of being judged, having their sexuality questioned, or being seen as 'weak'.	• Provide specific self-help materials for the LGBT+ community and signpost to community-specific services as available. • Advertise that the institution supports any person regardless of their identity or the perpetrator's identity using visual symbols where possible (Garvey et al., 2017; Marine, 2017).
9 **Sexual orientation** Lesbian, gay, bisexual (LGB) survivors may be reluctant to disclose for fear of being 'outed', thus losing control over who knows about their sexuality. LGB survivors may be concerned that the responder will not understand gay sex, minimise the experience as 'not real sex' or consider it less serious if the perpetrator is a woman.	• Where at all possible, have diversity in those members of staff trained to respond to disclosures, i.e., age, gender, race, sexual orientation, etc. • Provide specific self-help materials for the LGBT+ community and signpost to community-specific services as available. • Advertise that the institution supports any person regardless of their identity or the perpetrator's identity using visual symbols.
10 **Identity of responder/listener** Survivors may find it difficult to disclose to someone who is different from them in age, sexual orientation, race, nationality, religion or belief, age, class, or another characteristic. Survivors may find it difficult to disclose to someone of the same gender as the perpetrator. Students may be reluctant to disclose to staff,	• Where at all possible, have diversity in those members of staff trained to respond to disclosures, i.e., age, gender, race, sexual orientation, etc. • Provide online disclosing and reporting options. • Offer specialist responders who are independent of the student's department who students recognise as trained staff.

(Continued)

Table 4. *(Continued)*

Barriers	Solutions
particularly if they know them in another context for fear that the relationship may change.	• Provide student leaders with training on how to respond to disclosures so they can sign-post students to appropriate support, a signposting response only.
11 **Distrust in university response** Survivors may fear that the institution will (1) silence or ignore them, (2) retaliate against them and/or (3) protect the perpetrator(s). This is especially relevant in staff-student sexual misconduct or when the perpetrator is e.g., a successful student athlete, linked to institutional wealth or a staff member who has a high level of research finance capture.	• Ensure the institution has a clear and transparent policy for how disclosures and reports will be managed. • Have a named member of the executive team of the institution as responsible for addressing sexual violence. • Have an accessible internal but independent central office where disclosures can be made. • Communicate an explicit statement in institutional values statements, e.g., about the value of people over finances and no tolerance for retaliation or victimisation and demonstrate these values through actions. • Publicise statistical information on outcomes of the university's disciplinary response to include the numbers of cases and actions taken e.g., suspension or expulsion.
12 **Distrust of law enforcement** Survivors may be fearful of reporting to the police for fear of getting in trouble for other behaviour, worried that they will be further traumatised during a criminal	• Build a partnership with local law enforcement. • Include options to report to the police in induction talks, introducing police liaison officers, but be clear that reporting to

Table 4. *(Continued)*

Barriers	Solutions
justice process and fear the loss of control a criminal justice process may bring. They may also fear the police themselves. International students may distrust local law enforcement due to experiences in their home country.	the police is not the only option. It is most important to be guided by the victim-survivor and respect their wishes. • Signpost to Independent Sexual Violence Advisors (UK). • Note particularly for international students that a lawyer is not needed to make a report to the police.
13 **Not knowing how to disclose or what will happen** Survivors may not know who they can tell, where they should go, if they can remain anonymous, or what will happen during and after a disclosure and/or report.	• Include this information within campaigns, on the website and on signs/leaflets available for students using visuals such as flowcharts to demonstrate different options. • Include information on how to disclose in induction materials. • Communicate that the civil standard of proof will be used in any internal investigation into potential misconduct. • Offer online reporting tools, e.g., see Culture Shift's *Report + Support*.
14 **Fear of backlash, retaliation, or victimisation** Survivors may fear that the perpetrator may hurt them following a report or that their friends or family may turn against them. They may feel concerned that the academic department may mark their work differently or see them as a problem student, taking away academic opportunities.	• Make clear in the policy that retaliation and victimisation is not tolerated. Include information on how to report retaliation or victimisation. Provide information to Responding Parties and witnesses that retaliation is not tolerated. • Include information about confidentiality on the website, online reporting tool and on signs/leaflets available for students.

(Continued)

Table 4. *(Continued)*

Barriers	Solutions
15 **Disability** Survivors with disabilities may be at greater risk of not being believed due to individuals with physical disabilities being seen, incorrectly, as asexual. Individuals with mental health conditions may be concerned that the focus will be on their mental health and not the incident itself or that they may be asked or required to suspend their studies.	• Train disability support advisors on disclosure response; communicate they are trained. • Include students with disabilities in the development of campaigns (not just a featured photo). • Signpost to appropriate specialist support rather than only signposting to disability services.

We encourage readers to reflect on their own work environments to identify potential personal and departmental barriers. For example, working in an open plan office where there is no confidential space, lack of diversity in those who can receive disclosures, lack of information on support and report pathways and failure to model transparency when reports are made. By identifying local barriers, readers may employ practical solutions to reduce barriers. Every small change adds up and opens doors for survivors. One very easy and practical solution we encourage is that when staff are *trained and willing* to receive disclosures, they can use visual cues to ensure students and colleagues are aware they are able to receive disclosures. For example, an institution may choose to use a branded logo that is placed on a sticker, badge, email signature block, or staff online profile which informs the community that the member of staff is trained and willing to receive disclosures. It is important to note that not all staff who receive training will want to accept disclosures or are appropriate to fill this role. This can be for many reasons including primary survivorship (they were subjected to sexual violence), secondary survivorship (someone close to them was subjected to sexual violence) or possibly being resistant to this work – 'It's not my job.' However, there remains an institutional responsibility to provide training for all staff.

KEY PRINCIPLES IN DISCLOSURE RESPONSE

Principle 1: Empower Survivors to Choose How to Take Forward a Disclosure

Rape is often about power, control and domination, not necessarily about sexual gratification. When someone chooses to rape another person, they are taking that person's autonomy and control away. When a survivor discloses, it is essential to recognise their agency and to allow them to have control in making decisions on what to do next. The best way to give control back to a survivor and to empower them to choose what to do next is for the responder to offer non-directive signposting information on their reporting and support options. This means giving the survivor information on what is available without directing them to make a specific decision. 'Enabling survivors to make this choice on their own terms, without any pressure, should be of the highest priority of all institutions', (NASPA, 2017, p. 20). We regard this as essential in underpinning all policies and practices that are developed within HEIs.

Principle 2: Safeguard Survivors and the Wider Community

The institution needs to balance empowering those targeted by sexual violence to choose how to take forward a disclosure with safeguarding the survivor and the wider university community. Only in truly exceptional circumstances should the institution determine to contact the police against the wishes of the adult survivor. If the survivor's confidentiality is breached for safety reasons it should be done through a consultation with the survivor and should normally be based on imminent risk of serious harm to the survivor and/or third parties. Where a decision to breach the survivor's confidentiality and report to the police against their wishes is made, survivors should be given the option to be part of that conversation with the police from the beginning.

If the survivor is under the age of 18 years old, then the responder must follow their institution's safeguarding procedure. In the United Kingdom, there is a statutory duty under the Children Act 1989 and the Children Act 2004 (England and Wales), the Children Act 1995 and the Children and Young People Act 2014 (Scotland), and The Children (Northern Ireland) Order 1995 (Northern Ireland) to inform the police and local safeguarding authority if a child (anyone under the age of 18) discloses any form of sexual abuse or sexual violence. When it comes to breaching confidentiality based on age, there are two common pitfalls in this area which are highlighted in the examples below:

1. A 16-year-old girl discloses a 16-year-old boy raped her. Some may confuse the age of consent, which is 16 years old in the United Kingdom, to mean that they do not need to report this to the police or local safeguarding authority. The age of consent and the safeguarding age are not the same. Any allegation, disclosure or suspicion of child sexual abuse must be reported. A child is defined as a person under the age of 18 years.

2. A 16-year-old discloses they had 'sex' with their 30-year-old teacher from their school. The 16-year-old is not labelling this as rape and seemingly is discussing consensual sexual activity. However, in this case, despite the age of consent for sexual activity seemingly being met, the teacher is in a position of trust, so the age of consent here would be 18. This must be reported for safeguarding purposes per the Sexual Offence Act 2003. It is illegal for someone in a position of trust to engage in sexual activity of any kind with a person under the age of 18 who is in the care of their organisation, e.g., the school.

Principle 3: Ensure Staff Are Trained to Respond to Disclosures

In our experience, requiring students to only disclose to a specific group of staff is not a realistic or reasonable expectation and has the potential for silencing survivors by restricting who can receive disclosures. Therefore, we take a pragmatic approach. In the same way any member of staff who is informed of a student's disability or of a safeguarding issue is expected to respond appropriately, we recommend that all staff should have a basic knowledge – 'first aid response' – of how to respond to a disclosure which is in line with recommendations for universities from UN Women (2018a). By training all staff (including faculty), the institution: (1) raises awareness of sexual violence, (2) informs potential perpetrators (students and employees) that sexual violence is taken seriously creating a deterrent to perpetration and (3) provides a basic skill set for staff that can be used across wellbeing issues. A basic disclosure response does not qualify all staff as specialists in sexual violence, but rather helps them as 'first aiders' to respond in such a way that they can signpost to the correct staff and external agencies where more in-depth disclosures can be received and support can be provided.

HOW TO RESPOND TO A DISCLOSURE

In this section, we outline four key areas of a good disclosure response using the acronym BLOG:

1. Believe,

2. Listen,

3. Offer options and resources, and

4. Get support for yourself.

This guides the responder through four main points of how to respond and is easy to remember. In our experience teaching this response to students and staff, we find that many individuals can remember the acronym even a year later. This acronym does not capture all parts of a disclosure response, such as considering risk, the need for a private space or how to record the disclosure. Just as we find it helpful to use in training, we use it here to structure the conversation of a good response.

Believe

Believing a disclosure is considered international best practice in HE (USVreact, 2016). Beyond HE, police in various countries, the US military and the Federal Bureau of Investigation (FBI) start by believing disclosures (Lonsway & Archambault, 2016).

Based on our experience in this challenging field, we know that for some readers this may be the most controversial section of this book.

Many of our readers will simply see it as axiomatic that those reporting sexual violence should be believed, but others may disagree with this operating premise. The 'b-word' (believe) may be met with concerns and possible resistance. However, first responders to disclosures can and should believe those disclosing sexual violence. In this section, we will highlight the many reasons why this is imperative in a disclosure response.

For a university investigation, the individual receiving the first disclosure automatically has a conflict of interest and will not be engaged as an investigator or discipline decision-maker regarding the individual accused, i.e., the Responding Party. As soon as someone receives a disclosure, they need to be separate from 'due process', as they have acted in a support role by receiving a disclosure. Therefore, that person can believe the Reporting Party because they will not be involved in areas where, through believing, they may be seen to bias a process which is set up to establish the veracity of a report made to the university.

From a support lens, employees involved in supporting Reporting Parties can believe disclosures, e.g., counselling staff, ISVAs or SVLOs. The institution should not require proof or an investigation to offer support to a survivor, consider reasonable adjustments, or interim support measures. Institutions would (rightly) not require death certificates when students report the loss of a loved one. The student is believed and provided with appropriate support. The support the institution can provide sits somewhat separate from the discipline side where evidence is required to find misconduct, as action may be taken against another individual.

Reasons Why Believing Helps the Institution

Organisations that have a culture where survivors are not believed will be much less likely to receive disclosures and have knowledge of the prevalence of sexual violence happening within the community. When survivors are not believed they are silenced; perpetrators are empowered, and perpetration continues. Perpetrators are likely to tell their victims that no one will believe them. Laura Bates frames this clearly stating,

> *One of the saddest things about the silencing of women*
> *through shame, normalization, dismissal, disbelief and*
> *blame is that it has become so common that it is used as*
> *a controlling tool by abusers themselves... As long as*
> *we as a society continue to belittle and dismiss women's*
> *accounts, disbelieve and question their stories, and*
> *blame them for their own assault, we will continue to*
> *provide perpetrators with this powerful and effective*
> *threat. (2014, pp. 41–42)*

On the other hand, if the institution has a culture where survivors are believed – their voices are heard, a common barrier to disclosure will have been addressed. The institution will have more data to understand the issues in the community and will be able to use targeted preventive measures. Perpetrators may fear being caught because they know survivors will be much more likely to speak out, be heard and be believed – this is a deterrent to perpetration. The choice to believe survivors when they disclose makes an institution safer. Although incredibly beneficial to institutions, believing a disclosure is not principally about institutional gains.

Reasons Why Believing Helps Victim-Survivors

The most important reason why responders should believe a disclosure is because if a survivor is not believed during a first disclosure, research indicates this could have a detrimental effect on a survivor's recovery and stop them from seeking help (Campbell et al., 2001). They can experience delayed recovery and are at higher risk for developing physiological and psychological symptoms, including posttraumatic stress disorder (Campbell et al., 2001). The experience of re-traumatisation or, as it is sometimes referred to in the literature, 'second rape' will impact their mental health, physical health and their academic progress. They may withdraw from the institution and may even forgo a degree altogether, thus having an impact on their future earnings. Clark and Pino compellingly state,

> *Survivors who have a negative experience with police,*
> *who are not believed by officials at their school, or who*

are blamed even by their friends often describe the responses of unsupportive individuals as almost a second rape. That betrayal of a trusted institution compounds the already existing trauma. (2016, p. 84)

In comparison, by believing the survivor when they make a disclosure, the responder can increase that person's likelihood of seeking support and entering recovery with fewer physiological and psychological symptoms (Campbell et al., 2001). Therefore, the responder holds great responsibility in how they respond to a disclosure, as choosing to believe or not believe the survivor can help them or cause greater harm.

How to Believe

Believing a disclosure may sometimes be difficult as some stories, to the responder, may sound unbelievable. They may challenge the responder's view of the world or cause them to question what they know about a colleague or student. Often, negative responses to a disclosure are more about the responder and their very human reaction to try to make sense of something, rather than a reflection of the survivor's statement. Responding to a disclosure should never be about the responder. The responder is simply performing a role to offer a positive and supportive signposting response. However, the reality is we all have automatic thoughts, some helpful, some less so. To respond appropriately to a disclosure, the responder must remain focused on the victim-survivor and leave their own thoughts, morals, questions and feelings out of the picture.

Therefore, the responder should accept a disclosure without questioning it. Believe that what is shared is the Reporting Party's version of what has happened. The responder does not need evidence, proof, or corroboration. They are not part of the investigation or discipline process. The responder can validate the Reporting Party's feelings and may wish to say, 'I believe you', 'Thank you for telling me' and 'It's not your fault.' The responder should not judge the survivor, their experience, or their response.

The responder should not make assumptions about what happened, did not happen, or should have happened. With crime reporting in general the assumption is that we believe what is reported to us. However, some seem to make an exception with reports of sexual violence where it can be deemed socially acceptable to routinely have doubts about such reports. We do not worry about false reports of house break-ins, but some seem especially exercised about the possibility of false reports of sexual violence. This perhaps reflects what may be deemed as 'everyday misogyny'. In view of this, it is something that we need to address and cover in training and be mindful of in policy development.

What About False Allegations?

This is a very common question raised when discussing sexual violence in HE. A false allegation is when an individual deliberately fabricates a story of sexual violence when this did not occur. We note that it is an identified societal rape myth to believe that false allegations are common (CPS, 2021).

For the purposes of responding to a disclosure, the responder is not responsible for determining if the incident occurred or not. Their job, in a 'first aider' capacity, is to provide an appropriate and supportive response which includes believing, listening and offering non-directive information on reporting and support options.

For the purposes of investigation, statistically false allegations are thought to make up 2–10% of reports made to the police in the United Kingdom and in the United States (Ferguson & Malouff, 2016; Kelly et al., 2005; Lisak et al., 2010), with meta-analytic studies showing a false report rate to police of 5% (Ferguson & Malouff, 2016). Studies that

(Continued)

review false allegations use varied definitions of what counts as false and rely on police information where cases have found to be miscategorised as false reports, such as using that label when victims refuse to cooperate following witness intimidation. Recognising that sexual violence is reported at very low rates to begin with, the percentage of false allegations proportionately is a very small number compared to the estimated rates of sexual violence.

We do offer a word of caution, however. Perpetrators can use a tactic referred to as DARVO – Deny, Attack, Reverse Victim and Offender to deny responsibility and shift the blame to their victims. This can lead to false allegations, often counter allegations, made by perpetrators against their victim-survivor.

Listen

The second most important part of a positive disclosure response is listening to the survivor (Campbell et al., 2001). The responder should use active listening and communicate respect and empathy, not sympathy. The responder should be patient and not rush, allowing the victim-survivor to tell their story at their own pace (Sen, 2019). By listening to the survivor, the responder can better understand the reason they are disclosing which will aid in signposting to the correct services. Listening will also help the responder identify any safety or risk concerns that may mean the responder can offer a safety intervention.

Sometimes it is not easy to listen or to empathise. Expressing empathy is a skill. The responder must see the world as others see it, be non-judgemental, understand the survivor's feelings and communicate their understanding of that person's feelings (Wiseman, 1996). It can be difficult to listen when the responder is busy or when they hear a story where they think they would not have done what the survivor did or placed themselves in that situation. Active listening, coupled with empathy, are skills that should be included in disclosure training.

Offer Options and Resources

Most university staff are not the right person to support a survivor after an incident. The aim is to have staff trained like a first aider to signpost to the right services. In the same way that institutions expect staff to raise a safeguarding concern to their manager, staff should be expected to know the basics of where to signpost a survivor. This is accomplished through training, communication, management, policy and procedure and reinforcement.

Disclosure responses should be about empathising and sharing information. Non-directive signposting is key. The responder may have very strong feelings about what the survivor should do or not do. However, it is not the responder's choice. The responder can offer information about the options available, enabling the survivor to make an informed decision. From an institutional point of view, if the responder chooses what to do next for the survivor and the institution has a policy that says the survivor will be empowered to choose how to take forward a disclosure, the survivor would be able to make a complaint to the institution as the responder did not follow the policy.

Sexual Assault Referral Centres

If a victim-survivor discloses sexual violence involving physical contact, we recommend that the responder always signposts to their local Sexual Assault Referral Centre (SARC). A SARC can provide a range of services for individuals subjected to sexual violence. These services normally include access to a forensic medical examination, sexual health screenings, emergency contraception, medical care, specialist counselling and support from Independent Sexual Violence Advisors (ISVAs). SARCs normally serve individuals of all genders and ages and are free to all. Survivors can engage with the service with or without police involvement, and evidence can be stored for a period of time while the survivor decides whether they would like to make a report to the police.

The survivor needs to be in control of what they do next, and it is important to respect this dynamic. The responder may wish to say, 'It is your choice what you do next. Would it be helpful if I shared what options you have?' or 'Can I share with you the support available in the university and in the community?' The responder can then provide practical, non-directive information on reporting options and support services and provide handouts or links to local services. We recommend that survivors of physical sexual violence are always signposted to a SARC or similar service that offers forensic medical examinations and related services so that they may have the option to access that service should they choose to do so.

Survivors also need to understand their reporting options and understand that they can choose more than one option. The following outline reporting option examples:

- **Formal report to police:** If reporting to the police, in an emergency, the survivor or responder should call the emergency number. When it is not an emergency, the survivor can call the local non-emergency number, make a report at the police station or through the local specialist service, e.g., SARC.

- **Formal report to the university:** The responder can provide information to the survivor on how to make a report to the institution for further action under the university's policies and procedures. It is helpful if there are multiple pathways to do this, allowing for in-person and online reporting.

- **Anonymous report to the university:** Students may have the option to make an anonymous report through an online tool, app or hotline (NASPA, 2017). Staff may be permitted to file an anonymous report on behalf of the student. Typically, anonymous reports would be used to monitor trends and target prevention measures. In some cases, anonymous reports may require investigation at the discretion of the institution for safeguarding purposes.

- **Make no report and seek support:** Survivors may not want to report to either the police or university for many reasons. They can be signposted to internal and external support options. To access support, survivors should not be required to provide evidence of an incident or forced to make a report.

Promoting Support Services and Reporting Options

- Request service leaflets from local specialist services and promotional materials that can be shared in locations where students and staff can access them easily.
- Create an interactive webpage that provides accessible information regarding each service.
- Create posters, stickers, coasters, business cards and/or bookmarks with key services' contact information.
- Add key services' contact details to campus cards.
- Use visuals, e.g., flowcharts/diagrams, to represent reporting and support options.
- Check in with local services at minimum once per year before the beginning of the academic year to confirm services offered and contact details as these can change.

The following case study provides examples of unhelpful responses to a disclosure where the responder fails to use non-directive signposting.

Case Study: Mark and Mary

Example 1	Example 2
Taylor discloses to Mark that Ashley sexually assaulted her about a week ago at a house party. Mark believes that all potential	*Taylor discloses to Mary that Ashley sexually assaulted her about a week ago at a house party. Mary has dealt with cases before*

(Continued)

criminal offences should always be reported to the police for the purpose of public safety. Mark tells Taylor that she has to report the sexual assault to the police. Taylor is nervous about this option and is not sure she wants to do this. Mark helps her report the incident to the police. Eighteen months later, the police investigation ends in no further action. Taylor is given the option to have the university investigate a potential breach of policy if she makes a report against Ashley. Taylor's academic performance has declined, and she is about to enter the final year of her degree. Ashley is now a postgraduate student in her department. Taylor is unsure if she can cope with participating in a further investigation and feels defeated, as she is unsure if any disciplinary action will be taken against Ashley, as Ashley is well known in the department.

and knows that the police process can be traumatic, long, and often leads to no further action. Mary has not been impressed with how police treat survivors and feels strongly that Taylor should not report to the police. Mary tells Taylor how she feels and encourages Taylor to go to the university as an alternative to reporting to the police. Mary tells Taylor if she were in her shoes that this is what she would do. Taylor takes Mary's advice and does not report the incident to the police. Three months later, during the university investigation, Taylor decides she needs to tell the police because she continues to feel unsafe. The university investigation is paused, and the police investigation ends in no further action months later. Taylor blames Mary for encouraging her not to report to the police initially.

Discussion

In both examples, the university policy states that Reporting Parties will be empowered to choose how to take forward a disclosure. Employees are expected to offer non-directive signposting to all reporting and support options. Mark and Mary have both acted outside of the policy and made the disclosure response about their own opinions and experiences, rather than applying the procedures of the institution, negatively impacting Taylor and exposing the institution to risk of a complaint for procedural error. These examples are purposely set against each other to demonstrate the importance of having clear disclosure response guidelines for staff within the institution's procedure. For Taylor, depending on who she contacted, she received inconsistent responses. The only thing that was consistent was that Mark and Mary both made the disclosure about themselves and led Taylor down a path they thought she should choose. The best response would have been to offer non-directive signposting, to empower her to make an informed choice and to offer her the support regardless of the decision she made.

Recording a Disclosure

It is important to keep a record of any disclosure received. A Disclosure Recording Form (See Resource 4) is a tool that may be used to record a brief, non-judgemental, factual note of the information that was shared at the time of the disclosure. This is especially important if the disclosure is the first disclosure made to a professional and the Reporting Party chooses to make a report to the police. The police will be interested in speaking to the first person who received the disclosure. By recording the disclosure on a Disclosure Recording Form, the person who received the disclosure does not have to rely on their own memory of that conversation. It is best to provide a copy of the disclosure record to the individual who made the disclosure, allowing that person to have control over their data beyond how long an institution may keep the form. An example of a completed disclosure form is shown in Fig. 3 which returns to Taylor who in this example has received a more appropriate disclosure response from Juan.

Get Support for Yourself: Self-Care for the Responder

Disclosures will (and should) affect the responder. Whether the disclosure is a story about something that might be everyday or the most heinous event the responder can imagine, when someone trusts a

DISCLOSURE INFORMATION			
Date of Disclosure	9 November 2024		
Start Time	12:30	**End Time**	13:30
REPORTING PARTY the individual who was the subject of sexual violence			
Name	Taylor R.		
Gender	Woman		
Affiliation to institution	☑ Student ☐ Employee ☐ Visitor ☐ Other _____		
Department	Music		
If student, indicate year	☑ Undergraduate ☐ Postgraduate Year *first year*		
RESPONDING PARTY the individual reported to have committed sexual violence			
Name	Ashley P.		
Gender	Man		
Relationship to Reporting Party	peer		
Affiliation to institution	☑ Student ☐ Employee ☐ Visitor ☐ Other _____		
Department	Music		
If student, indicate year	☑ Undergraduate ☐ Postgraduate Year *third year*		

Fig. 3. Example of a Completed Disclosure Recording Form.

INCIDENT/S INFORMATION	
Date & Time of Incident/s	*31 October 2024 / 1 November 2024; around midnight*
Location of Incident/s	*Friend's house off campus*
Details about incident/s as disclosed by the Reporting Party	*Taylor disclosed that she went to pre's with her friends around 8PM and had a few drinks. Following that they left to a house party a few streets over where Taylor saw Ashley. They danced and drank together, and then Taylor started to feel "dizzy." Ashley offered to help her upstairs so she could rest. Taylor cannot remember what happened next, but reported that she woke up on a bed with Ashley undressing her. Taylor reported feeling "frozen" and that she did not know what to do. Taylor reported, "He began to touch me between my legs." Taylor's friend Mina walked in looking for her, and Ashley jumped away from Taylor. Taylor reported she wasn't sure how much Mina saw, but that she giggled and left the room. After Mina interrupted, Ashley said the mood was gone and left too. Taylor got dressed and made her way back downstairs. She found her friends and went back to her room. Taylor has been avoiding Ashley since then.*
Safeguarding issues identified & actions taken to address issues	*Ashley is in charge of an upcoming fieldtrip for the music society connected to their department. Taylor is supposed to attend the fieldtrip and is worried that Ashley will try something again with her or do it to someone else. Taylor turned 18 years old last month. Ashley does not supervise Taylor; however, the relationship during the fieldtrip is unclear. Taylor does not want her parents to know what happened and isn't sure she wants the department to know.*
Record the reporting & support options discussed & what, if any, decisions were taken by the Reporting Party	*Informed Taylor she can report to the police, the university, both, or take time to consider her options. Signposted her to the local Sexual Assault Referral Centre and informed her that she may be able to discuss reporting options with the Independent Sexual Violence Advisor. Signposted her to Student Wellbeing Office and to the sexual misconduct response manager. Taylor reported she wasn't sure if she wanted to make a report to the police or univeristy, but wanted to discuss her options. Supported Taylor to make an appointment with the sexual misconduct response manager. Provided copy of this note to Taylor.*

Fig. 3. (Continued).

Did you signpost to the (check all that apply)	☑ Sexual Assault Referral Centre
	☑ Police
	☑ Student Services
	☐ Specialist Counselling
	☐ University Counselling
	☐ Employee Assistance Programme
	☑ Other: *sexual misconduct response manager*
INDIVIDUAL WHO RECEIVED AND RECORDED THE DISCLOSURE	
Name	*Juan R.*
Title/Role & **Department**	*Harrasment contact, Equality and Diversity*
Contact Details	*Juan@uniemail.ac.uk or internal ext. 55555*
Date Recorded	*9 November 2024*

Fig. 3. (Continued).

responder with a piece of their story, it makes a mark. It is important for responders, and practitioners dealing with this daily, to reflect on strategies and skills to cope with hearing stories of sexual violence. Those who are managing staff who receive disclosures should consider how staff will be supported and how staff are offered a space to debrief and process emotions. Note this is not necessarily appropriate for a line manager to conduct as staff may feel their performance is being judged rather than being able to process their response to a disclosure.

The responder is encouraged to seek support when needed. They must recognise their own limitations and signpost the student to the appropriate services. Responders are expected to maintain professional boundaries with the Reporting Party and not attempt to fix or coddle them; boundaries are healthy for the responder and Reporting Party. Responders should avoid processing their personal feelings with the Reporting Party. Following a disclosure, the responder may process their feelings with a supervisor, counsellor, peer in a support network, or specialist service. We encourage the responder to keep the survivor's story private when seeking support and only discuss their own emotions and reactions to the disclosure rather than details of the case.

It is important that the responder take time to recognise how a disclosure affects them. Even if the responder has never experienced an incident on the sexual violence continuum or been close to someone who has, they still will likely be impacted. In some cases, this can have a significant impact on the responder. In Chapter 10, we discuss how being exposed to other's trauma can impact practitioners and this includes those acting as first responders. We recommend practicing healthy coping skills such as exercise, meditation, mindfulness, engaging in hobbies, talking to others and practicing a healthy work/ life balance. Healthy coping skills are only effective when practiced; this can mitigate the risks of being exposed to others' trauma. For more on this discussion, see the practitioner safety section in Chapter 10.

WHAT NOT TO DO

It is important to take a moment and highlight what responders should not do. Some of these were highlighted in the above section, e.g., do not make the disclosure response about the responder. Before concluding this chapter, we list a few key 'do-not's':

- **The responder should not contact the Responding Party.**
  Regardless of the Reporting Party's choice, it is completely inappropriate for the responder to inform the Responding Party of the disclosure. If the Reporting Party chooses to report to the police and the responder has already told the Responding Party, then the police will lose the opportunity to have the first conversation with that individual and the responder will have inserted themselves into the investigation. If the Reporting Party chooses to report to the institution, then the Responding Party will be informed by the appropriate person in the institution at the appropriate time in the process. If the Reporting Party decides to seek support only, the Responding Party still should not be informed by the responder.

The responder must follow the institutions' policy in this area, even if they know the Responding Party well.

- **The responder should not self-disclose personal experiences of sexual violence during a disclosure response.** They may feel this would be helpful to build rapport with the Reporting Party; however, it shifts the disclosure response to be about the responder rather than the victim-survivor, who is then placed in a helping position. In the same way, responders should not say they know how that person feels. Even if they had a very similar experience, no two experiences are alike, and it is not about the responder in that moment.

- **The responder should never ask victim-blaming questions.** Questions about 'why' the Reporting Party did or did not do something are not part of a good disclosure response. The responder is not an investigator and should not seek to try and understand what has happened to assuage their curiosity. Questions such as, 'How drunk were you?' 'Are you sure you didn't lead him on?' 'Why didn't you say no?' are all examples of victim-blaming questions which should not be asked. These questions will cause the victim-survivor to feel shamed and blamed, negatively impacting their recovery.

In summary, anyone could receive a disclosure of sexual violence, and preparing staff to respond appropriately ensures that staff follow the policy and do not cause additional harm to survivors. The guidance we have provided can be remembered as **BLOG**: Believe, Listen, Offer Options and Resources and Get Support for Yourself (University of Texas at Austin, USA; Durham University, England). There are many other acronyms that can be used to teach a good disclosure response, including:

- **BRAVE: B**egin by listening; **R**espect confidentiality; **A**sk what support looks like to them; **V**alidate them; **E**mpathise (Ryerson University, Canada)

- **SEEK: S**afe space to talk; **E**mpowering attitude; **E**mpathetic response; **K**nowledgeable about sources of support (Boston Area

Rape Crisis Centre; USVreact; University of Stirling, Scotland; Sussex University, England)

- **STRONG:** Start by listening – don't push for details; Tell them it's not their fault and they are believed; Respect confidentiality – explain when and how you will share the information; Options – provide them with the options of support available; No assumptions – reporting to the police may not be what they want to do; Get them to somewhere safe – make sure they are in a safe location away from the perpetrator (Keele University, England).

Ultimately, we end with wise words from Annie Clark and Andrea Pino:

> *If someone comes to you and tells you they have been assaulted, it is of utmost importance that you say that you believe them, and that whatever happened, it's never their fault. Some survivors find power in sharing details, in naming their experience, while others might not be ready yet, or may never choose to name what happened. It's critical that you offer a survivor options and let that person remain in control. They might make a different decision than you would make, but it is their choice all the same. (2016, p. 158)*

📖 Related Resources

- Start by Believing Campaign:

An international public awareness campaign by End Violence Against Women International, www.startbybelieving.org

- Video on Empathy:

Brené Brown on Empathy https://brenebrown.com/videos/rsa-short-empathy

10

CASE MANAGEMENT AND PRACTITIONER SAFETY

Sexual violence cases are unique in that they cannot sensibly, we would argue, be managed in the same way other non-academic or academic misconduct may be addressed in university settings. Dealing with a case of sexual violence is uniquely difficult and complex; handling the case incorrectly can lead to further, and potentially significant, harm to students as we discuss in Chapter 13. As we highlight throughout this book, staff working on sexual violence cases need to be appropriately trained, qualified and supported depending on the specific role they will play in a case. In the same way we need investigators and adjudicators to be trained in considering cases of sexual violence, case managers and those offering support to the students involved, particularly victim-survivors, must have the knowledge of sexual violence and how to work without re-traumatising survivors and/or escalating their risk of future harm. Therefore, specialist case management of sexual violence cases is key in the delivery of a comprehensive institution-wide approach as defined in Chapter 5.

In this chapter, we consider what specialist case management for sexual violence looks like in a university setting and highlight three key elements of a specialist case manager's role as well as tools case managers can use. In the second half of this chapter, we focus on practitioner safety identifying the unique risks of working in sexual violence response in higher education (HE) and how to mitigate for these risks.

CASE MANAGEMENT EXPLAINED

Prince and Franklin-Corben (2023) present seminal work on the importance of specialist case management for gender-based violence (GBV) cases in universities. They identify the core functions of GBV case management as:

- *The provision of information on health and support options, as well as other services;*

- *Coordinating access to and engagement with multiple services;*

- *Advocacy, which we define as informing and upskilling relevant stakeholders on the science of GBV and trauma-informed practice, with the aim of improving the quality of responses.* (p. 218)

They go on to outline the core tasks a specialist case manager will do at different points in a case as follows:

1. *Following a disclosure:*
   - *Provide information on support and reporting options;*
   - *Facilitate access to support, negotiating with relevant teams and service providers;*
   - *Identify risk and escalate to relevant decision-makers, providing specialist knowledge on risk and appropriate mitigation measures.*

2. *Following a formal report:*
   - *Ongoing risk identification, providing specialist knowledge to decision-makers;*
   - *Bridge communication between the investigator and the Reporting, Responding and Witness Parties, keeping parties updated throughout the process;*
   - *Co-ordinate and support the investigation process;*
   - *Ensure all parties have access to ongoing support, negotiating with relevant teams and service providers;*
   - *Liaise with the police where the Reporting Party has chosen to make a report to police.*

3. *Additional responsibilities:*
   - *Data analysis;*
   - *Input to the development of training packages.* (p. 222).

The Role of the Case Manager

A case manager supports the case from disclosure to appeal, keeping all parties safe and ensuring procedure is followed. Specialist case managers will have the ability to work calmly with high-risk cases while maintaining professional boundaries. Those who are not specialist may respond to high-risk cases reactively wanting to take control and make fast decisions due to being nervous about the complexity of the case and fear regarding safety concerns. Specialist case managers will risk assess each decision and work from a triage position, not reactively, but proactively, as they routinely manage caseloads with cases of varying degrees of risk. Inherit in the case manager role is a strict set of boundaries which prevents the case manager from offering support to one or both parties, but rather they signpost both parties to appropriate support. Case managers need to communicate, maintain and reinforce boundaries for the safety of all parties, including themselves as we discuss in the latter part of this chapter.

Case Manager as a GBV Specialist

Having a specialist case manager, that is, a case manager who has specific knowledge of sexual violence and a trauma-informed approach, is key in managing these cases well. A specialist case manager can be responsive to changes in risk, identifying when risk increases, and preventing the university response from escalating risk. For example, in cases of domestic abuse, the riskiest time for physical violence (specifically, homicide) is when the victim attempts to end the relationship with or leave the perpetrator. Informing a perpetrator of a report of domestic abuse can be a risky time for retaliation for the victim-survivor. A specialist case manager will be able to identify these risks and advise the organisation of the safest way to communicate this to a Responding Party, while having interim measures in place to protect the Reporting Party, and precautionary measures issued to mitigate the risk of the Responding Party's potential for retaliation. Specialist case managers will be skilled in conducting appropriate risk assessments with victim-survivors, have knowledge of referral pathways into various specialist services to meet the needs presented by either party in the case and be able to work from an empowerment model to support Reporting Parties in determining what support and reporting options they wish to pursue.

Case Manager as a Policy Expert

Part of case management is helping to 'future-proof' the case, by ensuring appropriate procedure is followed so as not to open the case up for a potentially successful appeal or challenge on procedural grounds subsequently. This includes the careful sequencing of the communicating of policy and procedures to the students involved, staff who may support the case or making decisions about the case and any other individuals who may become involved in the case. Case managers will ensure all parties understand the procedure that is being followed. The role involves the management of expectations on how an investigation and/or disciplinary process will work and the potential outcomes. Case managers will explain timeframes and provide updates to all parties involved, including any reasons for delays. Case managers can also be the key in supporting the improvement in policies and procedures by gathering feedback and recording case trends to inform policy and procedure development. For example, if students routinely express that they do not interpret a policy statement to have the same meaning that was intended, this can mean that the policy is written in jargon that it is not accessible to students and needs amending. Additionally, through monitoring case trends, it may mean that a policy can be amended to include more examples of misconduct, e.g. if a case manager can demonstrate through case trends that domestic abuse or dating violence is being disclosed by students, but not covered in policy, the higher education institution (HEI) may take that as evidence to update the policy to include domestic abuse or dating violence as a form of misconduct.

Case Manager as a Coordinator

A key part of a case manager's role is to coordinate and communicate with all parties and staff involved in a case. This can include not only providing information on the policy and procedure to be followed but also providing regular updates on the progress of an investigation, the outcome of the investigation and the outcome of any disciplinary process. This also means that case managers may not take on advocacy roles for individuals when managing cases where both parties are members of the university.

The case manager can communicate with the investigator and support communication between the investigator and parties to assist in keeping the investigator focused on the investigation and not distracted or impacted by case 'noise' that may bias their investigation. Noise here is referred to as information or issues that are not directly relevant to the investigation itself, e.g. communication from students' parents/guardians, legal representation or individual senior managers who may wish for a case to end with a certain outcome. The investigator needs to be focused on learning the facts of the case to determine if on a balance of probabilities, the alleged misconduct occurred. Any involvement of investigators with other communication could be deemed to bias their decision-making, e.g. if a parent of one of the students is making a plea on behalf of the student or a solicitor threatening legal action. This is not directly germane to the investigation process and should not be dealt with by the investigator themselves but by the case manager, who can shield the investigator from this and deal with these issues on behalf of the university or direct them to the relevant departments, e.g. legal services.

Case managers are also key in working in partnership with external organisation to ensure safe outcomes. This includes supporting referrals to specialist support that may not be available within the university support services or coordinating responses with multiple agencies, e.g. the police, local rape crisis, ISVAs/IDVAs, Multi Agency Risk Assessment Conference (MARAC), etc. For example, in a case where a victim-survivor is subjected to sexual violence while abroad, the case manager can support the response removing the burden from a Reporting Party, working with the university travel insurance, relevant embassy or consulate, and referring to appropriate support in the specific area where the victim-survivor is located.

Case Management Tools

Risk Assessment

A comprehensive institution-wide approach will require that all disclosures and reports are dealt with from a trauma-informed, survivor-centred, human rights-based, social justice–based and intersectional approach, and where misconduct is identified through due process perpetrator accountability. A key element we identified to ensure a trauma-informed approach is prioritisation of safety. From the point where someone is disclosing to making a report and through any disciplinary process, safety is key, and considering safety concerns can be done through a risk assessment.

When a report is made to the institution or the police, the institution needs to conduct a risk assessment. This is best conducted by a specialist case manager. This risk assessment should consider risk to the Reporting Party, risk to the wider university community, risk to any witnesses and risk to the Responding Party. Risk assessments consider whether there is potential further emotional, psychological, physical and/or sexual harm possible to the Reporting Party and/or other students or employees at the university. It also considers the likelihood of the risk of self-harm or suicide for the Reporting and/or Responding Party as well as any potential risk to the Responding Party, e.g. vigilante-type behaviour by others.

At the time of writing, there is not a standardised risk assessment tool HEIs are expected to use. Some are using risk assessment tools built for frontline practitioners in social care, police or health, e.g. *DASH (Domestic Abuse, Stalking and Harassment and Honour-Based Violence) Risk Checklist* (see, www.dash-riskchecklist.com). Other risk assessments available include Lime-Culture's *Sexual Misconduct Risk and Needs Assessment in Universities*, Culture Shift's *Report + Support Risk Assessment* and EmilyTest's *L.I.S.T.E.N. Risk Assessment* for first responders.

Key here is the importance of having a specialist or trained individual conduct the risk assessment with the Reporting Party. Risk assessments should not be conducted on a written report alone, as victim-survivors will often not write the full details of what has happened and not always realise that some behaviours are key in understanding risk (e.g. 'choking' or non-fatal strangulation). High-risk markers include – use of strangulation, use of a weapon/item as a weapon, perpetrator was a stranger, Responding Party threatened to kill self or others, Responding Party abused a pet/animal, escalation in behaviours and Reporting Party suicidal ideation.

Practitioners using specific risk assessments need to be trained in using the tool. If this is not available internally, then we recommend the institution include external partners in the assessment of risk including, e.g. the practitioners from the local Sexual Assault Referral Centre (SARC) or local Rape Crisis. Depending on the institution's partnership with these organisations, there may be a Memorandum of Understanding in place that will confirm how information is shared between the two parties. If external partners are included in this discussion, it should be clear beforehand what information will be shared, how it will be shared, how it will be used and how it will be stored (and for how long).

Universities have a vested interest in maintaining their reputation, but a risk assessment for individual cases should not include risk of reputational damage. In terms of 'risk', reputational damage is more a consideration at a strategic or corporate level. For example, the risk of reputational damage when purporting 'to take sexual violence very seriously' when it comes to public statements but not taking it especially, if at all, seriously as reflected in a lack of investment in staff and specialist training. The institution should surely not take precautionary action against a student based on reputational risk. Although reputational damage may be a form of misconduct captured in the institution's regulations, the potential for reputational damage should not, we would argue, be considered in the decision-making of precautionary measures.

A risk assessment can be used to (1) determine interim support measures to offer to Reporting Parties, (2) precautionary measures to impose on a Responding Party to allow for an investigation to proceed and (3) in determining an appropriate sanction when misconduct is found, e.g. based on the misconduct conducted and surrounding information risk of allowing a student to continue at the university, i.e., do they pose a further risk to other students.

Interim and Precautionary Measures

Based on the risk assessment conducted by the specialist case manager, this will inform the HEI what interim measures and precautionary measures may be used.

Interim measures are support measures offered on a temporary basis to a Reporting Party or Responding Party based on the specific needs of the case. These may be offered to a Reporting Party following a disclosure and/or to the Reporting or Responding Party during an investigation and disciplinary process. Examples of interim measures may include:

- **Emergency accommodation:** If the incident occurred in the Reporting Party's accommodation or if the perpetrator knows where they live, they may not feel safe to return. The HEI can offer emergency accommodation. If the Reporting Party is in university accommodation, the university may be able to permanently move the Reporting Party to new accommodation should they wish. If the Reporting Party is in private accommodation, the university may not be able to get involved in private housing contracts; however, the university can offer temporary accommodation while the Reporting Party arranges alternative accommodation or chooses to move into university accommodation if available. Note here that the Reporting Party should not be charged rent for such temporary accommodation as they will likely already be paying rent on their original accommodation.

- **Electronics:** During a police investigation, the police may take either Parties' laptops, mobile phones or the other electronic devices; these can remain in evidence for the remainder of the investigation. Therefore, one or both parties may not have access to a laptop/computer to access their learning materials online or work on assignments. The university may consider providing laptops to students to borrow during these times.

- **Academic:** Arrangements may be made to allow a student to access their studies remotely, have extensions on assignments and/or change the location of examinations.

- **Finance:** Students may experience a loss of earnings during a police investigation. Students should be signposted to information on hardship funds and other financial services and support during an investigation.

Precautionary measures are temporary, non-judgemental measures that are used to mitigate identified risk. For a precautionary measure to be non-judgemental, it should most effectively mitigate the risk while having the least negative impact on the Responding Party and should regularly be reviewed based on changes in the case to be responsive as risk changes. Precautionary measures must be proportionate to the risks identified. For example, the institution would not suspend a student for a one-off sexist remark made to another student. However, it would consider suspending a student if the student is accused of subjecting another student to a non-consensual sexual act. Fig. 4 provides an example of types of precautionary measures which may be considered in order of low-risk to high-risk cases.

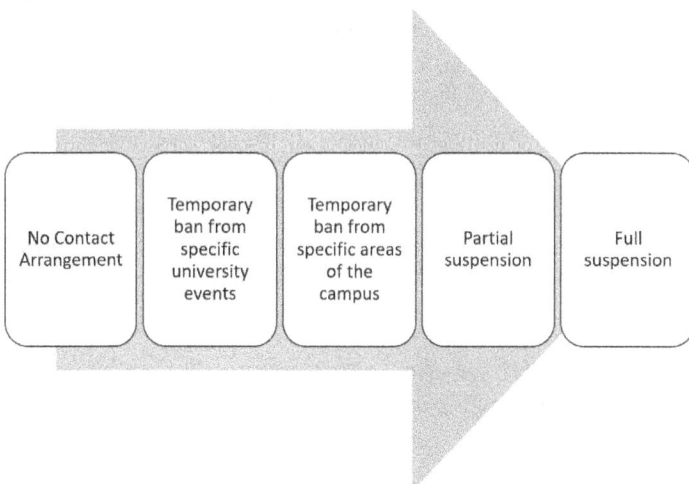

No Contact Arrangement | Temporary ban from specific university events | Temporary ban from specific areas of the campus | Partial suspension | Full suspension

Fig. 4. Precautionary Measures From Low-Risk to High-Risk Cases.

- **No Contact Arrangement:** This is a mutual arrangement applied to both parties as a precautionary measure to facilitate an investigation. This is the only precautionary measure we recommend applying to the Reporting Party. No Contact Arrangements stipulate that both parties will have no contact with each other including direct, indirect or third-party contact. It provides information on how to proceed should chance encounters occur (e.g., seeing each other on or off campus at a store). It is a temporary, non-judgemental measure. The consequence of breaching a No Contact Arrangement could be a disciplinary action separate from the investigation, or if the Responding Party breaches it, it could be added to the scope of the current university investigation. This is different than a No Contact Order which is a sanction; see Chapter 12 for more information.

- **Temporary bans:** The Responding Party may be banned from attending certain events, e.g. the Reporting Party's musical performances, or from certain parts of campus, e.g. the Reporting Party's academic department. Any bans from the university premises will have to be made in line with university regulations. For example, a Responding Party may be banned from entering university bars or sports facilities or the Reporting Party's accommodation block and academic department. Bans should be used when there is risk to that individual entering those areas. Risks may include emotional impact on the Reporting Party seeing the Responding Party, or that all allegations of misconduct happened when the Responding Party was drinking at the university bar. If the Responding and Reporting Party are in different departments, then banning the Responding Party from the Reporting Party's department will have little effect on the Responding Party while having a potentially significant effect on the Reporting Party's sense of safety.

- **Suspension:** A full suspension normally means that the Responding Party is banned from campus and cannot continue their studies while investigations are underway. The impact of a suspension on the Responding Party's academic progress should be balanced against the risks identified, and if a lesser precautionary measure is available to mitigate the risks, then it should be used first. Alternatively, partial suspensions may be used when needing to ban the Responding Party from large areas of campus and university events, but the Responding Party is allowed to continue their studies. Suspensions (in these situations) are non-judgemental and are only used to mitigate risk identified while an investigation is underway. Suspension decisions need to be transparent and well-evidenced. When suspending a student, the risk identified should be noted in the suspension letter to evidence the decision. Responding Parties should have a right to appeal a suspension and be given information about the appeal process at the time they are notified of the suspension.

All germane precautionary measures should be reviewed regularly. Any change or update in the case should spark a review of the precautionary measure to confirm it is still required and consider whether it should be removed, remain the same or be enhanced. Examples of when precautionary measures may be reviewed:

- Police investigation ends in No Further Action.

- Police investigation moves to charge Responding Party.

- University investigation concludes.

- Breach of current precautionary measure.

- Report of more allegations of sexual violence.

Online Reporting and Case Management Platforms

Key to good case management is reducing barriers to reporting and managing data well. Victim-survivors need to have options on how to disclose and/or report. Some will disclose in person to someone they trust. Others may not know who they can tell or may prefer not to disclose in person, so an online platform can be incredibly useful in helping victim-survivors access support and connect with specialist case managers. Here, we highlight a tool which does this along with offering case managers helpful tools such as a risk assessment and data trend monitoring features.

Good Practice Example: Report + Support, Culture Shift

Report + Support is an online reporting platform which gives HEIs insight to monitor and prevent sexual violence, bullying and harassment. The software allows students, staff and visitors to report any incident safely and access further support. Reporting Parties can choose to make named reports, request to speak to an advisor or make anonymous reports. Providing these options and having an online platform can assist in reducing barriers to disclosure for those who may not want to report to someone in person or not know who is available to receive disclosures. The university team receiving these reports can manage and follow individual cases with audit trails, logging case activities and utilising tools such as the built-in risk assessment. Additional value of this tool includes real-time data and in-depth metrics to get a deeper understanding of what is happening through the organisation. This access to data helps support the transparent reporting of trend monitoring information to university executives to support prevention and response initiatives.

For more information:
https://culture-shift.co.uk

Special thanks to Gemma McCall, Co-Founder and Chief Executive Officer of Culture Shift, for reviewing and approving this summary.

PRACTITIONER SAFETY

In the final section of this chapter, we focus on concerns that are directly linked to trauma exposure in the workplace. Practitioners working in sexual violence response in universities are routinely exposed to trauma. Although we might think of practitioners as specialist counsellors, ISVAs and case managers, for the purposes of this section, we include here those who receive first disclosures (first aiders/responders), those offering support to either the Reporting or Responding Party, investigators and discipline decision-makers too. A trauma-informed approach to sexual violence prevention and response work is not only used to safeguard victim-survivors and mitigate the risk of re-traumatisation but equally to mitigate the risks that come with being exposed to others' trauma.

When someone is exposed to another person's trauma, this is referred to as vicarious or secondary trauma. In the workplace, this can place practitioners at risk for compassion fatigue, vicarious traumatisation and/or secondary traumatic stress. Practitioners themselves may have their own trauma history and can also be at risk of re-traumatisation, which we discuss in Chapter 13. In Chapter 6, we discuss burnout which can occur working in sexual violence prevention or response work but is not directly related to exposure to trauma. However, we note practitioners can experience this too.

Compassion Fatigue

Compassion fatigue is when a practitioner loses empathy for those with whom they work. Someone experiencing compassion fatigue can feel emotionally exhausted, numb and/or physically depleted. A practitioner may begin to distance themselves from those suffering trauma as a protective mechanism (Preston et al., 2022). Sometimes, this can look like losing patience with students or being irritable with colleagues. Due to the practitioner's empathy being reduced, they may respond to victim-survivors in ways which unintentionally cause further harm (Perez & Bettencourt, 2023). Staff who repeatedly work with students experiencing emotional distress are prone to compassion fatigue (Raimondi, 2019).

Vicarious Traumatisation

When we are exposed to other's trauma, we can have a neutral or even positive response in how we see the world, e.g. focusing on the first aiders and being reassured in the good of people. Vicarious trauma-tisation, however, is a negative or harmful reaction from exposure to vicarious trauma with psychosocial symptoms including significantly altered perception of self, others and the world.

> *Long-term and repeated exposure to patients' traumatic lived experiences can cause disturbances in a clinician's cognitive schemas, including their beliefs that the world is safe and predictable, that people are generally benevolent, and that the self is worthy and protected. These disturbances in cognitive schemas are associated with changes in self-identity, worldview, and spirituality, and they are characteristic of vicarious traumatization. (Padmanabhanunni & Gqomfa, 2022, p. 2)*

Secondary Traumatic Stress

Secondary traumatic stress is when someone who is repeatedly exposed to secondary trauma experiences posttraumatic stress disorder–like symptoms without directly experiencing the events themselves. This may include, e.g. intrusive thoughts, avoidance, emotional numbing, hypervigilance, hyperarousal and nightmares (Hotchkiss & Lesher, 2018; Lynch & Glass, 2020; Padmanabhanunni & Gqomfa, 2022). 'The impact of secondary traumatic stress can be severe and debilitating.' (Lynch & Glass, 2020, p. 1044).

Mitigating Risks When Exposed to Vicarious/Secondary Trauma

As we can see, exposure to trauma in the workplace can lead to significant impacts on a practitioner. Unlike in regulated helping professions such as social work, where professionals are trained on how to mitigate the risks of vicarious and secondary trauma and demonstrate resilience in this work (Raimondi, 2019), not all practitioners in HEIs, particularly in the United Kingdom, are expected to have professional qualifications to work in student support. Therefore, it is even more imperative that (both senior and middle) managers support and safeguard practitioners from these risks. A practitioner experiencing compassion fatigue, vicarious traumatisation or secondary traumatic stress is not an individual issue but a reflection of institutional failure to protect staff. This not only can lead to harm to the employee but may well lead to poor services for students, staff sickness, high turnover rates and recruitment costs. It is bad for staff, bad for students and bad for 'business'.

Lynch and Glass (2020) studied secondary traumatic stress in student affairs staff in universities in the United States and found four factors which led to higher rates of secondary traumatic stress:

> ... lack of peer and supervisory support, lack of oppor-
> tunities to process and reflect on trauma support,
> unhealthy perceptions of what it means to be a profes-
> sional helper, and lack of confidence in professional's
> training and ability to engage in trauma support work.
> (p. 1061)

We conclude this section with ideas that managers and practitioners can consider to mitigate the risks of exposure to vicarious/secondary trauma which goes beyond token comments about self-care but actually embeds safeguards for the wellbeing of staff.

The Role of Management

There are several ways managers can mitigate these risks, and namely this is to create a safe and healthy working environment and awareness of these risks. Perez and Bettencourt (2023) highlight key actions that management can take to reduce these risks, including: (1) employing policies and practices aimed to enhance staff wellbeing, e.g. flexible time and wellness days, (2) equitable distribution of work, (3) compensating individuals when employees are acting up to cover more senior roles and/or when there are staff transitions all of which result in increased workloads, (4) encouraging staff to set and follow boundaries and (5) offering staff intentional mentoring and space for reflection on practice. Lynch and Glass (2020) argue that managers need to be trained in trauma-informed practices to develop trauma-informed philosophy of supervision, and senior leaders should use surveys or focus groups to understand how trauma is impacting practitioners within the HEI. They offer additional practical steps that can be used to mitigate these risks:

> *These leaders may also consider partnering with their human resources departments to explore equitable ways in which staff may be trained and supported in regard to dealing with student trauma. Examples of this may include exploration of compensation policies that cover a minimum number of visits for an outside counseling service, mandatory paid leave to recover from traumatic incidences that rise to a pre-determined threshold or restructuring of job descriptions to create boundaries and expectations regarding professional interaction with students experiencing trauma. (Lynch & Glass, 2020, p. 1063)*

In addition, managers can provide information to staff on compassion fatigue, vicarious traumatisation and secondary traumatic stress so they build an awareness of these conditions and can seek help if they notice early signs of these conditions.

Mindful Self-care

Self-care can sometimes be routinely relied on as part of a strategy to manage stress. It is hugely important; however, it cannot be used as a token action and should not be used as the only strategy to keep staff safe. Here, we discuss mindful self-care which can be used individually or collaboratively. Cook-Cottone and Guyker (2018) define mindful self-care as:

> *... an iterative process that involves (a) mindful awareness and assessment of one's internal needs and external demands and (b) intentional engagement in specific practices of self-care to address needs and demands in a manner that serves one's well-being and personal effectiveness. (2018, p. 1)*

Self-care often focuses on practising healthy coping strategies to manage stress, e.g. exercise, meditation, reading, dedicated time doing a favourite hobby and other activities that are good for one's mind and/or body. For coping strategies to be effective, it is helpful to practise these and to have a range of coping strategies for different forms of stress.

Self-care can be both an individual practice or practitioners can engage in collaborative self-care. Collaborative self-care can include engaging in group activities for the purpose of self-care and/or having accountability among practitioners to engage in self-care activities. For example, when closing a meeting and/or training, each attendee can state what form of self-care practice they will commit to intentionally practicing that day. The agreed commitment acts as a form of accountability which can encourage self-care practice when staff may normally skip that losing the opportunity to mindfully process or take a break from sexual violence work. Collaborative self-care can also enhance practitioner networks building a support system that can be professional and boundaried in the workplace.

Protected time for self-care is particularly important. We recommend that there is protected time within the workday for practitioners working with trauma to engage in individual or collaborative self-care. This is especially important as beyond working with others' trauma when being in role that deals with sexual violence daily, these employees outside of work have their own life stressors to manage. Therefore, a trauma-informed work environment will not expect staff to deal with the exposure to work trauma outside the workplace only. Within the workday, this space can helpfully be created to protect the work–life balance of practitioners. An example of protected time can be the implementation of **Wellbeing Hours**. This is an hour of protected time during one's working day once a week where the employee can focus on activities that enrich their mental and/or physical health to promote a healthy work–life balance for the prevention of compassion fatigue, vicarious traumatisation and/or secondary traumatic stress. This can also be useful for the prevention of burnout. Wellbeing Hours were implemented by the Welsh Government in 2018, where they greatly improved employee wellbeing scores (Morgan, 2018).

In addition, to creating protected space within the workday, encouraging staff to take mental health days or wellness days can be a useful tool as well. Staff exposed to trauma may be at higher risk for going on sick leave due to stress related to work. Rather than allowing staff to get to a point where they have to take long periods of sick leave, encourage the practice of 'Take time out, before you have to take time out.' In other words, take time off when stress is increasing rather than working to a point where one is so stressed or ill they are unable to work.

Trauma-Informed Supervision and Reflective Practice

Trauma-informed supervision is a key protective factor for practitioners routinely exposed to vicarious/secondary trauma (Padmanabhanunni & Gqomfa, 2022). Those working regularly with others' trauma will greatly benefit from supervision and/or reflective practice. Practitioners who are in regulated professions such as counsellors or social workers will already have a requirement to participate in any necessary clinical supervision. Supervision can be provided by a practitioner who is a supervisor, manager, mentor or even a peer in the same or similar field but not normally by the line manager. Supervision normally involves discussing issues arising from ongoing cases, considering decision-making in cases to ensure it is in line with sector guidance/policy, identifying and reflecting on lessons learned and considering the practitioner's own well-being and strategies to maintain this. Supervision can occur in one-to-one or group settings. Language is important, and some may find that the term 'supervision' may itself carry role assumptions; hence, some prefer to refer to the need for 'reflective practice' instead.

Reflective practice is an opportunity to build self-awareness of one's practice and consider any areas of improvement or lessons learned. Sometimes, we make mistakes. Practice is just that. It is not a science, and it is always developing based on research and feedback. So, what looked like 'good practice' in the 1990s in relation to how universities addressed sexual violence is now considered 'bad practice'. But part of that journey of development means that we must have space for learning and improving. We can learn and improve practice through receiving a complaint regarding a service delivered. But proactively, reflective practice can support practitioners and HEIs in developing better practice with or without complaints being made. To do this in a trauma-informed way means practitioners should be offered non-accusatory debriefing spaces for identifying lessons learnt (Klein, 2016). This is standard practice elsewhere where the importance of 'near miss' data is valued too. This can also include mentorship where new or less experienced staff are mentored by more experienced practitioners either within the same HEI or through a practitioner network.

Boundaries

Finally, we consider boundaries as another way to mitigate the risks of exposure to vicarious/secondary trauma. Managers should seek to set expectations and boundaries with practitioners and maintain these. Practitioners need to identify their professional and personal boundaries. An example of a professional boundary would be an investigator not acting in a support role with a distressed student they are interviewing but signposting the student to someone who can offer them support. An example of a personal boundary would be an investigator only working on a sexual violence case from their office on campus, not when remote working at home to avoid bringing vicarious/secondary trauma into one's home. This is very much an individual judgement – what is key is that it is a conscious individual judgement enacted reflectively. Once practitioners identify their boundaries, they need to communicate, maintain and reinforce these boundaries. And this is something that to be most effective really requires management support throughout the institution but especially perhaps with line managers of such specialist staff.

As we conclude this chapter, we highlight key take away messages. Case managers need to be trained specialists with a depth and breadth of understanding about sexual misconduct and sexual violence more generally. There is a need for a thorough understanding of the process of risk assessment and not simply a trained familiarity with a particular risk assessment tool, but rather a more nuanced and contextual understanding of the broader challenges when seeking to address our problems with sexual violence at universities. For case managers to do their jobs effectively, not unlike fire and safety officers, they need to do it with the freedom to enact the role professionally without prejudice and without undue instruction from line managers or other senior managers. We need to treasure such independence and trust their professional judgements. Practitioners are surely most likely to be safest when feeling supported and valued. Mistakes may be made, and it is crucial that there is an environment whereby such mistakes can be shared as early as possible so that any learning can be taken from the situation along with any efforts to rectify any such situations insofar as is possible. In general, there are more choices to rectify mistakes if reported straight away. Implicit to the arguments made around boundaries and professionalism in this chapter is a steer from us that it may be wise to select those from existing professions with a familiarity around risk assessment and what being part of a statutorily regulated profession means. Without the support and explicit leadership from senior managers at universities – to include governing bodies – it is unlikely that the role of case manager can be successfully enacted so crucially. Finally, leadership must support practitioner safety, as staff should not be harmed when responding to student sexual violence.

📖 Related Resources

- Prince, K. & Franklin-Corben, P. (2023). Case management as a dedicated role responding to gender-based violence in Higher Education. In C. J. Humphreys & G. J. Towl (Eds.), *Stopping gender-based violence in higher education: Policy, practice, and partnerships*. Routledge.
- *Safe lives dash risk checklist.* https://safelives.org.uk/resources-library/dash-risk-checklist/
- Steele, W. (2020). *Reducing compassion fatigue, secondary traumatic stress, and burnout: A trauma-sensitive workbook*. Routledge.

11

TRAUMA-INFORMED
INVESTIGATIONS

A higher education institution (HEI) can only investigate potential breaches of policy. The policy breaches, or misconduct, more frequently addressed tend to be academic in nature, e.g., plagiarism or cheating. Universities are generally very well equipped to investigate academic misconduct. However, many universities fail to understand sexual violence and do not conduct investigations that adequately investigate reports of this type. Sexual violence cases provide a challenge for university communities in view of the difficult and sensitive subject matter. Another difficulty is in terms of the sheer volume of such cases with university communities having some of the highest frequencies of sexual violence when, e.g., comparing students with other occupational groups. Universities do not determine if criminal offences have occurred, as this would be outside the institution's jurisdiction. Therefore, sexual activity without consent may be reasonably captured as sexual misconduct without designating this as rape or sexual assault, which is a matter for a criminal justice process to ascertain if desired by the Reporting Party.

For a university to have an effective policy against sexual violence, there must be the capacity to independently investigate such reports subject to the necessary consents from the Reporting Party, and if there is evidence to show that a breach of policy occurred, based on a balance of probabilities, consequences must be implemented. This demonstration of perpetrator accountability is required for a comprehensive institution-wide approach. In this chapter and the next, we discuss how an institution might conduct investigation, adjudication and disciplinary processes that are trauma-informed.

Until 2016, HEIs in the United Kingdom largely followed what was known as the Zellick report which was in short guidance from 1994 that advised universities not to consider misconduct which might also constitute a criminal offence through internal disciplinary processes. Thus, until 2016 universities did not have to, and were generally even encouraged not to, respond to sexual violence between its members. However, not all senior university managers were persuaded by such advice and indeed some argued for a different approach where university communities would take some level of responsibility for their problems with sexual violence on (and off) campus (see e.g. Towl, 2016). In October 2016, Universities UK and Pinsent Masons finally published new sector guidance based on the changes in the legislative framework in light of the Public Sector Equality Duty under the Equality Act 2010 and the Human Rights Act 1998 which shifted the policy landscape to require universities to investigate misconduct that might constitute a criminal offence as a potential breach of policy. However, the question of how an institution should investigate sexual violence has not been answered. In this chapter, we aim to present best practice in investigation techniques for sexual misconduct.

We recognise that many of the principles we present will be applicable internationally. However, the relevant legislative framework in a reader's home country will be necessary to consider when applying these principles. This guidance is not written for campus police investigating a crime, but rather investigators considering potential breaches of policy only.[1]

---

[1]For campus police, we recommend Busch-Armendariz et al. (2016) and Busch-Armendariz et al. (2018).

EFFECTIVE INVESTIGATORS

In Chapter 5, we discussed staffing requirements and the various options for resourcing investigators for trauma-informed investigations. We argued that regardless of who the investigators are, they must be trained in trauma-informed investigating techniques and have relevant knowledge of sexual violence and misconduct as discussed in Chapter 8. In this section, we build on those discussions and begin by considering the traits of an effective investigator.

Trained

Investigators must be appropriately trained and experienced to conduct the investigation. If investigators are inexperienced and/or untrained, the integrity of the procedure is at risk, trust in the institution to investigate reports of sexual violence will be reduced, and the risk of survivors being re-traumatised during investigations is increased. Effective investigators will understand sexual violence and the impact of trauma. Sexual violence is such that everyone may well have an opinion of what they believe sexual violence looks like, how one might act during an assault, what one should do to protect themselves from being attacked, who might be a victim, and how culpable or otherwise a perpetrator really is. However, these opinions may be based on widely held socictal rape myths. Just as we would not expect a layperson to investigate tax fraud without training in tax law and fraudulent behaviour, we cannot ask investigators to consider sexual misconduct based on a layperson's understanding of the issue. We would expect effective investigators to engage in continuing education on an annual basis. We cannot overstate the importance of making sure that investigators have appropriate training and support. In our view the time-honoured academic tradition of academics from any department simply being asked to undertake an investigation or matters of misconduct based on seniority is deeply problematic when it comes to matters of sexual misconduct.

Independent

Investigators should be independent of the parties involved in the investigation. If the investigators are internal, they should be from different departments than the parties involved. Investigators should be asked if there are any actual or possible perceived conflicts of interest before beginning an investigation.

Aware of Bias

Effective investigators will take steps to be aware of their bias and acknowledge that everyone has unconscious biases, or more starkly – prejudices. To accomplish this, we encourage investigators to engage in training and reflection to identify their own unconscious biases regarding race, gender, religion/belief, sexual orientation, socioeconomic status/class and rape myth acceptance. The latter is imperative. Investigators who identify which rape myths they believe are better able to challenge these and identify when this may impact upon a particular investigation.

For example, consider the rape myth that, 'The victim provoked rape and implied consent simply by their dress or flirtatious behaviour', (CPS, 2021; Myth 12 in Resource 5). If an investigator believes this myth, what are the implications for their investigation? The investigator might want to know what the Reporting Party was wearing at the time of the incident, and what the Reporting Party's intentions were in wearing a revealing outfit. If the Reporting Party presents to the investigation meeting in clothing the investigator deems as immodest, the investigator may judge the Reporting Party differently or assess her credibility differently.

There are many reasons why people believe rape myths. In this example, the investigator may have been taught this from a young age. Perhaps their parents instilled this into their upbringing which was then reinforced at school by teachers who measured the length of girls' skirts, and in their religion through messages that women should not cause men 'to sin' by their dress. Like many rape myths, it is easy to hold this as a source of self-protection, 'if women who dress a certain way are targeted, then by dressing differently, I won't be a victim.' However, rapists themselves have debunked this myth explaining that the act of rape has nothing to do with the person's attire and 'consent cannot be implied from the way a person dresses or flirtatious behaviour' (CPS, 2021; Myth 12 in Resource 5). This myth, like most, is used to excuse perpetrators and blame victims.

Regardless of why someone may believe a rape myth, it is important to note that rape myths are pervasive throughout our society, which contributes to why rape is so prevalent and accepted. Therefore, investigators must reflect on what their own biases are around rape myths, challenge these with facts and then own these biases while reviewing cases. If an investigator can identify their own unconscious bias or prejudices around rape myths and make these conscious, they can then: (1) improve their understanding by debunking rape myths with facts and (2) be more cognizant of their biases and logically consider how this is impacting their investigation.

Reflections on Rape Myth Acceptance

See Resource 5: **Tackling Rape Myths in Investigations and Discipline Hearings** then consider the following:

- Which rape myths seem reasonable?
- What is the evidence that refutes each myth?
- What is the alternative factual explanation?
- How might these beliefs enter your questions or behaviour toward the Reporting Party or Responding Party?
- Is the Responding Party (or witness) using rape myth acceptance to try to minimise or rationalise their actions?

Adapted from Busch-Armendariz et al. (2016)

Trusted

Effective investigators are trusted by the institution and the students. They have the relevant qualifications and are professional in their approach in working with all parties. They are approachable and build rapport with the parties during investigation meetings. They are above reproach. An individual themselves accused of and/or investigated for allegations of sexual misconduct should not act as an investigator into sexual violence.

Boundaried

Investigators work within the scope and boundaries of the investigation as dictated by the institution's policy. The scope of the investigation is based on the report linked to the policy. Effective investigators understand the scope of their investigation and their ability to investigate; they do not act as police (UN Women, 2018a). Investigators act as factfinders and access evidence that is made available to them by the parties involved or the institution. Investigators communicate their boundaries and limitations and do not attempt to move into support or advocacy roles for either party.

WHY INVESTIGATIONS NEED TO BE TRAUMA-INFORMED

A comprehensive institution-wide approach will be trauma-informed; this applies to investigations, adjudication and sanctioning. Under the Obama Administration, the White House released the *Not Alone* report (2014) that mandated that all institutions conduct trauma-informed investigations, thus setting a precedent for trauma-informed investigating in HE. It must be noted that under the Trump Administration the use of trauma-informed investigations was challenged. Upon closer review of the challenges noted, the issue was related to poor application of trauma-informed knowledge during investigations and failing to follow due process.

Trauma-Informed Investigation: Debate Versus Facts

In 2017, Emily Yoffe wrote an article in *The Atlantic* titled *The Bad Science Behind Campus Response to Sexual Assault*, asserting that the neurobiology of trauma was 'junk science'. Dr Jim Hopper responded in *Psychology Today* writing *Sexual Assault and Neuroscience: Alarmist Claims vs. Facts*, highlighting that the neuroscience does indeed confirm the neurobiology of trauma. ATIXA issued their position statement *Trauma-Informed Training and the Neurobiology of Trauma* in 2019 agreeing with some but not all of Yoffe's original points and agreeing with Hopper's points whilst advertising their products. Dr Kimberly Lonsway and Sergeant Joanne Archambault issued a *Statement on Trauma Informed Responses to Sexual Assault* on behalf of End Violence Against Women International, emphasising that the science underlying the neurobiology of trauma is robust and reliable (2019).

Ultimately, the current science confirms what is referred to as the neurobiology of trauma, and this is not specific to sexual violence only. For the purposes of a trauma-informed approach, seeing signs of trauma or not seeing signs of trauma does not mean there has or has not been misconduct. Trauma-informed investigation techniques help investigators to consider alternative possibilities for counterintuitive behaviour and provides a way to elicit more information from all parties involved. A Reporting Party could display signs of trauma, but the investigators would still need to confirm through evidence that the trauma experienced was by the Responding Party. Likewise, if the Reporting Party was not traumatised or did not exhibit signs of trauma, this would not mean that they had not been subjected to what they reported.

To conduct a trauma-informed investigation, we must understand how trauma can impact a victim-survivor and how this may affect or manifest in an investigation. An experience of trauma is subjective; therefore, we will not measure the impact that different forms of sexual violence have on individuals. What may be seemingly benign to one person could be devastating to another. Therefore, we recommend always using trauma-informed approaches as this (1) helps investigators gather and analyse more information, (2) helps investigators avoid wrongly misinterpreting trauma responses as signs of deception and (3) informs investigative processes (Henry et al., 2016; Lonsway & Archambault, 2019; Nolan, 2019).

The best way to highlight the importance of trauma-informed investigations is to share an example of what can happen when an investigation is not trauma-informed. We present this first, as we will critically assess this case study to apply trauma-informed techniques. At the end of this section, we will come back to this interview and consider how a trauma-informed investigation would have changed the investigative process.

Case Study: Jane Interviewed by Investigators Who Are Not Trauma-Informed

The following is an example of an investigation that is not trauma-informed and fails to adequately investigate an incident of sexual violence.

Jane, the Reporting Party, shifted in her seat, fidgeted and failed to make eye contact throughout the investigation interview. At one point, she described the reported non-consensual sexual act but did not express any emotion. Her voice was monotone, but she did not look even remotely distressed. During the interview, she shared new information that was not in her original statement; she changed her story. She described the door to the room being ajar but reported that she did not say anything or move during the incident. The investigators tried to get Jane to create a timeline for what occurred that night, but she could not answer simple questions about the order of what happened. Jane could not remember the layout of the room but was able to explain in detail how the Responding Party touched her. She reported having 'snapshot' memories. She presented as disengaged during the interview.

Upon review of this interview, the investigators were concerned about Jane's actions during the incident and the interview as many of her actions did not make sense to them if her statement was true. The investigators left the interview with the following concerns:

- *Why didn't she say no? She had every opportunity.*
- *Why didn't she fight back? She just laid there.*
- *Why didn't she try to get away? The door was partially open.*
- *How could she not remember the layout of the room when she was in there for hours? She conveniently remembers what he did and not much more.*
- *She can't get her story straight... There are inconsistencies in her written statement and interview.*

Based on that interview and the concerns they had at the end of the interview, the investigators determined that Jane was not credible due to inconsistent evidence, odd presentation in the interview and what they considered counterintuitive behaviour by the Reporting Party during the incident. They dismissed the case.

If the above case example is frustrating to read, we agree. Unfortunately, this reflects the reality of how cases can risk being mishandled when investigators are not trained in understanding sexual violence and fail to conduct a trauma-informed investigation.

Understanding trauma allows investigators to understand counterintuitive behaviour and consider alternative answers to the questions the investigators had in Jane's case. By understanding more about trauma, the investigators would have asked questions in a different way and possibly would have interpreted some of Jane's behaviours as a trauma response rather than counterintuitive behaviour. The impact of trauma itself cannot be interpreted as direct evidence of sexual violence but should not be used to discredit a Reporting Party as was done in Jane's case (ATIXA, 2019; Lonsway & Archambault, 2019). A trauma-informed approach provides investigative strategies that help investigators gather more complete and reliable information (Henry et al., 2016).

Trauma Response

We will now consider key areas that investigators need to understand to apply trauma-informed techniques. For this section we will primarily refer to Wilson et al.'s (2016) training bulletin *Understanding the Neurobiology of Trauma and Implications for Interviewing Victims*.

When an individual experiences a traumatic event, their brain responds through an autonomic (involuntary and unconscious) response. The brain, specifically the amygdala, detects a threat and triggers the release of chemicals into the brain and body to react to the threat. The person freezes briefly while the brain assesses the threat and determines which defence mechanism to use – Fight, Flight and other survival reflexes such as Dissociation, Tonic Immobility and Collapsed Immobility (this process is sometimes referred to as Fight, Flight, Freeze and Flop). This behaviour is unconscious and involuntary. When the brain determines that fight and flight are not options, the survival reflexes occur.

Dissociation is an adaptive mechanism where the person disconnects from what is happening. This may look like someone who is 'zoned out', 'spaced out' or non-responsive. Dissociation can happen during an incident or when retelling what happened. It can be misinterpreted by investigators and responders as deception or being uncooperative. It is perhaps best understood as a method of adaptation or coping and survival of a traumatic event.

Tonic immobility is a survival reflex where the individual is unable to move, speak or cry out; they are frozen. This can last for seconds or hours. Someone experiencing tonic immobility cannot escape, even if given the opportunity. This can occur when someone experiences, '(1) Extreme fear, (2) Physical contact with the perpetrator, (3) Physical restraint, and (4) The perception of inescapability' (Wilson et al., 2016, p. 18). It is sometimes referred to as 'rape paralysis'. Wilson et al. cite studies from 1993 to 2005 that show that tonic immobility occurs in 12–52% of sexual assaults. A 2017 study conducted in Sweden found that 70% of rape victim-survivors had experienced tonic immobility during their assault (Möller et al., 2017).

Collapsed immobility is similar to tonic immobility; however, the individual's heart rate and blood pressure can decrease, causing them to feel faint or even pass out, i.e., flop. The individual also experiences a loss of muscle tone compared to the muscle rigidity during tonic immobility.

Victim-survivors will not likely describe this clinical presentation to an investigator. They may describe feeling frozen or like they could not move. They may say they did not move or did not say anything or that they blacked out. Often, they are trying to make sense of what has happened. They are confused and do not understand why they did nothing. Victim-survivors often blame themselves for not resisting or trying to get away. It is important to note that victim-survivors already feel guilt and shame in relation to their behaviour, which is just as counterintuitive to them as it may be to the layperson. Rape Crisis Scotland launched the compelling *I Just Froze* campaign highlighting that it is common for there to be a mismatch in what individuals think they would do compared to what their brain chooses to do for them (see, rapecrisisscotland.org.uk/i-just-froze/).

Memory Production and Retrieval

During a traumatic event, the brain, specifically the hippocampus, can encode memories differently than how we normally create memories. Some traumatic memories may well be strongly encoded ('flashbulb memory'); however, many memories will be fragmented and encoded against sensory information such as smell, sound and sight and will lack contextual details such as timing. An individual who experienced the trauma may not be able to retrieve the memories in a linear way, but rather some memories may only be accessible in the first instance through a particular sense, e.g., hearing a song that was on the radio at the time of the assault. In addition, it may take time for the memories to be recalled which also explains why delayed reporting is common (Henry et al., 2016). This means that victim-survivors' stories may change as new memories are recovered. This can be misinterpreted as lying. In addition, memory production and retrieval can also be compounded by voluntary or involuntary substance use through alcohol, illegal or legal drugs at the time of the incident. Alcohol is the number one 'date rape' drug in HE. Individuals can voluntarily incapacitate themselves or be rendered incapacitated by a perpetrator. So-called, 'date rape drugs' such as Gamma-Hydroxybutyrate (GHB), Rohypnol, diazepam, ecstasy and ketamine can all cause memory loss, especially when mixed with alcohol.

Trauma Presentation

Following a traumatic incident, the victim-survivor can present with a wide range of emotions and behaviours (Busch-Armendariz et al., 2016). Flat affect, inappropriate laughter, crying, dissociation and even a calm and professional demeanour are all possible presentations. Victim-survivors may demonstrate their resilience during an interview; the presence of or lack of emotions does not confirm the legitimacy of a traumatic event. It is important to remember that a trauma response is a normal response to an abnormal experience; all responses are valid. The reason why this is important to note for the investigators is because the layperson may think, 'If it happened to me, that's not how I would act', or even, 'It happened to me, and that's not how I acted.' The reality is everyone will react differently, and it can be difficult to predict how individuals may act. This was highlighted well in the Netflix drama miniseries *Unbelievable* when the main character's foster moms think she is lying about being raped because she is behaving in a way which is very different from how they both responded after being subjected to sexual violence at different points in their lives.[2]

With this knowledge of how trauma can impact a victim-survivor and manifest during an investigation, the following are recommendations for conducting a trauma-informed investigation. Investigators must promote safety creating an interview environment that feels safe for the Reporting Party and in turn will make all parties feel safe (Henry et al., 2016). The interview room should be comfortable, preferably with comfortable chairs and couches rather than a table and hard chairs. Items such as stress balls, tissues, water and hot drinks can be made available. The location of the interview should be held in a neutral place so that all parties can attend their own interview without drawing attention to themselves as they enter and exit. Investigators should work to build rapport at the start of the interview, providing information about who they are, their role and allowing parties to know they can take breaks as needed. Investigators should avoid asking victim-blaming questions, such as 'Why did you let him in your room if you did not want to have sex?' or 'What did you expect would happen when you got into bed together?' Instead, investigators should focus on fact-finding, open-ended questions, such as, TED questions – Tell, Explain, Describe. Trauma-informed investigators may ask questions such as, 'Can you remember what you heard?' to elicit memories which may be encoded to sensory information. Trauma-informed investigators do not pressure the Reporting Party to create a timeline of events, but rather attempt to build a timeline of events from the information provided by the Reporting Party. Importantly, as highlighted by Lonsway and Archambault,

> *When interviewing techniques are based on an accurate understanding of trauma, and informed by the relevant neurobiological research, interviewers can ask questions in a way that is more in line with how traumatic memories are actually encoded, stored, and retrieved,*

---

[2]Based on the true story told by Ken Armstrong and T. Christian Miller in *An Unbelievable Story of Rape,* Available at: www.themarshallproject.org/2015/12/16/an-unbelievable-story-of-rape

and they can elicit more accurate information, which in turn can lead to more thorough evidence-based investigations. (2019, p. 14)

Now, we return to Jane's case and consider how the interview might have occurred if the investigators had been trauma-informed.

Case Study: Jane Interviewed by Investigators Who Are Trauma-Informed

The following is an example of an investigation that is trauma-informed.

Jane, the Reporting Party, shifted in her seat, fidgeted and failed to make eye contact at the start of the interview. The investigators explained their roles and the purpose of the interview. They worked to build rapport with Jane and reminded her that she could take as many breaks as she needed. At one point, she described the reported non-consensual sexual act but did not express any emotion. Her voice was monotone, but she did not look even remotely distressed. The investigators thanked her for explaining what she could remember and reminded her that she was in the interview room with them in a safe place. During the interview she shared new information that was not in her original statement; she changed her story. The investigators recognised that she may have recalled new information. She described the door to the room being ajar but that she did not say anything or move during the incident. The investigators asked Jane what she remembered about how she felt when she noticed the door was ajar. Jane reported she tried to move but could not. Jane reported feeling frozen and later felt stupid for not leaving when she had the chance. The investigators asked Jane to share what she could remember occurred that night and where possible to indicate any details around time or sequence she could remember. Jane was able to remember what occurred on the night out before going back to the room but could not recall the sequence of events beyond that point. She shared what she referred to as 'snapshots' of memories. Jane could not remember the layout of the room but was able to explain in detail how the Responding Party touched her.

The investigators recognised that Jane's story changed. The investigators considered the following during the interview:

- *She didn't say no. Was she able to say no? Did she say yes? Was there any verbal or nonverbal communication of consent?*
- *She didn't fight back. Was she afraid? Was she able to move? Did she feel able to move? Did the Responding Party threaten her or use any force against her?*
- *She knew the door was ajar. Was she restrained? Did she feel able to move? Did the Responding Party threaten her?*

Based on that interview, the investigators determined that a trauma response could be one explanation for some of Jane's behaviour during the incident and the interview. The investigators would interview the Responding Party and witnesses next to determine if there was any evidence that corroborated Jane's report.

INVESTIGATION MODELS

We recognise that there are different models for investigation and discipline used nationally and internationally based on legislation requirements and sector guidance. Investigators can be involved in different aspects of an investigation process based on the model chosen. We will briefly outline the possible roles for investigators and use one to further build our investigation model example.

Investigators can act as factfinders, only collecting evidence and providing a report to a disciplinary panel without any analysis or comment on the credibility of the evidence. As the investigator is

'What About the Trauma Response for the Responding Party? Isn't Being Accused Traumatic?'

Ultimately we cannot affirm or deny whether something is experienced as a traumatic event for anyone as this is a subjective experience. An investigation is likely to be anxiety inducing and highly stressful for the Responding Party, but we think that this is unlikely to compare with the SAMHSA's definition of trauma used in Chapter 5. To our knowledge there is no evidence to show that an internal university investigation has caused a Responding Party to fear for their life, to feel violated, to bring on acute stress disorder or post-traumatic stress disorder or create the physiological traumatic response that victim-survivors experience during rape. We do believe a report of sexual violence made against a Responding Party can have a significant emotional impact on the Responding Party and HEIs must offer appropriate support to the Responding Party (Murphy & Van Brunt, 2017). However, we would not wish to equate that with survivor trauma which seems to be far more clearly associated with a traumatic response overall, and by some measure.

the one who collected the evidence, they are likely best placed to speak to its credibility, so this option may be inherently flawed. Alternatively, investigators can act as factfinders and include analysis of evidence in their report with suggested findings of no further action or further action for consideration by a disciplinary panel. This provides separation between investigation, adjudication and sanctioning and may be the most balanced option. However, a disciplinary panel may not be proportionate for all levels of misconduct and the third option may be more appropriate for misconduct that is less invasive, e.g., verbal sexual harassment. Therefore, the third option sees investigators conduct a full investigation and make the final decision on the outcome of the case without the involvement of a disciplinary hearing. Institutions may already use more than one option depending on the type or level of misconduct. We note that there are other models where a disciplinary panel acts as the investigators rather than having an investigation conducted outside a hearing; however, this option does not allow for a trauma-informed approach, therefore we do not include it for our consideration.

For our purposes, we will focus on the second option, in which investigators investigate first to determine whether there is a case to answer for a further disciplinary process, as we find it is a relatively common approach to sexual violence investigations in HE. Due to the limited sector guidance in this area and particularly in the United Kingdom, where models have not been tested long enough to show best practice, we build on good practice identified in different areas. The key points of this chapter are that investigations must be trauma-informed and fair and transparent for the parties involved. Whereas university policy development may in recent years require an Equality Impact Assessment, it is by no means routine to check that policies are trauma-informed. Therefore, few universities may currently have trauma-informed policies to inform investigations.

Fig. 5 provides an example investigation model. Following a formal report made to the university (and any other relevant procedures, see Chapter 7), the investigators are assigned and receive the case. First, investigators must review the case based on the relevant policy and determine the scope of the investigation. The investigators will then enter the fact-finding stage of the investigation where they collect evidence and interview the relevant parties and witnesses separately, starting with the Reporting Party to confirm the scope of the investigation. This is also the stage where they may test the evidence, by providing evidence to both parties and requesting a response. After this, the investigators will evaluate the evidence and summarise their investigation in a report. If necessary, the investigators will participate in a disciplinary process as appropriate. During the investigation, it is likely that the investigators will rely on a case manager to communicate the progress of the investigation to the relevant parties.

Prepare

- Receive case file
- Confirm scope of investigation and draft plan for investigation

Fact-Find

- Interview all parties and relevant witnesses starting with the Reporting Party
- Gather evidence
- Test evidence

Evaluate

- Assess all evidence for validity, reliability, and integrity to determine credibility
- Weigh all evidence based on credibility
- Assess the evidence against the policy breach definition

Report

- Summarise investigation and findings in an investigation report (see Resource 6)
- Include recommendations where appropriate

Discipline

- Participate in disciplinary process if applicable
- Present investigation findings to disciplinary panel

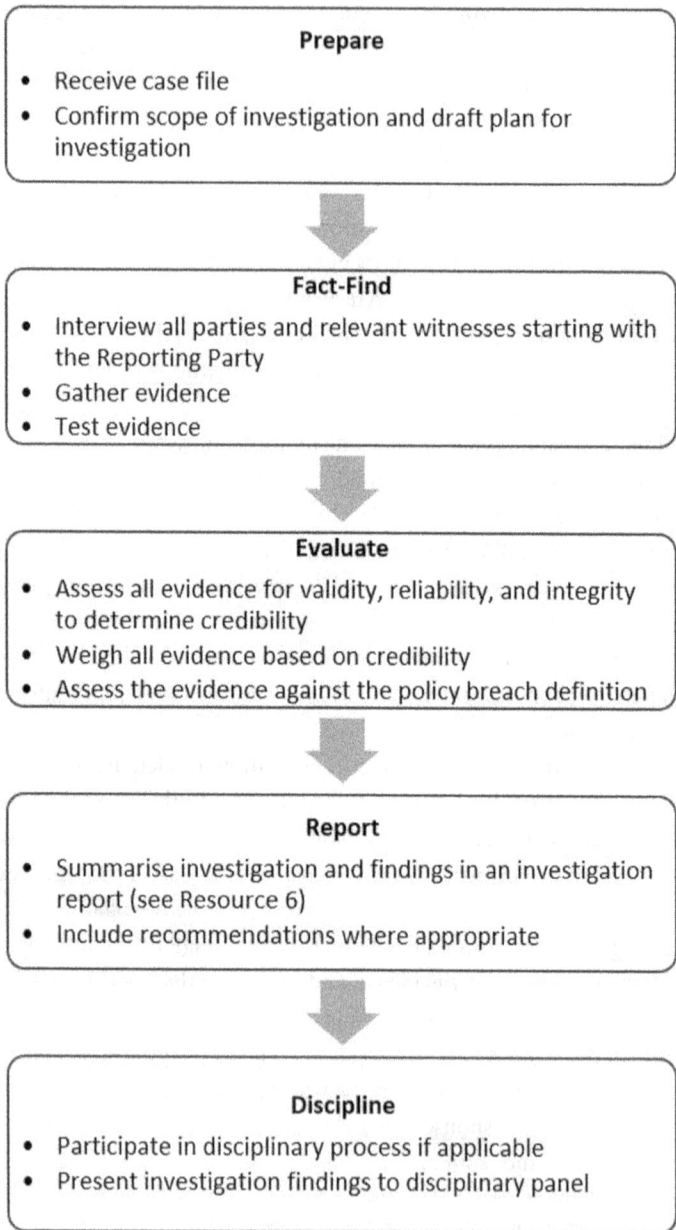

Fig. 5. Example of an Investigation Model.

COLLECTING EVIDENCE

Investigators are limited in the type of evidence they can access during an internal investigation. They cannot compel witnesses to provide evidence, conduct forensic medical examinations or forensic electronic analysis, nor can they obtain external closed-captioned television (CCTV). They are not qualified to interpret forensic reports. They can, however, access the following, which is a non-exhaustive list of examples of evidence that may be used in investigations within a university:

- Written statements,

- Emails/Letters,

- Text messages,

- Social media posts,

- Diaries/journal entries,

- Photos,

- Videos,

- Internal CCTV,

- Audio recordings,

- Phone logs,

- Campus building entry/exit logs,

- Letters from counsellors or doctors.

Witnesses

There are many types of witnesses that either party may identify during an investigation. Different kinds of witnesses have varying levels of importance in an investigation into sexual violence. The following are types of witnesses that may be used in a trauma-informed investigation (Sokolow et al., 2015):

- **Direct Witness:** An individual who observed or might have observed the incident/s or activity surrounding the incident/s. This person saw or heard the incident/s reported or saw and heard elements of what happened before or after the incident/s occurred. This is the most valuable type of witnesses if their statement is credible.

- **Outcry Witness:** An individual who knows details of the incident/s from the Reporting Party and/or Responding Party directly after the incident/s. This may be the first person to receive a disclosure from the Reporting Party. This may have been shared in person or via other communication tools. From a trauma-informed approach, an outcry witness may have learnt about the incident/s months or years later.

- **After-the-Fact Witness:** An individual who observed the reactions or changes in behaviour by either the Reporting Party or Responding Party. This witness may be particularly useful in investigations related to harassment, where demonstrating impact is important.

There are two types of witnesses that have little to no value in trauma-informed investigations.

- **Indirect Witness:** An individual who was later told about the incident/s by a third party.

- **Character Witness:** An individual who speaks to the general character of an individual but not to any aspect of the incident/s. The character of the Responding Party and Reporting Party is not in question. The investigation should be focused on gathering facts of the case to determine what was more likely than not to have occurred. Having the Responding Party's school teacher write a reference letter is not going to help the investigator to determine if the Responding Party did what was reported. Looking far and wide enough, anyone can easily produce a positive (or negative) reference letter. It is recommended that these witnesses are not permitted in an investigation or when identified, their statements/interviews are given less weight in the analysis of evidence.

We recommend that investigators interview all parties separately. The Reporting or Responding Party may wish to be accompanied by a witness; however, this may impact the integrity of the investigation meeting with that witness. Witnesses should only input into the investigation rather than receive information from the investigators about the report made. In cases where there are many witnesses, it may be useful to keep a list of everyone interviewed and their relationship to the parties and/or to create a map of how each person is connected.

COMMON DEFENCES AND INVESTIGATIVE STRATEGIES

In most investigations the Responding Party will offer a defence denying the report made against them. The Responding Party may seek to shift responsibility or blame to the Reporting Party or others involved in the incident. The Responding Party will likely say that the behaviour is 'out of character' for them, and therefore say they could not have done what was reported. In many ways this is all a very predictable territory. The Responding Party's intention or lack of intention to cause harm is not a defence (Sokolow et al., 2015). If the Responding Party did not know what they did was wrong, this is not a defence nor is it a mitigating circumstance. For example, 'I only touched her butt; it's not like I touched her breasts', is not a defence or mitigation. If the Responding Party was under the influence of alcohol or drugs, this is not a defence and should be considered an aggravating factor, which is discussed in Chapter 12.

The three most common defences used by Responding Parties are consent, denial and identity (Busch-Armendariz et al., 2016). In this section, we will outline each and discuss investigative strategies:

Identity defence: 'That sounds terrible, but it wasn't me!'

The Responding Party denies being involved in the incident and believes it is a case of mistaken identity. They may even deny being present at the time of the incident. In the university setting, this would most often be used if the Responding Party and Reporting Party did not know each other before or at the time of the incident. Based on experience, this is less common due to the small community scale of some universities. However, this defence may be used more often at larger universities, in more urban university campuses or where multiple institutions are in proximity. When the Responding Party uses this defence, the investigators need to establish if the Responding Party is correctly identified. Investigators would seek to gather evidence, e.g., view internal CCTV if events happened on university premises, speak to witnesses who witnessed events before, during and/or after the incident who may be able to identify the perpetrator and confirm if this is the Responding Party or not. Additional evidence such as photos, videos, screenshots of social media messaging may all be useful in identifying the perpetrator. If the Responding Party is correctly identified, then their credibility is undermined.

Denial defence: 'I don't know what you're talking about. That never happened! All we did was talk.'

The Responding Party denies that the reported non-consensual sexual activity or incident/s occurred. The Responding Party may deny all or some parts of the allegation using justification or minimisation. They may argue they said the reported remark, but that the meaning was misunderstood and deny intending to cause harassment. They may confirm one sexual act, but deny another, e.g., admit to penetrating the Reporting Party's vagina, but not their anus. The investigators need to establish whether the reported sexual misconduct took place. Investigators will seek to speak to direct witnesses, outcry witnesses and after-the-fact witnesses. They will likely review contact between the parties after the incident, screenshots of social media messaging, emails, journal entries and CCTV.

Consent defence: 'Of course, we had sex. It was the best sex of our lives!'

The Responding Party admits to some or all sexual activity and reports it was consensual. This may well be the most common defence used in university sexual misconduct cases. When the Responding Party uses this defence it is necessary for the investigators to conduct a consent analysis looking first to confirm that the Reporting Party had freedom to consent, capacity to consent and finally provided consent (See Fig. 6, which is derived from the rubric developed Black et al., 2017). This analytic will guide the questions the investigators ask and when they ask them. It will later help the investigators to analyse the evidence when determining their findings. It is helpfully ordered in a specific way to

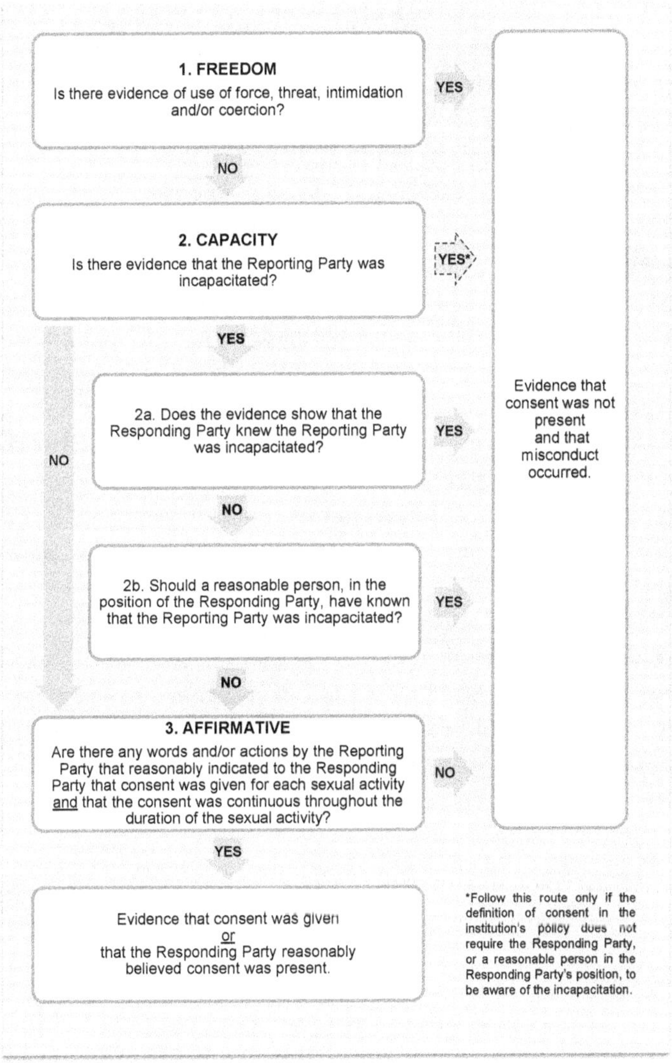

1. FREEDOM
Is there evidence of use of force, threat, intimidation and/or coercion?

YES

NO

2. CAPACITY
Is there evidence that the Reporting Party was incapacitated?

YES*

YES

2a. Does the evidence show that the Responding Party knew the Reporting Party was incapacitated?

YES

NO

NO

2b. Should a reasonable person, in the position of the Responding Party, have known that the Reporting Party was incapacitated?

YES

NO

3. AFFIRMATIVE
Are there any words and/or actions by the Reporting Party that reasonably indicated to the Responding Party that consent was given for each sexual activity <u>and</u> that the consent was continuous throughout the duration of the sexual activity?

NO

YES

Evidence that consent was not present and that misconduct occurred.

Evidence that consent was given
or
that the Responding Party reasonably believed consent was present.

*Follow this route only if the definition of consent in the institution's policy does not require the Responding Party, or a reasonable person in the Responding Party's position, to be aware of the incapacitation.

Source: Graphic derived from Black et al. (2017).
Fig. 6. Consent Investigation Flowchart.

keep investigators on track and not to be distracted by other issues the Responding Party or witnesses may wish to raise, e.g., the Reporting Party's sexual history. The analytic essentially deconstructs the definition of consent which allows the investigators to consider each element of the policy definition. The analysis begins with checking for freedom, because a 'yes' given under force, threat, intimidation or through coercion is not freely given and therefore cannot be consent. If the investigators confirmed the Reporting Party said, 'yes' first, they might forget that they must first confirm the Reporting Party had freedom to agree. If a Reporting Party had the freedom to consent, investigators next need to check to see if the Reporting Party had capacity to consent. Just like a 12-year-old does not have capacity, someone incapacitated due to substance use cannot consent even if they provide an 'enthusiastic' yes. If a Reporting Party had the freedom and capacity to consent, investigators then need to determine if there is any evidence that the Reporting Party provided any verbal or non-verbal confirmation of consent. For this strategy, it is imperative that investigators are trained in understanding consent and able to assess signs of force, intimidation, threat, coercion, incapacity and substance-induced incapacity during an investigation. Like in previous strategies, evidence from witnesses, social media, contact between the parties and CCTV may be used. Witness statements in relation to the Reporting Party's capacity are useful. Investigators will want to speak with witnesses who were with the Reporting Party before the incident. Witnesses may be able to speak to how much alcohol (or drugs) a Reporting Party consumed, what type of alcohol/drug was consumed, over what period and how the Reporting Party was presenting.

INTERVIEW TECHNIQUES AND TIPS

The following interview strategies are drawn from a range of resources (Black et al., 2017; Busch-Armendariz et al., 2016; Sokolow et al., 2015; University of Pennsylvania, 2012; United Educators, 2021). Interviews should be held in comfortable spaces that are private. At the start of the interview, investigators should provide introductions ensuring that the role of everyone in the room is explained (including an accompanier). It should be made clear that breaks can occur during the interview when needed. Investigators should allow the interviewee to ask any questions at the start. We recommend that in all interviews with the Reporting

Party, Responding Party and witnesses, that investigators use open-ended, non-judgemental and non-leading questions, e.g. 'What are you able to remember?' Investigators should avoid compound questions where they are asking for multiple things and rather aim to ask questions one at a time. They should allow interviewees sufficient time to respond.

When working with the Reporting Party, investigators should be mindful that Reporting Parties may not be able to recall linear accounts of events and there may be variation to what they can recall over time. Investigators should avoid victim-blaming questions. If they ask a question that sounds victim-blaming, they should acknowledge this and then reframe the question. For example, 'How drunk were you?' may come across as victim-blaming. However, to understand if the Reporting Party had capacity to consent, the investigators will likely need to understand how drunk they were. A simple reframe would be, 'It is helpful to know if you consumed any alcohol/drugs before or during the incident to understand your ability to give consent. Please describe any alcohol and/or legal or illegal drugs you used that night.' This may be followed up with clarifying questions to understand the type of alcohol/drug, amount and over what period this was consumed.

When working with all parties investigators need to continue to remain neutral and non-judgemental. It is not appropriate to approach the interview as 'good cop and bad cop', and questions should not be asked in an accusatory way. The tone is one of curiosity to find the truth of the case and the particular set of circumstances.

It is good practice to assume the Responding Party will respond with a consent defence and given that what differentiates consensual sexual activities and sexual violence is consent, exploring consent with both parties is important. Investigators should seek to ask questions of both parties (and possibly the witnesses) to understand whether the Reporting Party had the (1) freedom and (2) capacity to consent and demonstrated (3) affirmative consent. When considering freedom, the investigators may ask the Reporting Party specific questions around whether they were forced, threatened, intimidated or coerced by the Responding Party. Likewise, they may ask the Responding Party specific questions as to whether they used force, threats, intimidation or coercion on the Reporting Party. When discussing force, one possible defence is that a Responding Party may report that physical force was part of consensual sex act, e.g., in a BDSM (bondage, discipline/domination, sadism/submission, masochism) or kink relationship. If this is reported, the investigators would then need to explore whether consent was given for physical force, e.g., asking 'How did you know the Reporting Party was consenting and continuing to consent to [specific action] being used?' It is likely that in this case, the Reporting Party will have already highlighted the physical force as not consensual. Moving on to consider capacity, the investigators will likely ask about substance use as discussed previously and how the substances affected the Reporting Party's condition or behaviour. The investigators should ask the Responding Party to describe the substances used by the Reporting Party and how the Reporting Party was presenting. Likewise, the investigators should ask witnesses about the Reporting Party's presentation to determine whether it was reasonable that the Responding Party would have known the Reporting Party was incapacitated if this is evidenced. Finally, if there is evidence to show that the Reporting Party had the freedom and capacity to consent to sexual activity, then the investigators will ask questions to understand if there were any words or actions by the Reporting Party that indicated consent was given to each individual act and that this was continued and not withdrawn. Some questions that might help frame this include: 'Did you discuss consent?' 'How did you communicate expectations for sexual activity?' 'Did you discuss safe sex?' 'What was the timing of any agreement to sexual activity?'

Before ending an interview, we recommend that investigators offer the interviewee a break to gather their thoughts and reflect on what they have discussed with the investigators. Investigators should offer the interviewee an opportunity to share any last thoughts or ask any questions before concluding, e.g. 'Is there anything else you would like to share?' Reminders about confidentiality and any no contact arrangements can be provided. In addition, investigators should provide the interviewee with information about the next steps of the process. Finally, investigators should always remind the interviewee (even witnesses) that they can access support if needed following the interview and direct them to the appropriate service within the institution.

RECORD KEEPING DURING AN INVESTIGATION

The investigators should ensure that all aspects of the investigation are recorded, including all interviews. Institutions may choose to use note-takers in the meeting, ask investigators to take their own notes or audio/video record the meetings with the consent of the attendees. Audio/video recordings may impact individuals' comfort level in discussing the incident/s, but likewise adding a note-taker in the room can make it more difficult too. If recordings are used, it is important that a clear policy for who has access to the recordings, how these are stored and when they will be destroyed is communicated to the interviewees. All attendees of the interview must consent, preferably in writing, to the recording before this should be used. If written notes are taken, attendees should have the option to review and comment on the notes prior to finalising the notes. Notes/recordings of meetings should be considered confidential.

ASSESSING CREDIBILITY

Investigators (and adjudicators) will need to assess credibility to weigh the evidence and determine whether it is more likely than not that there is a case to answer for a disciplinary panel or that a breach of policy occurred. Assessing credibility means to weigh the reliability and accuracy of each piece of evidence presented in an investigation in light of all evidence (Henry et al., 2016). The investigators should use the same scale as the balance of probabilities for credibility. In other words, credible evidence will sit on the scale at 51–100%, but once it is at 51%, it is considered credible. In cases that are commonly referred to as 'he said/she said', the assessment of credibility is key. A decision on the balance of probabilities can still be established if the credibility assessment shows that one of the parties' evidence is more credible than the other (Henry et al., 2016). Investigators will look to corroborate evidence and will consider the source of the evidence, the content and how plausible the evidence is (Henry et al., 2016). Questions to consider are whether the statement makes sense looking at the whole of the evidence. What facts have been verified? Which account makes more sense based on all the evidence? Could a witness, Reporting Party or Responding Party have seen or heard what they reported, or should they have seen or heard more? For example, if a witness reports seeing the Responding Party leave the Reporting Party's accommodation, but at the time it is verified that the witness was not in town and would not have been able to see this, their evidence will not be credible. It is also useful to consider how biased or neutral a witness may be. However, it must be noted that just because someone is close to one party, does not automatically mean they are not credible.

It is important to highlight information that does not add to or subtract from the credibility of the noted party. The Reporting Party's past sexual history is not relevant to the investigation or their credibility and should not be considered as part of the investigation or adjudication processes (UN Women, 2018b). In addition, the Reporting Party's behaviour such as delayed reporting, having consensual sexual activity with the Responding Party previously or flirting with the Responding Party should not impact on the assessment of their credibility as delayed reports are expected and consent is specific to the time, place and activity and can always be withdrawn (Sokolow et al., 2015). In addition, the reputation of the Responding Party as an outstanding student or accomplished athlete should not impact on the credibility assessment (Sokolow et al., 2015). The protected characteristics of either party should not be considered when assessing credibility.

REPORT WRITING

Once the investigators have completed the investigation, it is necessary for them to write a report detailing their investigation and findings. This report will be provided to the Reporting Party, Responding Party and if required the individual/s responsible for adjudicating on the case, i.e., disciplinary panel. Witnesses are not provided with the investigation report or informed of the findings of the investigation.

The report should include (1) relevant background information, (2) an explanation of the scope of the investigation, (3) specific allegation/s connected to the policy definitions which are being investigated, (4) detailed discussion of the evidence, (5) a credibility assessment of all evidence, (6) summary of findings from the investigation for each allegation referring to evidence, (7) conclusion finding for further action or not and (8) any additional recommendations as required. See Resource 6 for an investigation report template.

From a trauma-informed approach, it is important investigators present information about a trauma response in the report. Investigators should document how the Reporting Party described their experience using their exact wording where possible. Investigators can document the Reporting Party's demeanour with objective wording without interpreting, e.g., 'the Reporting Party spoke in a monotone voice and did not make eye contact' (IACP, 2005; Lonsway & Archambault, 2019). If the Consent Analysis was used, include how it was used in the report and document fear, force, threat, coercion, intimidation and/or incapacity and/or lack of evidence of consent (Black et al., 2017; IACP, 2005). It is important to document the credibility assessment so that it is clear to the reader how different evidence was weighed based on this. In other words, if the investigators did or did not believe a witness was truthful, how they came to this conclusion should be documented (Henry et al., 2016).

Where possible, use the Reporting Party and Responding Party's own words rather than paraphrasing to ensure there is no change in the meaning of their statements. If the evidence shows non-consensual activity, then avoid wording that implies consent, e.g., fondling, caressing, performing, engaging in and instead use descriptive words to describe the actions that occurred, e.g., touched breasts, put penis in Reporting Party's mouth (Archambault & Lonsway, 2019).

Investigation reports should be written in past tense and in a neutral tone avoiding any language that may apply bias. When discussing information presented by either party or a witness, the words 'reported', 'stated', 'explained' or 'said' help ensure that no unconscious bias or misinterpretation is added to the information. Words that should be avoided include 'claimed', 'alleged' or 'complained'.

✗ Rita complained that Kelly sexually harassed her. Kelly claimed that they never did what Rita alleged.

✔ Rita reported that Kelly sexually harassed her. Kelly stated that they never did what Rita reported.

By using neutral language throughout the report, the reader can read the information without any inflection or bias added by the author. All conclusions and recommendations should logically follow from the preceding investigative sections of the report.

SHARING THE INVESTIGATION OUTCOME

When the investigators have finalised their report, they would normally submit this to the case manager or whoever authorised the investigation. The case manager should provide the outcome of the investigation and discuss any next steps with both parties in separate meetings. Where possible, these meetings should be scheduled on the same day in different locations to avoid the parties meeting. If the Responding Party is not permitted on university premises due to precautionary measures implemented before or during the investigation, the case manager can provide this information through a remote meeting. The parties should be allowed to be accompanied but not legally represented at that meeting. Where possible, the case manager may choose to arrange an appointment with the university counselling service following the meeting for one or both parties depending on the outcome of the investigation and any wellbeing concerns the case manager has identified. These appointments may be offered in person or via video/telephone. If there are next steps, such as an option to request a review and/or disciplinary process to be followed, as much information as possible should be provided to both parties about what happens next. Both parties should be informed of when they will next receive information.

INTEGRITY OF THE INVESTIGATION

Normally, at the conclusion of the investigation, both parties will be given the option to appeal or request a review of the investigation findings as outlined in the relevant policy or procedure. An appeal or review can normally be requested on the following grounds: (1) a procedural error that could have had a material impact on the outcome, (2) new evidence that was not previously available for good reason or (3) the outcome was unreasonable given the evidence provided. Following the conclusion of the appeal/review stage of the process, the individual who has requested this can receive a Completion of Procedures letter (England and Wales) or case closed letter. Note, that some universities will not allow an appeal until the conclusion of the disciplinary process, and due to current guidance set by the OIA, Reporting Parties are unlikely to be given the option to appeal the disciplinary outcome (OIA, 2018a).

The appeal or review request is one way to check the integrity of investigations. This is initiated by one of the parties involved in the case and this reviews one investigation. Lessons learnt can be gleaned from a review request; however, there will be no trends or comparison identified. A more comprehensive way to check the integrity of investigations is to conduct an internal audit. An audit may review length of time of investigations, adherence to procedure, application of balance of probabilities, consistency in approach and record keeping. An audit allows the university to capture trends and lessons learnt and check that the procedure is being followed correctly.

In this chapter, we have provided information on the need for trauma-informed investigations highlighting the basics of the neurobiology of trauma. We have discussed the traits of effective investigators and offered beginning strategies to develop trauma-informed approaches. More so than anywhere else in this book, we would highlight that reading this chapter alone does not qualify someone to conduct a trauma-informed investigation. Investigators must be trained and experienced to do this. The purpose of this chapter is to highlight key elements of a trauma-informed investigation noting often overlooked elements of this type of investigation when HEIs run investigations into sexual violence without the proper framework and training. It is our hope that this chapter has sparked interest in developing trauma-informed investigation approaches, caused senior leaders to consider the resource they are dedicating to investigations and encouraged practitioners that there are already tools and training available for the sector rather than feeling like they need to reinvent the wheel. For those using external investigators, we encourage HEIs to challenge the investigators to run trauma-informed investigations to get the best outcome for all parties involved.

Related Resources

- Norcliffe, C. & Pescod, A. (2023). Investigation and interviewing: Responding to formal reports of sexual violence in higher education. In C. J. Humphreys & G. J. Towl (Eds.), *Stopping gender-based violence in higher education: Policy, practice, and partnerships*. Routledge.
- NHS Lanarkshire EVA Services. (2015, April 30). Trauma and the brain: Understanding abuse survivors' responses. *Vimeo*. https://vimeo.com/126501517
- Black, N. et al. (2017). The 2017 ATIXA whitepaper: Rubric for addressing campus sexual misconduct. *ATIXA*. https://www.atixa.org/resources/atixa-2017-whitepaper-the-atixa-rubric-for-addressing-campus-sexual-misconduct/

12

THE DISCIPLINARY PROCESS

Higher education disciplinary processes are often best suited to respond to academic misconduct such as plagiarism and cheating where the higher education institution (HEI) is, in a sense, the injured party. There is a great deal of expertise on such academic matters accumulated over many years and reflecting a key area of core business of an HEI. By contrast, levels of expertise in relation to sexual violence, or sexual misconduct, tend to be very low at universities. And this presents some real administrative and moral difficulties. The administrative processes can be found wanting because they are often designed and applied without a consideration of the dynamics involved with sexual misconduct. Morally, the problem seems to us to be that if we know students to be at a relatively high risk of being subjected to sexual violence, then it is surely incumbent upon us to seek to put in place institutional prevention and protection programmes.

Responding to non-academic misconduct that is against another student or member of staff can present challenges to our administrative procedures. In this chapter, we build on Chapter 11 and recommend that these two chapters are read closely together. We highlight some key principles of good practice for disciplinary procedures and discuss options for benchmarking sanctions against different forms of sexual violence. We argue that creating sanctioning guidelines for adjudicators and publishing this material provides for increased transparency of the process and fairer procedures. If communicated correctly, sanctioning guidelines can also be a tool for prevention by acting as a deterrent for some potential perpetrators.

PRINCIPLES FOR DISCIPLINARY PROCEDURES

Natural justice is at the core of any disciplinary procedures ensuring that procedures are fair, timely, and conducted by impartial parties. The Office of the Independent Adjudicator for Higher Education (HE) in England and Wales or 'OIA' (2018a) sets out eight key principles for disciplinary procedures as part of their good practice framework. We summarise and expand on these as follows:

1. **Accessibility:** Discipline procedures should be clearly written, visible and available to all students and staff using plain language free from jargon. They should include information on how to access advice and support and allow students to appoint a representative.

2. **Clarity:** They should outline what behaviours constitute misconduct and what actions will be taken in response to reports of potential breaches of policy, including how sanctions may be imposed. Information regarding what may be considered as mitigating, aggravating and compounding factors should be outlined.

3. **Proportionality:** Precautionary measures, procedures and sanctions should be proportionate to the alleged misconduct. We discussed precautionary measures in Chapter 10, so we note here that procedures also need to be proportionate. For example, it would likely be disproportionate to hold a disciplinary hearing for a one-off inappropriate comment of a sexual nature made in jest. Developing sanctioning guidelines that outline the minimum and maximum sanctions available for types of misconduct can help discipline decision-makers in applying proportionate penalties for misconduct.

4. **Timeliness:** The discipline process, including the investigation, should be concluded as quickly as possible, normally within 90 calendar days. More complex cases may require additional time; however, any delay in the process should be promptly shared

with both parties, and explanations for delays should be provided as transparently as possible. Case managers can support
the timeliness of investigations and disciplinary processes by
providing students (and staff) with reasonable timelines for
providing statements during each process, e.g. seven days.

5. **Fairness:** Procedures need to be fair, balanced, transparent and
consistent for all parties, ensuring the burden of the proof is
placed on the institution not the Reporting or Responding Party.
Support should be available for all parties, and students should
be permitted a support person to accompany them into all
meetings/hearings. Decision-makers must be properly trained.

6. **Independence:** Investigators and adjudicators should have no
previous involvement with the case and should be independent
of both parties, including their academic departments, thus
avoiding actual or perceived conflicts of interest.

7. **Confidentiality:** Appropriate levels of confidentiality should be
maintained to facilitate the investigation and discipline process,
and this should be outlined in the procedure.

8. **Improving the student experience:** Procedures should promote
positive behaviours while safeguarding the student and staff
community. The disciplinary outcomes should be monitored to
capture lessons learned to improve services and to ensure that
good practice frameworks are being followed.

Can Students Have Legal Representation in Discipline Hearings?

The OIA (2018a) states (seemingly in relation to Responding
Parties only):

> *Students who have access to well-trained and
> resourced student support services will not nor-
> mally need to seek legal advice, although they
> may wish to in serious cases. It is good practice*
> *(Continued)*

> *for providers to permit legal representation in com-*
> *plex disciplinary cases, or where the consequences*
> *for the student are potentially very serious. (p. 9)*

and

> *Disciplinary procedures are internal to a provider*
> *and should not be unduly formal. It will not nor-*
> *mally be necessary for a student or the provider to*
> *be legally represented at a disciplinary hearing, but*
> *it is good practice for the procedures to permit this*
> *where there are good reasons. (p. 18)*

The High Court's decision in *AB v. University of XYZ [2020] EWHC 2978 (QB)*, and confirmed again in *AB v XYZ [2023] EWHC 1162 (KB)*, affirmed that criteria set in *R. v Secretary of State for the Home Department, ex parte Tarrant [1985] QB 251*, should be used to consider if legal representation should be allowed in university discipline hearings, albeit the case referenced was a prison disciplinary proceeding. The Tarrant criteria is: (i) the seriousness of the charge, (ii) whether any points of law are likely to arise, (iii) the capacity of the prisoner [student] to understand the case against them, (iv) procedural difficulties, (v) the need to avoid delay and (vi) the need for fairness between the prisoner [student] and those making allegations.

The High Court's decisions along with the OIA guidance confirm that there is no absolute right to legal representation at discipline hearings, but decisions to allow legal representation should be made on a case-by-case basis considering fairness and natural justice (which focuses on the rights of the Responding Party).

Given this, we briefly note concerns of allowing legal representation into university internal disciplinary proceedings into potential breaches of policy, i.e. misconduct:

- **Adversarial:** This further pushes universities into adversarial disciplinary procedures instead of inquisitorial procedures.

- **Economic:** Legal representation is costly and discriminatory and may serve to disadvantage students who cannot afford this. Therefore, what responsibility does the HEI/HE sector have to ensure that all students have access to legal representation should they require this?
- **Unequal:** If the Responding Party has legal representation, is the Reporting Party permitted legal representation? The Reporting Party is only a witness in their own case once the Responding Party is taken to a discipline process, so it is likely that the Reporting Party as a witness would not be permitted representation. If they were permitted this, then the question regarding whether they can afford this stands. Reporting Parties are automatically disadvantaged if the Responding Party has legal representation and the Reporting Party does not. This leads us back to the question asked in point #2.
- **Criminal justice drift:** Finally, and possibly most importantly, this is pushing HEIs into creating mini-criminal court proceedings rather than conducting civil internal procedures into breaches of policy, i.e. misconduct. See Cowan and Munro (2021) for a detailed discussion of this issue and the implications of this. And this is an especially important point if we are mindful of the track record of criminal justice procedures and processes in monumentally failing to satisfactorily address sexual violence with perpetrators only very rarely ending up being imprisoned.

Including the Reporting Party in the Process

A principle that is missing in the OIA guidance is the expectation of equitable rights for both parties in the discipline process. Traditionally, while a case is being investigated, it is part of the de facto complaint process. At this stage, the procedure has as its focus the Reporting Party, albeit that both the Reporting Party and

Responding Party have equitable rights in the process. If the complaint is upheld, the HEI would be expected to offer a remedy to the Reporting Party for the impact the Responding Party's behaviour had on the Reporting Party (OIA, 2018a). When it moves into a disciplinary process, the focus is on the Responding Party and the Reporting Party becomes a witness in their own case rather than a main actor. Therefore, while it is a complaint (or report), there are two members of the university community involved: the Reporting Party and the Responding Party. When it moves into a discipline process, it becomes the Responding Party's process, with the Reporting Party as a witness. HEIs must balance the complaints process, which involves two students with the disciplinary process that is against one student while still involving and providing a fair outcome to the Reporting Party. In England and Wales, this model is embedded into current sector guidance (see e.g. OIA, 2018a; 2018b).

It must be noted there are fundamental issues rooted in this model which take away rights from the Reporting Party once it moves into the discipline stage, meaning the process is no longer fair for both parties. It makes it appear like the ombudsman favours Responding Parties over Reporting Parties. For example, during the discipline stage, the Reporting Party does not see all the evidence presented in the hearing, so if new information is submitted that was not dealt with in the investigation/complaint, there is no opportunity for this evidence to be tested with the Reporting Party. A Reporting Party could have their complaint upheld followed by the same case being dismissed in a discipline process without having any opportunity to challenge new evidence.

Another example of this model inherently being set firmly against those subjected to sexual violence is that following the conclusion of the investigation into the complaint, both parties would normally have a right to request a review or appeal the outcome (depending on the language of the institution). However, following the outcome of a discipline process, only the Responding Party has a right to appeal the outcome because even though it is the Reporting Party's case, in this stage, it is the Responding Party's process only. The OIA guidance currently states:

> *If the student who made the complaint is dissatisfied*
> *with the outcome of the disciplinary process, the pro-*
> *vider should inform them what steps they can take. A*
> *witness in a disciplinary process cannot appeal the*
> *outcome of that process, but they may be able to*
> *make a complaint under the student complaints pro-*
> *cedure if they have concerns about how the matter was*
> *handled, or the outcome. (2018, para 166)*

If there were procedural errors or new evidence submitted that led to a discipline outcome where the case was dismissed or the Responding Party remained in the vicinity of the Reporting Party on campus, the Reporting Party would not have a right to appeal this decision. The only recourse at that stage would be to make a complaint to the HEI, and it is highly unlikely that the outcome of a complaint against the service the HEI provided would lead to a change in another student's discipline outcome. Worryingly, it is not even a requirement that the Reporting Party receive the outcome of their own case once it goes to a discipline process, but rather the expectation is that the Reporting Party be given 'some resolution' and the HEI 'should offer them a remedy for the impact' (OIA, 2018b, p. 24). This is different in the United States, where the Title IX of the Education Amendments Act of 1972 (Title IX) and The Jeanne Clery Disclosure of Campus Security Policy and Campus Crime Statistics Act (Clery Act) require institutions to provide both the Reporting Party and the Responding Party with written information about the outcome of any sexual violence report including any sanctions imposed and both parties have the right to appeal the discipline decision (Clery Center, n.d.).

If a comprehensive institution-wide approach is truly applied to the disciplinary process, the involvement of the Reporting Party is required. Disciplinary outcomes need to remedy the harm that occurred when misconduct is found, and the Reporting Party's desired outcome must be considered to do this. We argue that in the case of sexual violence, the Reporting Party and Responding Party should have equitable rights in the disciplinary process and challenge regulators, the sector ombudsman and organisations producing sector guidance to work to make these procedures fairer for both parties.

Separating the Three Stages of Discipline

As noted in the previous chapter, the investigation, adjudication and sanctioning stage of disciplinary proceedings must be separate (Begin et al., 2023; Henry et al., 2018). It is necessary to create procedures that will not conflate these processes. The investigators should not choose the sanctions, and the discipline decision-makers, or adjudicators, should not re-investigate the case. There needs to be separation to ensure that cases are managed appropriately, fairly and in a trauma-informed way.

It is necessary in terms of procedural justice, to create a disciplinary process that separates adjudication and sanctioning. Adjudication is determining on a balance of probabilities whether a breach of policy occurred. Sanctioning is used to determine the appropriate penalty for a breach of policy while considering mitigating, aggravating and compounding factors. If adjudicators are concerned about the potential sanction at the time of determining whether the misconduct is proven, this can bias the decision-making. An example of this might be when the adjudicator decides that they do not think expulsion is the correct response to a policy breach of a non-consensual sexual act, and therefore, they dismiss the case against the Responding Party. In the Criminal Justice System (CJS), that is an example of jury nullification. Another example of conflating these two processes would be if mitigating factors are heard during the adjudication stage of the discipline process then used erroneously to dismiss the case. Mitigating factors which we outline later in this chapter should not be used to determine if a breach of policy occurred (Begin et al., 2023). A third example would be using the quantum of evidence used to determine a breach of policy to then choose the severity of penalty, e.g. 51%–49% resulting in a lesser sanction than a case found at 80%–20%. We explore this later in this chapter.

Ultimately, the process should be a trauma-informed investigation where, based on the civil standard of proof, the investigators determine if there is a case to be heard. A discipline panel then should receive the case and determine if, based on a balance of probabilities, there is evidence to confirm misconduct has occurred. If evidence demonstrates it is more likely than not that misconduct occurred, then the adjudicators will move into the sanctioning stage of the discipline process to hear any mitigating, aggravating or compounding factors to help them determine the best outcome for the case. In the United States, some HEIs will separate these two stages completely having one panel confirm the breach of policy and a separate discipline panel determine the appropriate sanction/s (Begin et al., 2023).

ADJUDICATION

During adjudication, the discipline decision-maker/s must allow the evidence to lead to the conclusion rather than interpreting evidence to match a desired or expected conclusion. The same standard of proof should be used for all disciplinary cases, regardless of the type of misconduct or the Responding Party identity or status. Unconscious biases such as believing one student because of the nature of their degree, say medicine or theology, is something to be mindful of when adjudicating cases. The standard of proof cannot change. If we apply this differently to different students be it, e.g. medical students vs history students, home students vs international students, white students vs Black students, straight students vs gay students, we would be creating a system that is structurally and inherently discriminatory. We would be valuing one type of student over another, which is surely wrong. We cannot wisely privilege one discipline or profession or identity over another. In the same way, we cannot change the standard of proof based on the type of misconduct. We cannot use 51% for physical assault and 75% for sexually touching someone without their consent. There must surely be parity across all disciplinary procedures.

If the criminal offence was determined through criminal proceedings, the HEI would not be expected to re-investigate and adjudicate on the case. Policies can be written so that confirmation of a criminal offence can automatically mean a breach of policy. Therefore, only the sanctioning stage of the process would be necessary. A caution is a confirmation that a criminal offence occurred, and therefore, a breach of policy is confirmed, so the case would only need to be considered at the sanctioning stage. As a reminder, if a case in the CJS ends in No Further Action, not guilty or an acquittal, a breach of policy can still be investigated and considered as the decision regarding misconduct is conducted at the civil standard of proof.

SANCTIONING

'The evidentiary analysis of whether a policy has been violated should be entirely separate and independent from the evaluation of what sanctions are appropriate given a particular set of circumstances' (Henry et al., 2018, p. 23). In other words, the sanctioning stage of the process should not be impacted by the amount of evidence that led to the decision that the policy has been breached. Whether the standard of proof was met at 51% or 85% is irrelevant when determining the sanction. Once the civil standard of proof is met at 51% the policy breach stands. If the discipline panel provides a lesser sanction due to evidence that found a breach at 51%, they are ultimately demonstrating their lack of confidence in the evidence, disagreement with the civil standard being applied and using this as a mitigating factor while undermining the integrity of the procedure (Begin et al., 2023; Henry et al., 2018).

There are three types of sanctions that can be used in response to non-academic misconduct in HE: punitive, developmental or restorative. These sanctions can be used separately or in combination. An example of a punitive and developmental sanction being used together might be a Responding Party who receives a reprimand and is asked to write an essay on the impact of their behaviour on the Reporting Party and the university community.

Sanctions should be proportionate, relational, remedy the effect of the misconduct and consistent, considering mitigating, aggravating and compounding factors that may be present (Begin et al., 2023; Henry et al., 2018). Relational means that sanction stops the misconduct, prevents reoccurrence and remedies the effect of the misconduct. Consistent means the sanction imposed is comparable with sanctions imposed in past cases of a similar nature.

Punitive sanctions are negative consequences proportionate to the misconduct, e.g. expulsion, exclusion for one year, ban from parts of the campus, restrictions on activities, a no contact order or reprimand. Punitive sanctions may impact on the Responding Party's academic progress. Beyond expulsion, which stops the Responding Party from furthering their academic work at the institution, other sanctions such as exclusion for one year, bans from parts of the HEI's premises or even No Contact Orders can impact on their academic engagement. This does not mean that sanctions should not be imposed. If they are proportionate and remedy the harm caused, they should be used. The Responding Party's ability to successfully achieve a degree should not auto- matically result in a lesser sanction. Rather, case managers can work with departments to facilitate access to facilities needed for academic progress within the parameters of the sanction/s imposed (Daniel & Logsdon, 2015). For example, arrangements can be made for the Responding Party to meet with staff in an alternative location on campus if they have been banned from the location where the member of staff has an office. In some cases, propor- tionate sanctions will mean that the Responding Party cannot receive their degree, e.g. expulsion.

Developmental sanctions are activities to help the Responding Party understand why the behaviour is a problem e.g. reflective writing exercises or training (Murphy & Van Brunt, 2017). These are particularly important to consider, especially when the Reporting Party specifically requests leniency for the Responding Party's sanction but wants the Responding Party to learn that their behaviour was not acceptable and caused harm. When considering asking Responding Parties to attend training or counselling ses- sions, we recommend that these are reframed from being a sanction, but rather a recommendation or steps required before someone who has been excluded from the institution for a period of time is able to reintegrate into the community. It is important to note that the HEI cannot dictate how someone engages in counselling. If the sanction includes attending training, this training needs to be provided by the HEI, otherwise the student will likely be unable to complete this requirement or recommendation.

Restorative sanction, often referred to as Restorative Justice (RJ) or approach, in its simplest form is an action to pay back the community or injured party for the harm done. RJ requires the Responding Party to accept responsibility for the harm caused, i.e. admit guilt, and helps them remedy the harm they caused (Murphy & Van Brunt, 2017). Uniquely different from punitive and developmental sanctions, RJ may be used as a resolution process, a victim impact process, a sanctioning process or a reintegration process (Koss et al., 2014). Both parties volunteer to participate, but in the case of sexual violence, it is led by the Reporting Party wanting to engage in RJ.

Restorative sanctions can be seen in other types of misconduct where the Responding Party apologises for the harm or pays to fix damaged property. RJ used in sexual violence or domestic abuse, however, requires trained RJ practitioners to conduct a restorative conference safely. The use of RJ in sexual violence and/or domestic abuse is highly controversial because if done incorrectly, it may present a high risk of causing increased harm to the Reporting Party. We advise significant caution when considering this approach as we would not want Reporting Parties to feel pressured into this process. However, contributors to the field argue that victim-survivors want this form of justice as an option (Karp et al., 2016; Keenan, 2018; McGlynn & Westmarland, 2019). Specialist training for facilitating cases of RJ in sexual violence cases is required (beyond basic restorative justice training), helping prepare the practitioner to respond to concerns about risks of re-victimisation, re-traumatisation, and power imbalances (Keenan, 2018). RJ processes must also consider intersections of racism and other forms of discrimination and that these barriers may impose to the Reporting Party being able to fully engage in the RJ process (Scott et al., 2017).

We advise caution in HEIs using RJ in incidences where a potential criminal offence has occurred before criminal proceedings have considered the case. The Responding Party must accept responsibility (i.e. guilt) for harm caused. If the Responding Party does this without legal advice in the case of an incident that may involve a potential criminal offence, the Reporting Party may report this to the police. Now the concern here is not that of the Reporting Party seeking criminal justice outcome following an internal outcome. The concern is ensuring that the Responding Party is aware of the meaning of admitting a breach of policy through an RJ process. We have not found substantial guidance on how to manage this and feel it is prudent to caution the use of this in these cases currently until further research and guidance is available. As we are not specially trained RJ practitioners, we present this as an option for HEIs to consider but hold that this must be done correctly and safely.

Creating a Sanctioning Guide

We will use the following examples of punitive sanctions to discuss developing sanctioning guidelines for a disciplinary process. This section predominantly builds on the work of Henry et al. (2018). A sanctioning guide promotes proportionality, consistency and transparency. For the purposes of prevention, this can act as a deterrent for potential perpetrators. It can also reduce barriers to disclosure and reporting if Reporting Parties have an idea of the possible outcomes of taking a case forward. In addition, it supports discipline decision-makers in fulfilling their role on behalf of the institution if the HEI has set a guide for them to follow.

- **Formal Warning:** This is a written warning placed on the student's record for a set period noting the behaviour that was unacceptable, as well as actions to be taken if the behaviour is repeated or if behaviour of a similar nature occurs.

- **Written Reprimand:** This is a written letter placed permanently on the student's record outlining the misconduct which occurred and noting this did not meet the standards of the policy or code of conduct. This may also note actions to be taken if the behaviour is repeated or if behaviour of a similar nature occurs. This may be noted in response to reference requests that ask about the student's conduct record.

- **No Contact Order:** This requires the Responding Party to have no direct, indirect or third-party contact with the Reporting Party. It requires the Responding Party to remove themselves from situations where chance or incidental encounters occur in reasonable time. This can remain in place for the remainder of the Responding Party's time at the university.

- **Conditions/Restrictions:** These are sanctions imposed on the student that require them to do certain things or ban them from certain activities, positions or locations on campus. An example of a condition is requiring the student to change accommodation when staying in accommodation managed by the HEI. An example of a restriction is banning the student from entering the Reporting Party's academic department.

- **Exclusion:** This is where the student is barred from the institution for a set period, e.g. one academic year. The student is not expected to continue with their studies during this time and is stopped from entering the institution's premises or events during this time. This may be referred to as suspension from studies by some HEIs. For our purposes, we use suspension to describe non-judgemental precautionary measures and exclusion to refer to a sanction.

- **Expulsion:** The student is permanently removed and banned from the HEI, stopping their academic progress at the institution. This may be referred to as permanent exclusion by some HEIs.

Using these sanctions as an example, we have demonstrated suggested sanctioning guidelines in Fig. 7 for different forms of sexual violence. In developing sanctioning guidelines, it is important to consider the severity of misconduct to develop the sanctioning range. Keep in mind the impact on the Reporting Party and the need to create flexibility to move within the range depending on the specifics of a case.

Mitigating, Aggravating and Compounding Factors

Sanctioning guidelines allow discipline decision-makers to have a starting point to apply appropriate sanctions. They then consider mitigating, aggravating and compounding factors to determine the

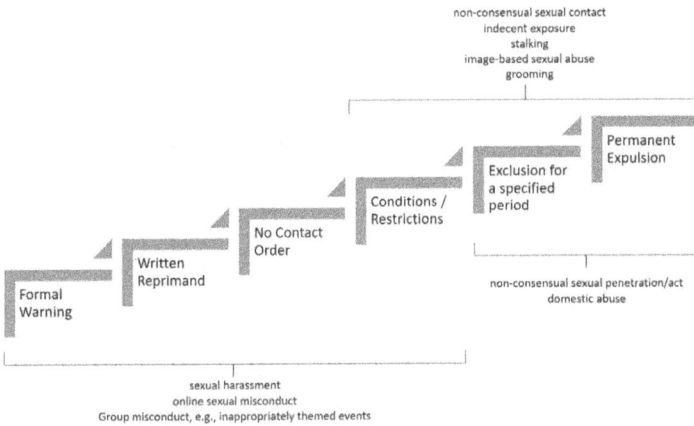

Fig. 7. **Example Sanctioning Guidelines.**

most appropriate discipline outcome. These factors are not always relevant to determining evidence of misconduct; however, they should be considered if misconduct is found before determining the appropriate sanction/s.

Mitigating factors may allow the discipline decision-makers to move to a lesser sanction within the scale. For example, for sexual harassment, the sanctions of formal warning (the lowest level sanction) to conditions or restrictions (the highest level sanction) are available. Mitigating factors such as a request for leniency by the Reporting Party and the Responding Party expressing genuine contrition will allow the decision-makers to use a formal warning as an appropriate and proportionate outcome. Alternatively, if **aggravating factors** are present, such as the Responding Party refused to stop even though they were told the behaviour was unwanted and the Responding Party displays no remorse, the decision-makers may use more enhanced restrictions, such as banning the Responding Party from the Reporting Party's academic department, as a proportionate sanction. If **compounding factors** are present, such as this is the second time the Responding Party has been disciplined for this type of behaviour, the decision-makers can then move to the next part of the scale and consider exclusion or expulsion as an appropriate sanction (Table 5).

Table 5. Mitigating, Aggravating and Compounding Factors in Sexual Misconduct Cases.

Mitigating Factors	Aggravating Factors	Compounding Factors
• Request for leniency by the Reporting Party with no coercion or retaliation by the Responding Party identified • Genuine contrition by the Responding Party • The Responding Party admitted the misconduct at the earliest opportunity. • The Responding Party attempted to make amends following harassment (this is NOT to be considered in cases of domestic abuse as this is part of the abuse pattern.)	• Request for enhanced sanctions by the Reporting Party for safety reasons • The Responding Party used force, violence, threats or intimidation. • The Responding Party used drugs or alcohol to intentionally incapacitate the Reporting Party. • The Responding Party was under the influence of alcohol or drugs at the time of the misconduct. • The Responding Party refused to stop behaviour after consent was denied/revoked. • There is an ongoing hostile environment. • The Responding Party shows no remorse. • Evidence that misconduct was planned • Misconduct caused physical or mental injury or illness.	• The Responding Party has a prior history of misconduct recorded following due process. • The previous misconduct was of a similar nature. • Cumulative breaches within one case, e.g. the Responding Party breached the policy multiple times in a single/multiple incident(s) with the same/multiple Reporting Parties, and/or the Responding Party breached multiple policies.

Sharing Information on Outcomes and Sanctions With Both Parties

We take the view that the Responding Party's misconduct towards the Reporting Party's mind and body means that data about the sexual misconduct are intrinsically linked to both parties. Our strong recommendation is that Reporting Parties and Responding Parties receive information regarding the outcome and sanctions (if imposed) as modelled in HE in other countries.

Universities UK (UUK) published data sharing guidance in 2022 that argued that universities should not have blanket policies to share or not share outcomes and sanctions in harassment cases but should decide on a case-by-case basis. Still the strategic guidance stated the purpose of the guidance was to help HEIs 'have the confidence to share more information on outcomes and sanctions with reporting parties where it is appropriate and reasonable to do so' (UUK, 2022a, p. 6). We tend to see more conservative decision-making about sharing data occur in relation to staff misconduct; however, guidance in relation to sharing outcomes regarding staff sexual misconduct more widely (not specific to HE) appears to be more in favour of sharing than the approach taken with students. The Equality and Human Rights Commission in relation to sexual harassment in the workplace states:

> ... wherever appropriate and possible, if a complaint is upheld then the complainant should be told what action has been taken to address this, including action taken to address the specific complaint and any measures taken to prevent a similar event happening again in the future. If the complainant is not told what action has been taken, this may leave them feeling that their complaint has not been taken seriously or addressed adequately. (2020, p. 76)

Similarly, the Advisory, Conciliation and Arbitration Service (ACAS) states, 'You should consider on a case-by-case basis whether to tell the person who made the complaint about what disciplinary action, if any, has been taken. **You should tell them if you can.**' (2021, section 12, our emphasis).

The purpose of the sanction is to stop the misconduct, prevent reoccurrence and remedy the effect of the misconduct. If HEIs choose not to share the outcome and sanctions with the Reporting

Party, what remedy are they offering to the Reporting Party? Saying 'we are taking the appropriate discipline action' is not a remedy. It provides no assurance to the Reporting Party and allows them no information on managing their own safety. They will not know if the Responding Party will be back in their university accommodation or lecture hall. If the Responding Party has been restricted from parts of the University, excluded for a period or even expelled from the HEI, but continues to attend university-related events, the Reporting Party will not know that the Responding Party should not be there. The UUK argument for not sharing the outcome and sanctions with the Reporting Party is the risk to the Responding Party should the Reporting Party share that information widely. However, there is no concern regarding the converse risk of the Responding Party sharing that outcome when a case is dismissed and the risk to the Reporting Party of being stigmatised as a malicious or false accuser (Cowan et al., 2024). Cowan et al. (2024) helpfully argue that HEIs and HE sector guidance prioritise Responding Party privacy above that of the Reporting Party. The same level of protection is not afforded to the Reporting Party, who's private information is often shared widely, and in the cases of complaints or reports that are dismissed, no protection is provided to the Reporting Party not to be seen as a malicious complainant. For brevity, we offer an excerpt from a speech to highlight just how unequal Reporting Party and Responding Party data are treated traditionally in UK sexual misconduct processes in HE.

🎤 'Me and My Body'

Pretend I'm a student.

I disclose to a member of staff that I have been subjected to sexual violence.

That a responding party has penetrated **my vagina** with his penis **without my consent**.

I disclose that to a member of staff, and she or he now knows my story about **me and my body**.

If I report that to the university, more members of staff now know about **me and my body**.

A risk assessment is conducted, and more members of staff know about **me and my body**.

The investigator gets to know the minute detail of everything I can remember about what happened to **me and my body**.

And then... universities have a *blanket policy* to share my data with the Responding Party, and he gets to see my full report about what I said that he did to **me and my body**.

The witnesses get to know that I am a Reporting Party in a sexual violence case.

At the end of the investigation, I am told if it is upheld or dismissed.

And if it is upheld, I lose all rights in the next part of the process.

It goes to a discipline process and at best, I'm a witness; at worst, I'm told the university will take the appropriate disciplinary action.

The discipline panel is more staff, and even student representatives, who I've never met, who have not been part of *my* process, who get to hear about **me and my body**.

I'm asked maybe to submit an impact statement about what's happened and **my PTSD, my inability to concentrate, my inability to sleep, the impact on my work and my academic progress** – that is shared with the Responding Party.

And then a decision is made on whether a breach of policy has occurred, and the Responding Party has a finding of founded or not founded.

If founded, there will be sanctions imposed and some universities will come back to me and say we found misconduct, but we're not going to tell you the sanction.

Very few universities will actually tell me, the Reporting Party, the sanction.

That sanction is based on the Responding Party penetrating **my vagina** with his penis **without my consent**.

(Continued)

And the reason why universities will not tell me...

Is because they will say it is the personal private information of the Responding Party, and I cannot know that about *him*.

But everybody in that process, from the point of disclosure to discipline, got to know about **me and my vagina** and what happened to me **without my consent.**

My privacy was not protected, and my rights, the equality and human rights I have as a student, were never balanced with that.

Excerpt of speech delivered by Clarissa J. DiSantis as part of the Guidance on Sharing Data in Harassment Cases Panel at the Universities UK Tackling Violence, Harassment and Hate Incidents 2022 Conference on 3 March 2022.

APPEAL OPTIONS

It is important that policies and procedures are followed correctly. If there is a procedural error or irregularity, the outcome of a discipline process can be subject to appeal and if upheld, the discipline imposed can be removed or lessened. The Responding Party must be informed of their rights to appeal including the grounds of appeal and the timeframe for doing so. As we have previously noted, and quite remarkably, the OIA does not advise that the Reporting Party should have a right to appeal the discipline outcome; however, we encourage the sector to consider changing this to offer equitable rights to both parties in the process as is modelled in HE in other countries. After all, if a Responding Party is disciplined for sexual violence, it is because they subjected a student or employee to sexual violence, not the university. If the discipline outcome is not dealt with properly or the outcome is unreasonable leaving the Reporting Party without safe access to their education, currently Reporting Parties have no remit to appeal or challenge this. Therefore, it could be argued that we are not fulfilling our duty under the Public Sector Equality Duty of the Equality Act 2010 to ensure students can study in environments free from the fear of harassment.

In this chapter, we have discussed principles for disciplinary processes that although are specific to England and Wales hold true for other locations as good practice. We have emphasised the need for separate investigation, adjudication and sanctioning stages highlighting pitfalls for when these are conflated. We have considered punitive, developmental and restorative sanctions, noting the need for more research and guidance on the latter. We have considered how an HEI could develop sanctioning guidelines to support the delivery of discipline outcomes and culture change on a wider level. As a final note, we highlight the training mentioned in Chapter 8 to note that in the same way that it is expected the investigators will be trained appropriately to consider cases of sexual violence, discipline decision-makers must understand sexual violence and trauma and how this may impact on discipline decisions to ensure appropriate and safe discipline outcomes.

Related Resources

- Cowan, S., Munro, V. E., Bull, A., DiSantis, C. J., & Prince, K. (2024). Data, disclosure and duties: balancing privacy and safeguarding in the context of UK university student sexual misconduct complaints. *Legal Studies*, 1–20. https://doi.org/10.1017/lst.2024.9
- Begin, N. et al. (2023). *The 2023 ATIXA guide to sanctioning student sexual harassment violations in higher education settings.* ATIXA.
- Cowan, S., & Munro, V. E. (2021). Seeking campus justice: challenging the 'criminal justice drift' in United Kingdom responses to student sexual violence and misconduct. *Journal of Law and Society, 48,* 308.

13

WHEN UNIVERSITIES GET IT WRONG

A number of studies appear to provide evidence to indicate that it is not just perpetrators who harm students, but university officials responding to sexual violence also harm victim-survivors through taking no action to protect them or by taking inappropriate action (Bedera, 2023; Bloom et al., 2023; Cruz, 2021; Hales, 2023; Lorenz et al., 2023; Sall & Littleton, 2022; Shannon, 2022; Sidelil et al., 2022; Smith & Freyd, 2013). In this chapter, we present examples of *what not to do* to raise awareness of practices and errors which can significantly harm victim-survivors and exacerbate the trauma they have already experienced. And we recognise that much of what we include in this chapter may well be routine practice in many institutions. Our concern about this is that for all intents and purposes, such institutional leadership teams are enabling perpetration by actively or passively not addressing it.

Although university staff may make errors in relation to Responding Parties which may be addressed through an appeal process or complaint to the ombudsman (e.g. Office of the Independent Adjudicator for Higher Education in England and Wales or 'OIA'), the evidence for university officials routinely harming victim-survivors grossly outweighs evidence of harm caused to those accused of sexual misconduct. Albeit there is often much focus on such potential harms. We are purposeful in placing a magnifying lens on when universities fail victim-survivors. We explore re-traumatisation, resistance tactics used against victim-survivors and institutional betrayal. We critique sector guidance which perpetuates these issues and draw upon documented stories to demonstrate where universities have failed victim-survivors.

Sadly, the examples we offer of when universities get it wrong are by no means exhaustive, but we aim to highlight some common pitfalls. It is our hope that through naming these and explaining how they occur, we can assist university administrators in providing safer responses for victim-survivors that do not cause further harm. To begin this discussion, we are guided by Nina Funnell's pointed view on university priorities, which includes a quote from man who reported sexual violence to his university:

> But university reputation and income should not take priority over the wellbeing and safety of students, and processes that retraumatise rape victims or deter reporting are only protecting and enabling offenders. As one victim from Wollongong University said: "Make no mistake, I consider the events of my sexual assault and this university's response to be equally despicable. There is a shocking correlation between someone not listening to you say 'stop' and an organisation not listening to you scream 'help'." (2017)

RE-TRAUMATISATION

A key element of the comprehensive institution-wide approach is to be trauma-informed, mitigating the risk of re-traumatising victim-survivors. Re-traumatisation is defined as:

> ... the re-experiencing of thoughts, feelings or sensations experienced at the time of a traumatic event or circumstance in a person's past. Re-traumatisation is generally triggered by reminders of previous trauma which may or may not be potentially traumatic in themselves. (Office for Health Improvement & Disparities, 2022)

Re-traumatisation can be caused by poor practice, untrained staff, being forced to retell trauma stories multiple times, victim-blaming responses and investigations that are not trauma-informed. It can impact the individual's mental health, physical health and academic or work performance and progression. Victim-survivors are often re-traumatised by the reporting and investigation process in universities, workplaces and the criminal justice system (Bedera, 2023). Next, we consider resistance tactics used against victim-survivors and institutional betrayal – all of which can cause re-traumatisation in victim-survivors.

RESISTANCE TACTICS USED AGAINST VICTIM-SURVIVORS

In Chapter 6, we outlined eight forms of resistance tactics used to block, stall or dismantle prevention and response initiatives for addressing sexual violence. In this chapter, we return to the eight tactics and consider how these are used directly against victim-survivors to maintain the status quo and cause them further harm, often resulting in re-traumatisation.

Denial

Denial used against victim-survivors takes many forms, but at the core, it is denying the victim-survivor's lived experience. This can include denying knowledge of a perpetrator's actions or wilful ignorance, as identified by Page (2022), not to know about these behaviours. Denial can also include denying that the misconduct is sexual in nature, i.e. ignoring the victim-survivor's experience of the behaviour as sexual and finding for the perpetrator's version that the behaviour was not sexual (Page, 2022; Schulz et al., 2022). This form of denial goes to minimise the victim-survivor's lived experience and has been referred to as a form of institutional gaslighting (Lorenz et al., 2023).

Multiple studies show survivors are regularly denied as conveyors of knowledge and their testimony is deemed unreliable (Page, 2022). We highlight in Chapters 11 and 12 that failure to conduct trauma-informed investigations can often lead investigators and/or discipline decision-makers to find the Reporting Party's counterintuitive behaviour, gaps in memory, delayed reporting and/or inconsistent statements to be used to discredit them rather than to open lines of enquiry that allow for consideration of a trauma response. Later in this chapter, we will provide additional examples of reasons why victim-survivors are often discredited over perpetrators and consequently, not believed – regardless of evidence presented.

Disavowal

Disavowal is when university administrative and managerial staff refuse to recognise their responsibility to act. When disavowal is used against a victim-survivor directly, this is often refusing to accept a report for a variety of reasons, e.g. the assault happened off-campus, not during university business, or the assault must be reported to the police before the university will consider it. If a higher education institution (HEI) has a policy that they will not accept reports related to sexual violence that occur off university property, they are automatically disadvantaging a large portion of their community. Given most rape occurs in private, e.g. someone's home, having this policy in place directly disadvantages most students and employees who do not live on campus. It ignores technology-facilitated abuse unless it specifically occurs on universities' virtual learning environments (VLEs). It can often be used to ignore abuse that occurs in connection with university-related events but that are not technically on university business, e.g. after hours at conferences or field trips. Sexual violence that does not occur physically on campus will still impact a victim-survivor's safe access to their education or workplace if the perpetrator is a member of the university community. It is shocking that quite so many governing bodies seem to allow Vice-Chancellors to calmly relinquish any responsibility for sexual misconduct which takes place 'off campus'. This would seem like a somewhat bizarre demarcation in any other area of student well-being practice. For example, if a student experienced a mental health crisis, we would not ask if this occurred on or off campus. We would rightly focus upon the impact and what we could do to help.

Inaction

Inaction directed towards victim-survivors is simply taking no action to prevent sexual violence and/or to respond to a disclosure or report. It can include, e.g. not putting precautionary measures in place during a police or university investigation, not providing access to support, refusing to investigate or failing to impose meaningful sanctions when misconduct is found. University inaction in such cases may well impact upon lowering future reporting rates when we need reporting rates to increase.

Appeasement

Appeasement is placating or pacifying the victim-survivor without taking any action. An example of appeasement is telling a Reporting Party that the appropriate discipline action will be taken, but then taking no or inadequate disciplinary action against a Responding Party and often not informing the Reporting Party of what action was or was not taken under the guise of General Data Protection Regulation (GDPR). Again, such duplicity and institutional deceit does not serve the interests of Reporting Parties nor those thinking of reporting. However, such appeasement unequivocally serves the interests of Responding Parties.

Appropriation

Appropriation is simulating change while covertly undermining it, and this can be used in myriad ways against victim-survivors. Examples of appropriation can include when a university has a sexual violence policy in place, but university officials subtly or overtly discourage victim-survivors from reporting, make the reporting process inaccessible or make the procedure for investigation and discipline convoluted, overly lengthy and/or to disadvantage Reporting Parties. Appropriation can also include having untrained staff responding to disclosures, investigating sexual violence reports and/or acting as discipline decision-makers for sexual misconduct. And this point about untrained discipline decision-makers is especially important to emphasise because even if a university employs skilled investigators, all such nuanced and informed work can effectively be neutralised by untrained and uninformed discipline decision-makers at the end of what can be a lengthy process. No decision-maker in relation to cases of sexual misconduct should be without training in the area, but they should minimally have access to expert advice. A lack of expertise and training in those who are responsible for managing sexual misconduct investigations and discipline processes can result in unjust outcomes (Bedera, 2023; Lorenz et al., 2023; Page, 2022).

Co-option

Co-option is using the language of progressive frameworks and goals for reactionary ends or to maintain the status quo, and when used against victim-survivors directly, this can often be seen as prioritising the needs of the Responding Party over the needs of the Reporting Party. This can be seen when university officials are more concerned about the impact of an investigation on a Responding Party than consideration of the impact of the investigation on the Reporting Party and any potential compounding impacts of the reported sexual violence and trauma response. In other words, the impact of the investigation on the Responding Party is prioritised over the harm the Responding Party caused to Reporting Party, and no attention is given to the impact of the investigation on the Reporting Party. Co-option can commonly be seen at the sanctioning stage of a case, where the impact to the Responding Party's future is prioritised over the Reporting Party's future. Co-option is also seen when universities allow Responding Parties to make countercomplaints against Reporting Parties, without knowledge of Deny, Attack, Reverse Victim and Offender (DARVO) tactics and without consideration of the Responding Party potentially using the university's procedures to cause further harm to the Reporting Party. This is commonly seen in cases that involve domestic abuse where a Responding Party will allege the Reporting Party 'was violent too'.

Repression

Repression is reversing or dismantling a change initiative and can be seen when changes are made directly to impact victim-survivors, for example, removing access to specialist services from internal support options, adding delays to investigation/discipline procedures, removing rights for Reporting Parties in university policies and procedures, making it harder to report and creating more convoluted procedures if they had been more transparent in the past. Repression can also be removing precautionary measures and/or sanctions from a Responding Party that were keeping the Reporting Party safe without offering alternative safety measures. For example, fully suspending the Responding Party from the university, but then lifting the suspension and allowing the Responding Party to return to campus following an appeal of the suspension before an investigation is completed, or allowing the Responding Party to appeal an expulsion and this being lifted without allowing the Reporting Party who is impacted by that decision to participate in the appeal process. After all, the Reporting Party was likely considered a witness only to the discipline process to begin with, meaning they would not (albeit unjustly) then be included in the appeal process under current OIA guidance (See Chapter 12 for more on this issue). Defunding services through say not replacing staff is another method which may be used to quietly undermine such services.

Backlash

Backlash is an attacking or aggressive response against victim-survivors. This can be seen when retaliation and/or victimisation is used following a disclosure or report. This can be in how Reporting Parties are treated during investigation and discipline procedures by those conducting the procedures, but it can also include other staff acting against the victim-survivor or stopping them from accessing opportunities as a way of punishing them for making a report. Victimisation can be subtle and difficult to prove, including not just what people say but what people do not say in a reference or academic opportunity.

INSTITUTIONAL BETRAYAL

All eight forms of resistance discussed can result in victim-survivors experiencing institutional betrayal and re-traumatisation. Institutional betrayal is when the institution 'acts in a way that betrays its member's trust' and 'exacerbates the interpersonal trauma of the initial sexual assault' (Smith & Freyd, 2013, p. 120). In a university setting, this phenomenon is when an HEI fails to support victim-survivors following disclosures of sexual violence and exacerbates the trauma of the initial sexual violence through its actions or inactions (Bedera, 2023; Hales, 2023; Hannan et al., 2021; Pinciotti & Orcutte, 2021; Shannon, 2022; Sidelil et al., 2022; Smith & Freyd, 2013). It is sometimes referred to as a 'second rape' or secondary victimisation when victim-survivors are denied help by their community after sexual violence and are presented with victim-blaming attitudes and practices (Campbell et al., 2001).

Institutional betrayal is based on the trust of the member being broken by the institution's actions. Interestingly, Shannon and Bull (2024) found that not all victim-survivors trust the institution to begin with but are more likely pushed into a position of what they found was 'unwilling trust' given the need to engage with the institution to have perpetrators held accountable and/or to access safety measures. Lorenz et al. (2023) explain that a student is dependent on the HEI for education and safety creating a dependency or 'trust' in the institution. Dependency may be more suitable in describing the relationship between a victim-survivor's connection to an HEI compared to trust. After all, if a student has been subjected to sexual violence by a member of the HEI community, then the HEI has not succeeded in maintaining a safe learning environment for the student; any trust could already be broken at that point. However, the student, now a victim-survivor, must depend on the HEI to take the appropriate action to keep them safe during an investigation and to hold the perpetrator accountable.

Institutional betrayal is widely associated with difficult reporting processes, poorly conducted investigations, mishandled disciplinary procedures and minimising or covering up sexual violence (Bedera, 2023; Shannon & Bull, 2024; Sidelil et al., 2022). Examples of actions which cause institutional betrayal can include failing to acknowledge sexual violence, failing to act on behalf of survivor's interests, victimisation of Reporting Parties following a disclosure or report of sexual violence, inaccessible reporting procedures, treating Reporting Parties from marginalised groups differently and allowing untrained staff to manage reports and disciplinary procedures (Lorenz et al., 2023). Bloom et al. (2023) found that postgraduate students' experiences of institutional betrayal also included 'passing the harasser' where the perpetrator (an employee) was not held accountable for their behaviour and was able to move between institutions and continue harming students. In addition, postgraduate students are not always given adequate support and resources as prevention and response initiatives were often tailored to undergraduate students. Institutional betrayal was also found not only in the poor responses to sexual violence but when universities had not taken any action to prevent sexual violence (Smith & Freyd, 2013).

Whether victim-survivors start off trusting the HEI or are placed in a position where they need to trust the HEI, the inactions and actions of HEIs where victim-survivors are not safeguarded or are blamed for the sexual violence can lead to significant harm. The impacts of institutional betrayal are great as it exacerbates the victim-survivor's trauma symptoms (re-traumatisation) and can put them at higher risk for posttraumatic stress disorder, anxiety, depression, dissociation, sleep disturbances, sexual dysfunction, physical health problems, declined academic performance and disengagement from activities within the university (Bedera, 2023; Hannan et al., 2021; Lorenz et al., 2023; Pinciotti & Orcutte, 2021; Smith & Freyd, 2013).

> When universities fail to fully consider and include the rights and interests of reporting parties, or fail to implement trauma-informed processes that aim to reduce harm, this can amount to an 'institutional betrayal', and sends a message to the wider campus community that reporting or disclosing sexual misconduct to the university is likely to re-traumatise. (Cowan et al., 2024, pp. 19–20)

Additionally, students will share their experiences of how the university treated them. This will cause other students not to trust the university, and reporting rates will likely decline (Rogalin & Addison, 2023). It will also inform would-be perpetrators of how cases are handled and will demonstrate a lack of perpetrator accountability. Therefore, not only do the HEI actions which cause institutional betrayal harm victim-survivors directly, but they perpetuate sexual violence in universities; it is a failure in the areas of prevention and response (Sidelil et al., 2022).

FACILITATORS FOR BETRAYAL AND RESISTANCE

Studies show there are multiple reasons why university administrators fail victim-survivors (Bedera, 2023; Cruz, 2021; Lorenz et al., 2023; Rogalin & Addison; Sall & Littleton, 2022; Shannon, 2022). Bedera (2023) studied how university administrators rationalise unjust outcomes and how gender stereotypes guide the rationalisations specifically in sexual violence cases within universities in the United States. Bedera identified three themes in why universities may betray victim-survivors: (1) financial decision – concern of civil litigation or impact on reputation which could impact prospective students, alumnae or donors, (2) gender – holding a man accountable could threaten patriarchal traditions, for example, when male-dominated organisations prioritise men's sport and (3) too complicated – 'orchestrated complexity' where cases fit in the 'too hard' box. Lorenz et al. (2023) found that self-protection was a common reason for institutional betrayal – whether that was from liability, financial risk, reputational risk or protection of managers and administrators who feared losing their jobs. Sall and Littleton (2022) found that HEI's desire to protect their reputation and have low numbers of rape documented resulted in most investigations being ruled as inconclusive. Shannon (2022) found that when the perpetrator is valuable, then the victim-survivor is expendable; thus, perpetrators can weaponise their status to harm with impunity if the HEI prioritises reputation over survivor wellbeing. In that study, examples included a professor perpetrator being more valuable than the student victim-survivor, a high performing male athlete perpetrator being valued over the female athlete whose athletic performance declined following sexual violence and valuing mathematics and physics male student perpetrators over female student victim-survivors studying history.

Some have considered the disconnect between HEI efforts to respond to sexual violence and victim-survivors' experiences of institutional betrayal (Cruz, 2021). And this was a striking finding of the SUMS consulting evaluation (Baird et al., 2022) of progress (or more accurately a distinct lack of it) with the implementation of the Office for Students' (OfS's) *Statement of Expectations* exhortations. In the United States, sexual violence investigations and disciplinary procedures are expected to be conducted as impartial processes. Impartiality meaning the students involved have equal forms of representation and rights. However, many universities have altered this to mean Title IX administrators should be 'neutral', empathising with both parties, regardless of wrongdoing. Cruz found that to be 'neutral', university administrators forced themselves to become 'numb' to the trauma stories of sexual violence and minimised men's sexual violence against women as 'making a mistake'; this minimisation of the harm allowed university administrators to better cope with exposure to vicarious trauma and act in a 'neutral' manner.

> *However, by focusing on neutrality, administrators are in conflict with the goals of Title IX. The definition of the word neutral is, 'not engaged on either side.' Title IX exists to eliminate sex discrimination, which means it is necessary to take a side: the side against discrimination. The problem with neutrality is that its proclivity is to do nothing. (Cruz, 2021, p. 379)*

Gendered Double Standards, Rape Myths and 'Himpathy'

There are also identified facilitators for betrayal and resistance that are specific to cases where the Responding Party is a man and the Reporting Party is a woman using gendered double standards, gendered rape myths and himpathy (Bedera, 2023; Cruz, 2021; Rogalin & Addison; Weaving et al., 2023).[1] Gendered double standards and societal rape myths can often be seen in decision-making in cases where male perpetrators are prioritised over their female victim-survivors. Rape myths absolve perpetrators of guilt while blaming victims. We caution readers to look out for the following gendered double standards and/or rape myths within cases to prevent these from being used to bias decision-making:

- Excusing a man for raping a woman because he was drunk at the time of the assault but holding the woman responsible for being raped because she was drunk.

- Viewing women as 'too hysterical' – emotional and irrational – to be trusted with defining an act of sexual violence (Bedera, 2023).

- Believing women are vindictive, liars, to be punished for not following gender norms, attention-seeking or seeking revenge.

- Treating women as aggressors who are attacking men and hurting them by accusing them of sexual violence.

- Believing men's violence against women is 'not that bad' while a man being accused of sexual violence could 'ruin his life' (Bedera, 2023).

These examples are not an exhaustive list but represent some gendered double standards and views that are (1) deeply sexist and (2) are used to minimise and justify the perpetrator's behaviour absolving them of guilt while blaming or even villainising women victim-survivors.

A study in the United States into the rationalisations of Title IX administrators found that Title IX administrators were not specialist, did not take the job with the expectation of dealing with sexual violence, learned about sexual violence through informal mechanisms in the workplace and used hysteria and himpathy to justify rationalisations of institutional betrayal (Bedera, 2023).

---

[1] See Chapter 6 for a full definition of this term and further discussion.

> ... *all reports fit into one of two categories: (1)*
> *women's overly emotional misinterpretations of a*
> *sexual encounter that did not merit university interven-*
> *tion, or (2) violence so severe that no university action*
> *could reverse a survivor's life-long trauma. As a result,*
> *administrators rationalized that refusing to sanction*
> *perpetrators of sexual violence was moral – they*
> *could do nothing to help a survivor, but they could*
> *protect a perpetrator's education. (Bedera, 2023, p. 37)*

In this first quote, we see the university administrators see women as overreacting due to 'emotional misinterpretations of a sexual encounter' rather than considering whether the sexual encounters in question were consensual or not, immediately dismissing them as not deserving of university intervention, while at the same time dismissing sexual violence that they see as having life-long impact on victim-survivors, as they are too severe for the university intervention. In this quote, we see the university administrators prioritising the perpetrator's future, as they see victim-survivor as already harmed but the perpetrator as someone they can prevent from harm.

In this same study, administrators 'regularly described the act of being accused of rape as equally traumatizing to being a victim of rape' and focused their sympathy on the perpetrator, not the victim (Bedera, 2023, p. 8). They focused on the struggles perpetrators faced from being accused of sexual violence while not considering the impact of violence on the lives of the victim-survivors. In this study, investigators focused questions on seeing perpetrators as a whole person but often did not do this with victim-survivors. Administrators in this study felt that sanctioning a male perpetrator of sexual violence was 'immoral and cruel'. Women's futures were not viewed as worthy of protection. This is particularly used when women fail to perform the 'perfect victim' role. If they tell multiple people what happened to them, express anger, share their story on social media, complain that the university is not keeping them safe or acting quickly enough, instead of seeing their actions through a trauma-informed lens, they can be valued as 'unworthy' for not acting the way the university administrators want them to act (Bedera, 2023). Dodson et al. (2020) found that individuals who highly value loyalty (vs betrayal), authority (vs subversion) and purity (vs degradation) can perceive women who report sexual misconduct as 'unjustly tarnishing the lives and careers of the male accused' (p. 33).

Rogalin and Addison (2023) argue that himpathy is especially used when the men who have been accused of sexual violence 'hold a privileged status (white, middle- to upper-class, "cisgender", heterosexual)…' (p. 69). A key driver for himpathy is to protect dominant men's interests (Manne, 2021). Weaving et al. (2023) found that those with stronger motivation to maintain the gender status quo/hierarchy provide milder punishments for perpetrators of sexual violence. Cruz (2021) argues that as it is rare for the public to hold men accountable for sexual violence, university administrators too can be influenced by this making it difficult to challenge the culture that is sympathetic to men who perpetrate sexual violence and silences women who are subjected to sexual violence:

> When [the university administrator] explained why a woman who was sexually violated wouldn't be happy if her perpetrator was found guilty of misconduct, she justifies that the victim's life was already ruined, and now the perpetrator's life will also be ruined. She said, 'It doesn't feel good knowing two people are walking away with a lot of hurt.' Within her explanation she does not take into consideration power and that one person assaulted another. In [the university administrator's] construction of how the victim feels, there is no room for the victim to find any sense of justice in seeing the person who harmed her held accountable. Similarly, when administrators share that 'no one is ever happy,' they equate being unhappy about being sexually assaulted with being unhappy about being found responsible of sexually assaulting, and don't explain why they see the two as being equal. (Cruz, 2021, p. 378)

Prioritising men's futures and believing that only men can be harmed through a sexual violence disciplinary process is 'inaccurate and dangerous' (Bedera, 2023, p. 19).

Counter-complaints and Victimisation

In the studies noted earlier, when women were accused of sexual violence by men, the women did not receive the same response by university administrators to attempt to protect their futures, even when the complaints were retaliatory (Bedera, 2023). Counter-complaints are common tactic used particularly when perpetrators use DARVO – Deny, Attack, Reverse Victim and Offender – tactics. We remind readers that when an investigation or discipline process has an outcome of 'dismissed' or 'not founded' or in the Criminal Justice System (CJS) there is a verdict of 'not guilty', this does not mean the report was a false allegation.

We also note that women who report sexual misconduct in the workplace face retaliation for reporting misconduct, whereas men accused of sexual misconduct rarely are dismissed and are less likely to be targeted to resign than their victims (Dodson et al., 2020). Dodson et al. (2020) found that perpetrator sympathy can motivate retributive actions, e.g. victimisation, sympathy for perpetrators leads to lesser sanctions for the men and harsher punishments for victim-survivors.

CASE STUDIES

Sexual violence prevention and response work in the United Kingdom HE sector truly began in 2016. At the time of writing, there is scarce research on how universities are treating Reporting Parties and victim-survivors for student perpetrated sexual misconduct, but from the exposes the practice is not good. There are countless stories we could consider in this section, from 2015 American documentary film *The Hunting Ground* to Emily Drouet's story told through EmilyTest and hundreds more. For brevity, we note a few cases below.

In 2021, Al Jazeera's Investigative Unit published *Degrees of Abuse* – a series of powerful videos, podcasts and an interactive webpage with a wealth of data from 164 freedom of information requests presenting overwhelming evidence of UK universities failing women in academia by protecting student and staff perpetrators of sexual violence. Along with presenting harrowing stories of how these women were treated while the perpetrators were protected, their study found that between 2017 and 2020, 83% of complaints of sexual violence made by students did not result in disciplinary action for the Responding Party (Al Jazeera, 2021). Part of their findings revealed that universities had refused to allow reports made against the same Responding Party to be heard together, thus ignoring patterns of behaviour and dismissing cases as he-said-she-said. They also found that cases took months to years to be heard.

We next look at a specific case of stalking that occurred at a university in England. The information for this case described below comes from the news coverage from *The Guardian* (Batty, 2019) and BBC (2019). A man pled guilty and was convicted of stalking and image-based sexual abuse offences that he had perpetrated against his ex-girlfriend. Both were students at the same university, and she had reported him to the police and their university. The magistrate's court imposed a 12-month community order and a restraining order banning him from contacting the woman he had harmed. The university required the woman to attend the university's disciplinary hearing and give evidence regarding the offences. They allowed him to continue studying at the university and required both students to sign a no contact agreement. The woman was quoted describing how the university's decision impacted her, '... And the university's decision made me feel worthless, like my safety wasn't important at all. It felt as though they couldn't see the harm of the emotional abuse' (Batty, 2019). The university responded to the journalist noting they worked to ensure the safety of students and had taken action to begin a review of their disciplinary procedures following a petition that was raised regarding this case. In this case, we see a decision made based on a perpetrator pleading guilty to multiple criminal offences and a conviction of said offences occurring in criminal court. As a decision was made in a higher court, it would not be necessary to rehear evidence on the civil standard to determine if the allegations occurred. Without knowing the full details of the case, we cannot comment on why the university felt it was appropriate to allow a convicted stalker to return to campus where the woman he had stalked studied or why they felt it was appropriate to place the burden of breaching a no contact agreement on the victim-survivor too rather than issuing a No Contact Order on the Responding Party only. However, we can say this outcome of this case does not appear to prioritise safe access to the education for the woman who had been subjected to stalking and image-based sexual abuse.

Case Spotlight: Feder & McCamish v Royal Welsh College of Music and Drama

Two women, Sydney Feder and Alyse McCamish (who waived their right to anonymity), won their cases against the Royal Welsh College of Music and Drama who they reported failed to properly investigate the reports of sexual misconduct that had been perpetrated against them by the same male student. The Court found the College's liability was a result of nine key failures, and the College was ordered to pay £19,000 in damages and court costs.

Recorder John Halford at Central London County Court ruled on October 5, 2023, that HEIs have a **duty of care** to students to carry out reasonable investigations when students report sexual misconduct. HEIs must take reasonable care by taking reasonable:

- Protective steps.
- Supportive steps.
- Investigatory steps.
- Disciplinary action (where applicable).
- Steps to communicate reasonably with Reporting Parties.

(*Continued*)

> **(Feder and McCamish v Royal Welsh College of Music and Drama, 2023)**
>
> **For more information:**
> Feder and McCamish vs Royal Welsh College of Music and Drama (County Court, October 5, 2023), https://wonk-he.com/wp-content/wonkhe-uploads/2023/10/5-10-23-Feder-and-McCamish-v-RWCMD-FINAL.pdf

HOW SECTOR GUIDANCE FAILS VICTIM-SURVIVORS

Our concern is that current sector guidance in England and Wales is not preventing institutional betrayal, resistance tactics used against victim-survivors or re-traumatisation. We argue that in some cases, it is actively encouraging it. The glaringly obvious concern is that sector guidance creates a system that allows Reporting Parties to be systematically disadvantaged in investigation and disciplinary procedures as they have fewer rights than Responding Parties (see Chapter 12 for more discussion on this).

There is criminal justice drift which is moving the sector to more adversarial mini-criminal court-style hearings with fewer protections for victim-survivors than even the criminal justice system provides, e.g. victims' rights through the Victim's Code (Ministry of Justice, 2024). As a reaction to case law (*AB vs University of XYZ (2020)* EWHC 2978 and *AB vs University of XYZ (2023)* EWHC 1162), HEIs are more readily allowing legal representation for Responding Parties in disciplinary cases. And of course, this will protect the wealthy who can readily 'lawyer up', while disadvantaging Reporting and Responding Parties who do not have the means to seek legal representation. Prof Sir Steve West, the Vice-Chancellor of the University of the West of England and former President of Universities UK, said:

> As expulsion is a penalty, parents of the accused often start to raise the stakes by hiring a lawyer. It is a power game, because usually the victim has no representation, and I think it is completely unacceptable and unfair. (Fazackerley, 2023)

We agree. And university leaders can make choices about the extent to which they decide to permit the involvement of legal representatives in their institutional processes – we would strongly advise against the routine involvement of legal professionals in internal university processes to determine breaches of policy.

Even the pathway for Reporting Parties to get to the OIA in England and Wales is not equal to that of the Responding Parties. It is not clear where the expertise on sexual misconduct is at the OIA – we are not aware that they draw upon any such expertise. A student normally can only make a complaint to the OIA if they have a completion of procedures (COP) letter. To be given a COP letter, the student needs to have completed all available internal procedures with the university. For a Responding Party, this simply requires appealing the outcome of the disciplinary process. Once the appeal is completed, the HEI will issue the COP letter, and the Responding Party can make a complaint against the HEI through the OIA. However, for Reporting Parties, their pathway is more convoluted. If the investigation into the report made by the Reporting Party dismisses the case, then the Reporting Party may be given an option to request a review of that decision. At the end of that process, the Reporting Party can be issued with a COP letter. However, if the investigation finds there is a case to answer and the case is moved to a disciplinary process (away from the complaints process), the Reporting Party no longer has any access to internal procedures but would not necessarily be issued a COP letter at this point. If the Reporting Party was dissatisfied with the outcome of the disciplinary process, because, e.g. the discipline hearing dismissed the case or used a sanction that did not meaningfully hold the perpetrator accountable and remedy the harm caused to the Reporting Party, then there is no right for the Reporting Party to appeal. Their only option would be to make a complaint to the university or not. Through that complaint process, they would then need to appeal the outcome of the complaint process if the outcome was not satisfactory (which is very likely as a complaint against the service the university provided would very likely not have any impact on the action taken against the Responding Party). From there, the Reporting Party would be issued a COP letter and be able to make a complaint against the university with the OIA. Likewise, when a Responding Party makes a complaint to the OIA, the OIA can require the university to rehear a discipline case – making this decision with no input or care regarding the impact this will have on the Reporting Party. However, when a Reporting Party makes a complaint to the OIA against a university, the OIA would not require the university to rehear the case against the Responding Party. This is because the OIA sees the discipline process as belonging to the Responding Party only.

We highlight in Chapter 12 that sector guidance on data sharing prioritises Responding Parties' privacy over Reporting Parties safety and privacy (See, Cowan et al., 2024 for a full discussion). Sector guidance also remains overly cautious and tends to offer no formal mechanisms for information-sharing between institutions regarding student and staff sexual misconduct facilitating 'pass-the-perpe-trator'. And at the time of writing, there is lack of oversight/regulation of HEIs in this area.

PREVENTING BETRAYAL AND RESISTANCE

The aim of this chapter is to explicitly highlight *what not to do*. The rest of the book primarily focuses on what to do and how to do it. In Chapter 14, we spotlight the Gender-based Violence (GBV) Charter from EmilyTest which was developed to support universities in pre-venting failing students. However, we cannot sensibly end this chapter without highlighting a few key points on actions university officials can take to prevent institutional betrayal and resistance.

HEIs must actively raise awareness of sexual misconduct victimi-zation, improve support services available for victim-survivors and provide transparency in reporting, investigation and disciplinary procedures (Moore & Mennicke, 2020). Moore and Mennicke (2020) recommend one way for universities to mitigate potential institutional betrayal is 'universities could consider engaging in iter-ative investigation into whether they are handling claims of sexual misconduct in fair and just ways', (p. 380).

Clear guidance on the principles of trauma-informed practice needs to be embedded in guidance. It is not enough to use 'trauma-informed' as a buzz word. Equal rights and mitigating for himpathy and rape myth acceptance need to be embedded into guidance. Current guidance does not address these issues allowing for universities to continue to make these mistakes.

Finally, we note that the HE sector has a long history of what is referred to as 'pass the perpetrator' where an employee or student who has committed sexual violence moves between institutions often without anyone at the new institution having knowledge of this. This is hugely problematic for risk assessing admissions applications. Given evidence that serial perpetration of sexual violence in universities is common, allowing students (and employees) to move to institutions without factual references that the individual left during an investigation into sexual misconduct or that they were found to commit sexual misconduct simply means those individuals can move to a new institution without further safeguards in place. In the United Kingdom, academic transcripts do not list discipline sanctions, including expulsion. Therefore, no information is shared with the new institution. University HR departments are well placed to show some leadership on this point whereby they could choose to insist on a reference from the HR department of the previous institution when making appointments. That would be a quick inexpensive win for any leader who is serious about addressing their problem with sexual misconduct at universities. To this point, we highlight the Misconduct Disclosure Scheme as an example of good practice and highly recommend university leaders demonstrate their leadership by having their HEI join this scheme.

Good Practice Example: Misconduct Disclosure Scheme

The Misconduct Disclosure Scheme was launched in January 2019 to address the specific problem of known sexual abusers moving between organisations undetected. The Scheme is currently implemented by over 280 organisations worldwide including three UN agencies (UN population Fund, UN High Commission for Refugees and the UN Office for Project Services), several of the most renowned organisations operating in

(Continued)

the humanitarian and development sectors (e.g. Oxfam, CARE, Save the Children, Islamic Relief and the British Red Cross), as well as a growing number of private sector organisations. HEIs internationally have long faced problems with staff moving institution during investigations into GBV or harassment. The Misconduct Disclosure Scheme helps to address the problem of 'pass-the-perpetrator'. Between 2019 and 2023, the scheme resulted in 385 rejected hires.

The Scheme consists of two main commitments, a commitment to:

1. systematically check with previous employers about any sexual harassment issues relating to potential new hires and
2. respond systematically to such checks from others.

By joining, HEIs will:

- demonstrate a public commitment to address the specific issue of repeat perpetrators of GBV moving between organisations;
- reduce the risk of GBV in the institution, by supporting safer hiring decisions by reducing employing abusers;
- demonstrate the preventative duty to prevent sexual harassment of employees in the workplace in line with the Worker Protection (Amendment of Equality Act 2010) Act 2023.

For more information or to join the scheme:
https://misconduct-disclosure-scheme.org

The 1752 Group, DiSantis, C. J., Bezzolato, E., & Price-Jones, G. (2024). *Briefing note no. 4: Why higher education institutions should join the misconduct disclosure scheme.* https://1752group.com/briefing-notes/

With special thanks to Gareth Price-Jones, Executive Secretary of the Steering Committee for Humanitarian Response, Elena Bezzolato, MDS Coordinator, and Anna Bull, co-founder of The 1752 Group for reviewing and approving this summary.

As we conclude, we note that the point of addressing sexual violence in higher education is to ensure students and employees can access their education and workplace safely, not to protect the university. However, the university *is* protected as a by-product of keeping students and staff safe. University policies and procedures to prevent and respond to sexual violence should prioritise safety, mitigating for the risk of re-traumatisation, resistance and institutional betrayal.

📖 Related Resources

- Al Jazeera. (2021). *Degrees of abuse.* https://interactive.aljazeera.com/aje/2021/degrees-of-abuse/index.html
- Bedera, N. (2023). I can protect his future, but she can't be helped: Himpathy and hysteria in administrator rationalizations of institutional betrayal. *The Journal of Higher Education*, 95(1), 30–53. https://doi.org/10.1080/00221546.2023.2195771
- Drouet, F., & Gerrard-Abbott, P. (2023). EmilyTest: From tragedy to change. In C. J. Humphreys & G. J. Towl (Eds.), *Stopping gender-based violence in higher education: Policy, practice, and partnerships.* Routledge.

14

LEADERSHIP AND PARTNERSHIPS

So much of the work to prevent and respond to sexual violence in universities is delivered by student-facing practitioners and trainers within a higher education institution (HEI). However, no work is sustainable without support from leadership at the highest levels of the organisation, and the most effective and highest quality initiatives will likely be developed and possibly delivered through secured partnerships with external organisations. In this chapter, we highlight the necessity of leadership to truly address sexual violence in higher education (HE) and discuss opportunities for partnership working to enhance prevention and response initiatives.

LEADERSHIP

Probably one of the more disconcerting truths around addressing our problem with sexual violence at universities is the capacity for denial of the problem – or at least assertions that we are indeed prioritising this area of work despite all the evidence to the contrary. For example, in the guidance provided by the Committee of University Chairs (CUC) to governing bodies, they boldly state that "Most Universities already prioritise action in this area..." (2022, p. 10). This seems to us to be misleading and at odds with the evidence perhaps with some notable exceptions. As we have seen elsewhere in this book, it is the student body that has provided the leadership in making headway in addressing our problems with sexual violence in HE (See Dickinson and Blake, 2023, for a history of student leadership contributions). University leaders have largely not provided the leadership necessary. It is probably fair to say that there remains a significant leadership deficit in this area of policy and practice across the sector. However, on a more positive note, the CUC guidance concludes by noting that "A university that fails to take action to address issues of harassment risks its reputation, its relationship with students and local communities, and its long-term sustainability," (CUC, 2022, p. 10). This is an important shift – on reputation. Previously, concerns about "reputational risk" seemed more associated with the problem of being found out that there was indeed a problem rather than a focus on student safety and wellbeing. Any public admission of a problem with sexual violence was seen as leading to potential reputational damage for even having the problem itself. Some things are perhaps starting to change with more risk associated with the doubling down denial of the past. But change is frustratingly slow despite the labours of activists, Students' Unions and staff wanting to enact changes so that we reduce our problem with sexual violence in the sector; the potential to do so is huge. So, it is a prize worth working for.

The broader context of the leadership lacuna is set in the context of the regulatory environment. At the time of writing, the Office for Students (OfS) are about to release information on regulation in this area. The resignation of the Chair in combination with the installation of a new government have perhaps contributed to something of a policy flux – hence, we anticipate writing about this once any such new policy directions have become clearer. Our hope is that there will be a tightening of regulation to require institutions to take some key steps to tackle their problems with sexual violence. For student-on-student sexual violence/misconduct, we would anticipate that there would need to be pecuniary incentives for organisations to demonstratively, rather than ritualistically, "take the problem seriously". We have views on staff-to-student sexual misconduct too and how to address such matters; however, for the purposes of this book, we keep our focus on student-on-student sexual misconduct and refer readers to the work of The 1752 Group for information on staff sexual misconduct.

Showing Leadership

Vice-Chancellors and their executive leadership teams are well placed to show leadership in addressing their problem of sexual violence at universities. Despite this, many appear to have chosen not to bother even to the extent of ensuring that the very minimalist OfS *Statement of expectations for preventing and addressing harassment and sexual misconduct affecting students in higher education* herein *"Statement of Expectations"* (2021) is delivered upon. This of course maybe reveals a broader governance problem within HE related to how leaders are held accountable. We do not see any evidence of governing bodies having held university executive leadership teams to account – perhaps they similarly lack any such motivation for change? And yet as mentioned above, there does seem to have been a shift in very recent years to be more risk averse in relation to being found wanting in this area rather than to be found out for having a problem. It is now a very open secret that universities have significant problems with sexual violence. It seems to us that this is not a problem of capacity or ability but rather one of motivation. Hopefully, if confirmed, new regulation will go some way to help motivate university leaders with showing such leadership. Student activists have been heavily motivated to address the issue with a high number having been subjected to sexual violence themselves. The burden to ensure universities are places where students and staff can access their education and workplaces safely should not be placed on students and/or victim-survivors – it should remain with university leadership.

Executive Leadership

One element of the role of leaders is to recognise when changes need to be made and to convey to their followers or wider community the (urgent) need for the change. The case for change is very powerful indeed, especially in view of the high rates of the perpetration of sexual violence at universities. What we do know is that there are comparatively high concentrations of perpetrators of sexual violence at universities. It may well be that they are quite a different population from imprisoned sex offenders which much of the forensic psychological field has focused upon in support of claims about "what we know about sex offenders". So, there may be a need for academics to start providing some academic leadership in identifying the differences and commonalities between student sex offenders and imprisoned sex offenders who may have perpetrated sexual violence in other contexts. There may, of course, be some overlaps between the two groups over time. But we want more from leaders than merely academic leadership; there are broader civic duties that we may reasonably expect, and we outline some ideas below which we hope will be helpful for any university leaders who want to make a difference in this vital area of student safety. One easy leadership win is to allocate responsibility for tackling sexual misconduct to a member of the executive team who can report to the governing body and their executive team termly to indicate the extent of the problem and progress tackling it. In general, we would recommend the Pro-Vice-Chancellor for Equality, Diversity and Inclusion or the Pro-Vice-Chancellor for Education or their equivalence. Of course, there will be some variability between institutions on nomenclature and the configuration, and structure of senior teams and leaders will be informed by that too.

Leadership Actions

In this section, we outline key actions university leaders can take to demonstrate a commitment to addressing sexual violence within their HEI. The OfS *Statement of Expectations* seems to us to be a good starting point for leaders as a checklist to inform any audit of current practices. What is important to understand is that the *Statement of Expectations* sets the bar at a level well below what many student or staff activists would want. Nonetheless, it is a good starting point in that few will be meeting all such expectations at this juncture as evidenced in the evaluation report for the OfS of the implementation of the *Statement of Expectations* (see Baird et al., 2022).

Leading academic institutions is a difficult and demanding role. We all need help at times. And this is so in such a specialist area as sexual misconduct at universities. Rather than rely upon generic auditors to audit the progress against the *Statement of Expectations*, we would advise working with a specialist or a specialist organisation. To this point, we offer the *Gender-based Violence (GBV) Charter* from EmilyTest as a useful tool that university leaders can consider when seeking independent evaluation of prevention and response initiatives.

✿ Good Practice Example: GBV Charter, EmilyTest

In 2016, undergraduate law student Emily Drouet died following a campaign of abuse and violence by her boyfriend, whom she met during her first year at university. Fiona Drouet, Emily's mother and founder and CEO of EmilyTest, advocated to the Scottish Government for adequate provisions to be implemented in universities and colleges regarding GBV prevention, intervention and support, following the identified failings at Emily's university. However, despite these efforts, there remains no independent scrutiny of the sector in this area.

The GBV Charter is an award, the first of its kind, allowing HE and Further Education (FE) institutions to take the "Emily Test", which involves meeting minimum standards aimed at preventing tragedies similar to Emily's. It establishes minimum standards and excellence in GBV prevention, intervention and support by prompting institutions to consider, *"Would your policies, procedures, and practices have saved Emily's life? Would your institution pass the Emily Test?"*

The Charter provides a framework, alongside guided coaching, for HE and FE institutions to effectively prevent, intervene and respond to GBV in line with best practice and national guidance, while also celebrating progress outwardly. It comprises the following five principles, encompassing over 40 minimum standards that institutions must meet:

1. Open and Learning.

2. Educated and Empowered.

3. Comprehensive and Connected.

(Continued)

4. Equal and Inclusive.

5. Safe and Effective.

To facilitate the implementation of this framework, EmilyTest supports institutions through one-to-one coaching, resources, training and opportunities to share best practices within the sector.

For more information:

www.emilytest.org/charter-about

Drouet, F., & Gerrard-Abbott, P. (2023). EmilyTest: From tragedy to change. In C. J. Humphreys & G. J. Towl (Eds.), *Stopping gender-based violence in higher education: Policy, practice, and partnerships.* Routledge.

With special thanks to Fiona Drouet MBE, Founder and Chief Executive Officer of EmilyTest, for reviewing and approving this summary.

Perhaps, the single most impactful decision that a senior leader can make to address this area is to appoint a full-time specialist who understands the area. Such staff may, for example, come from a range of health and social care backgrounds. The appointment of a specialist demonstrates an awareness of the complexities of this challenging area while also providing a resource for senior leaders on informing policy and service development.

Prevention and response work should be evidence-informed, considering research and local data. Data collected need to be widely, regularly and routinely shared so the whole university community can see that if there is a report of sexual misconduct what action is taken and what support is available, e.g. the Reporting Party will receive appropriate counselling and academic adjustment support where needed, and perpetrators are held accountable for misconduct.

Next senior leaders can commission biannual prevalence campus climate surveys to get a measure of the extent of the problem while also providing a baseline from which to measure any improvements over time as various policies and processes are implemented. Additionally, such data can inform interventions – it may be that there are "hot spots" for sexual misconduct in the institution. It is important to get data on these rather than to rely upon the default of rumour and university informal networks or gossip. So, for example, it may be that there are places or activities more or less associated with higher prevalence rates of sexual misconduct. One place to start looking is in relation to sport. Again, there is empirical evidence of particular problems with sport with, e.g. one study highlighting rugby as a sport with a particular problem with sexual misconduct and "laddish" behaviour (Phipps & Young, 2012). But it won't be likely by any means to be just one sport – it may be that there are different characteristics with team than individual sports, but each would be anticipated to import problems into any university community. An awareness of such issues may well be part of the selection process for any Director of Sport and related senior staff working in the student sport arena.

Open days are a great opportunity to send messages to potential perpetrators of sexual violence that there is a strong encouragement of reporting, and that those found to have committed sexual violence face sanctions. One way of illustrating this is to share the publicly available data and for a member of the executive team to present such information to prospective students and their parents on open days.

In the academic world, we tend to be good at researching or commenting upon what changes others may wish to make in a range of domains for improvements of various kinds. We are perhaps less good at looking at ourselves and how we may need to change. We are not unique in this respect; nonetheless, it is important that we recognise that we are part of the problem. Sexual violence is not perpetrated by one "bad apple" but is perpetuated by the structural inequalities within communities which is why a social justice-based approach is embedded into the comprehensive institution-wide approach we recommend.

University leaders can set the professional standards of all staff, given academia does not have regulated professional standards like other professions, e.g. medicine, social work and teaching. Professional standards can include prohibiting close personal and intimate relationships (including one-off sexual activity) between staff and students to mitigate for abuse of power. Normative exemptions to this (e.g. in HE in the United States) would be (1) if the relationship existed prior to the implementation of the policy and there was no conflict of interest, coercion, or favouritism present; (2) if the relationship existed prior to a change in either partner's status as student or employee, which then resulted in a violation, and there was no conflict of interest, coercion or favouritism present; or (3) the Vice-Chancellor, or delegate, could retain discretion and authority to grant exemptions in other individual situations that appear to be "exceptional" according to her/his/their professional judgement. We would recommend that the Vice-Chancellor seek specialist advice when considering an exemption request if needed. Having this ban on staff–student relationships conveys an important message – that power inequalities and professional boundaries are acknowledged and adhered to – it says to the wider community what the values of the institution are and feeds into role expectations in terms of the focus being on research and education (Towl & Humphreys, 2021). It also elevates the professional standards of university staff to match those of regulated professions, where concerns of potential for abuse of power are safeguarded through professional boundaries.

Any institutional strategy aimed at tackling sexual violence is incomplete without clear policies in relation to alcohol. The introduction of minimum pricing for units of alcohol may be one element of such policies along with the availability of subsidised soft drinks. Where there are events which involve the consumption of alcohol, the institution should plan for increased reporting of sexual misconduct. Annual sporting dinners or graduation events can each be hot spots for sexual misconduct.

University leaders should take actions to decrease barriers to disclosure of sexual violence and encourage and welcome reports of sexual violence, recognising this will support Reporting Parties in accessing support and aid in prevention. If reporting is the "new norm", it may well deter some perpetrators while also ensuring that there is counselling and educational support in place for those subjected to sexual misconduct.

We recognise that many universities have international partnerships to support study abroad, internships and international research projects. Another area needing careful consideration is in relation to these types of partnerships often led by international offices or those concerned with setting up placements or opportunities for students (and staff) in other countries. Such partnership working needs informed vetting from the perspective of student safety. Routinely rates of sexual violence and the policing of it in other countries need to be understood before sending students on such placements. Ensuring that partnership organisations have policies and procedures in place and clear prevention actions is key when considering student safety. Where international organisations lack these measures, HEIs can work in partnership to mitigate risk to students and staff studying and working abroad. University leaders must also recognise the converse is that international students from other countries may be an especially vulnerable group insofar as there may be cultural barriers to reporting and a lack of clarity around UK law and university policies and procedures around matters of non-academic student misconduct (Humphreys & Towl, 2023b).

We conclude this section of the chapter with a non-exhaustive checklist of leadership actions in Table 6. These are a starting point for university executives to demonstrate leadership in addressing sexual violence in HE.

Table 6. Checklist of Leadership Actions.

Leadership Actions	Completed
1. Appoint a full-time sexual violence prevention and response specialist.	
2. Allocate executive responsibility to the appropriate Pro-Vice-Chancellor (or equivalent), including sexual violence on the strategic risk register.	
3. Commission and enact a biannual prevalence campus climate survey.	
4. Focus prevention initiatives on areas where there are known problems, e.g. "Freshers" week, sport, fieldwork.	
5. Vet international partner institutions carefully in relation to their policies and prevention measures related to sexual violence.	

(Continued)

Table 6. *(Continued)*

Leadership Actions	Completed
6. Invest in specialist support for victim-survivors to access through the HEI rather than waiting on community waitlists, e.g. specialist counselling through the local rape crisis service delivered at the university (paid for by the university).	
7. Appoint in-house trauma-informed investigators or retain the equivalent through vetted external investigating firms.	
8. Deliver an annual trend monitoring presentation to the governing body to include characteristics and numbers of cases and actions to be taken as a result of analysed trends (See Resource 2).	
9. Audit and evaluate prevention and response work to assess whether initiatives are having a positive effect on culture change and campus safety. To have this done independently, see, e.g. the EmilyTest *GBV Charter*.	
10. Prohibit close personal and intimate relationships (including one-off sexual activity) between staff and students to mitigate for abuse of power, noting relevant exemptions.	
11. Encourage increased reporting by reducing barriers to disclosure and making reporting pathways clear.	
12. Ensure that there is a comprehensive institution-wide programme of staff and student training aimed at preventing and responding to sexual violence.	
13. Join the *Misconduct Disclosure Scheme* (see Chapter 13) to ensure that when recruiting staff at ALL levels, there is a check with previous employers about any sexual harassment issues relating to potential new hires and respond systematically to such checks from others.	
14. Publicly acknowledge that gender-based violence is a concern within the university and that perpetrators will be held accountable for this behaviour which will not be tolerated. Share anonymised outcomes of sexual violence discipline processes with the entire HEI community to demonstrate this.	
15. Work in partnership with local organisations on shared prevention and response goals and drawing on the expertise of partners: e.g. County councils, NHS, public health, sexual health clinics, SARCs, rape crisis, police and, of course, Students' Unions and Trade Unions.	

PARTNERSHIP WORKING

We recommend that HEIs not work siloed from local organisations and expertise. Partnership working should be valued and encouraged as the best practice. This includes building partnerships with external organisations and internal academic departments or research groups. When partners have the same aim, it is easier to work together to accomplish the goal.

Working With External Partners

As highlighted in the Advance HE minimal safeguarding recommendations shown in Chapter 5, it is expected that HEIs will work collaboratively with local partners (Baird et al., 2019). One of the first and crucial steps is to create a partnership with local services – i.e. local government, police, Rape Crisis, Sexual Assault Referral Centres (SARCs) and other local or national specialist services who will serve victim-survivors and may work with perpetrators.

Partnerships may be formal or informal; however, we recommend formal partnerships with key services, i.e. Rape Crisis, SARCs and the police. A formal partnership may include a Memorandum of Understanding (MOU) detailing what services each partner will provide, how information will be shared and an expected service-level agreement. Formal partners may have a seat at the table on task forces or operational groups. Often these services will be well-placed due to their expertise to provide feedback on the development of policies, procedures, trainings and campaign work. Partners may have expert trainers available to deliver training sessions to staff and/or students. We recommend HEIs pay for any consultancy or services partners provide, e.g. training, counselling or advising, as appropriate. This is important for at least two reasons. First, such partners are rarely as affluent as university bodies. Often, they are charities with uncertain funding streams. In other words, this is both a moral (it is the right thing to do) and practical (we help ensure that the service stays afloat) imperative. Second, we would anticipate that academics and other university staff would anticipate receiving pay for services; we should surely do the same with partners when we benefit from such services, e.g. specialist staff training services. As a further resource for this discussion, we note that in Humphreys and Towl (2023), Part III of that edited volume focuses solely on building partnerships to stop GBV in HE and offers examples of successful partnerships UK HEIs have developed. Well worth a read.

In addition, HEIs may consider developing partnerships with nearby institutions depending on the institutions' geography. If the university is the only university in town, this may be less of a priority; however, in cities with multiple universities, it is likely that students will spend time with students of nearby institutions. Consideration for how student misconduct may be addressed across institutions is key. In addition, institutions may share resources, conduct joint campaigns, conduct campus climate surveys and compare results, and ensure that police and specialist services are equipped to support each institution. A partnership may include jointly supporting specialist services in the local area who serve the institutions' students and staff.

Working in Partnership Within the HEI Community

We can learn a lot from the student body. Student activists internationally have provided the sector leadership on raising the issue of the need to address sexual violence at universities while also keeping it very much on the agenda (See, for example, Clark & Pino, 2016; Dick & Ziering, 2016; Dickinson & Blake, 2023; NUS, 2011). There may student groups focused on sexual violence prevention and/or supporting those subjected to sexual violence. Giving these groups a voice in university task forces or operational groups is key. Students' and victim-survivors' voices should be part of any development and evaluation of prevention and response initiatives.

Although Students' Unions and local branches of Trade Unions are technically external organisations, we include them in this section as part of the HEI community as their members are made up of an HEI's students or employees. Students' Unions have the benefit of a legacy of having led in this area along with the power of peer persuasion. This is a potent mix and one that the whole university community may benefit from working with. Likewise, local branches of Trade Unions can be useful in promoting campaigns and advocating for culture change.

HEI and student leaders need to work in partnership to address sexual violence. One approach to conveying a commitment to such partnerships is to provide the necessary resources to Students' Unions to support their ability to lead in specific areas such as student-led campaigns, peer support and peer-facilitated training. The elephant in the room here is that university leaders have not historically shown leadership in this area; the uncomfortable truth seems to us to be that as a sector, we have largely left it to the student body. This speaks loudly culturally and maybe underlies the point so oft stated that it is difficult to get senior leadership teams truly on board with such work. Therefore, a commitment by senior leaders to work in partnership with student leaders can greatly support prevention and response work and send a very powerful and positive message to the whole university community.

Finally, noting the importance of working within the university community collaboratively, we highlight the great potential that we have as HE communities in view of the expertise and talent among staff including administrators, professionals and academics. HEIs will have experts in-house who can lead on conducting campus climate surveys and develop evaluations for prevention education programmes. From our experience in this field, it is probably the most common error in institutions working in this area – home-grown expertise is not drawn upon, and often there is working in silos of university administrators vs academics. Especially in the broader context of existential concerns about sector finances, it seems especially important to draw upon existing expertise across the institution and across into existing external partnerships. HEIs may have schools or departments with professional groups such as social workers or authorities on social policy whose expertise could be used in the development of institutional policies and practices. There may be dedicated research groups focused on GBV within the organisation. Working in partnership across an institution, rather than in silos, can support the development and success of a comprehensive institution-wide approach.

As we conclude this chapter, we recognise that partnerships can only be impactfully developed and maintained through the support of leadership. Although social change is most often formed through grassroots efforts, we implore universities leaders not to burden students and staff, victim-survivors and activists with the responsibility of creating safe university communities. The burden belongs to university leaders. In Chapter 6, we highlight how HEIs can resist prevention and response work to sexual violence. We note in that chapter a motivation for resisting positive cultural change is maintaining the status quo, so as not to threaten gained positions of power. Instead, we challenge university leaders to see addressing sexual violence in their HEI as a way to demonstrate their positive leadership of the organisation. For leaders to most effectively lead, we need to be role models – to model good practice. Leaders must speak with as much pride about student safety as institutional research and educational achievements. **To permit is to promote – if we permit an enabling culture of sexual misconduct characterised by high prevalence rates, then in effect, we promote it.** Those leaders who do best in this area will have great partnership-building skills and recognise that it is only by working with others that we can maximise our impacts in both reducing prevalence levels and also providing support where there are cases of sexual misconduct alongside investigatory and disciplinary processes covered in more detail elsewhere in this book. It takes a comparatively rare leader to be able to stand above and beyond current practices to see the prize of not just a safer university environment but safer futures for students as they emerge from university and go into and influence all our futures – what could be more fulfilling than that?

📖 **Related Resources**

- Towl, G. & Humphreys, C. (2021, April 22). How to do more than the bare minimum on harassment and sexual misconduct. *WONKHE*. https://wonkhe.com/blogs/how-to-do-more-than-the-bare-minimum-on-harassment-and-sexual-misconuct/
- Committee of University Chairs. (2022). *Tackling harassment and sexual misconduct: Guidance for Chairs and*

Governing Bodies. https://www.universitychairs.ac.uk/2022/05/18/cuc-guidance-for-chairs-and-governing-bodies-tackling-harassment-and-sexual-misconduct/

- Humphreys, C. J. & Towl, G. J. (Eds). (2023). Part III: Partnerships (Chapters 17–21). In *Stopping gender-based violence in higher education: Policy, practice, and partnerships.* Routledge.
- Humphreys, C. J. & Towl, G. J. (Eds). (2023c). Stopping gender-based violence in higher education: Policy, practice, and partnerships. Routledge.

15

CONCLUDING THOUGHTS AND RECOMMENDATIONS

In writing this second edition of this book, we have tried not to shy away from the difficulties in getting universities to address sexual violence. We have offered practical guidance on what universities can do to prevent and respond to sexual violence in their communities but also deliberately spent time discussing what not to do.

We have watched HEIs move on from 'it's not our problem' or 'it doesn't happen here' to a position where the need for action is increasingly being recognised. And it is an indication of some progress that the time of doubling down on denial is seen as riskier than being transparent about our problems for governing bodies of universities at least. However, action and material delivery of change has been glacial in the 2020s to date. The moral momentum since the 2016 publication of the UUK's *Changing the Culture* report and the 2021 OfS *Statement of Expectations* seems all but lost. Sexual violence is happening in every HEI in the world (see e.g. Everyone's Invited for examples of universities in the UK https://www.everyonesinvited.uk/submissions/schools-list-2022), and the #MeToo movement is exposing this issue more and more each day (see e.g. Me Too Rising at metoorising.withgoogle.com).

As we hope is evident from this book, the time to do this work is now. We need to embed a comprehensive institution-wide approach that is trauma-informed, survivor-centred, human rights-based, social justice-based, intersectional and hold perpetrators account-able for their actions. We need to address these issues at the indi-vidual, relationship, community and institutional levels of HEIs. At the institutional level, we need to address the strategic, tactical and operational aspects of this work.

In the powerful words of author and survivor Chanel Miller in her personal account of the sexual violence she was subjected to in *Know My Name*, Miller highlights the impact of institutions' failing and inaction:

> *The assault harmed me physically, but there were bigger things that got broken. Broken trust in institu-tions. Broken faith in the place I thought would protect me. Their apathy, their lack of apology I could live with, but what troubled me most was their failure to ask the single most important question: How do we ensure this does not happen again? They had treated my assault like a singular, isolated incident... Brock was not one bad apple, he just threatened to expose the greater, underlying issues of sexual violence on campus. Stanford should have taken the opportunity to conduct a systematic review of procedures and pol-icies. To make sure that when a victim is harmed, there are services in place to take immediate action. To re-evaluate safety on campus. To make survivors feel supported. They should have said, It mattered, what happened to you. (Miller, 2019, pp. 296–297)*

For us, the above quote succinctly captures a great deal about the HE sector where there is an increasing recognition that we are not doing enough, soon enough, if ever. The quote also puts into context how many of us working and/or studying in HE may ourselves become institutionalised and habituated to the everyday sexism or racism of institutional life. We hope we have successfully explained that sexual violence is not just about an individual 'bad apple' but rather it is indicative of a broader institutional and institutionalised problem which we are all in some way part of as members of our institutions. Just as with racism and sexism, institutional culture change is required to truly prevent sexual violence and intersecting forms of discrimination in our communities.

Those who hold rape myths may very well not know about them, such is the nature and power of a myth. We need not restrict our discussions to so-called 'unconscious biases' – a term widely used in the HR industry to be a polite version of prejudices at the level of the individual. We need to look at the institutionalisation of prejudice (e.g. institutionalised sexism and racism) which we can see baked into the sector which creates the structural inequalities which perpetuate sexual violence. Such institutional prejudices are reflected in outcomes as well as processes, but the underlying processes can be hard to identify and change. But it can be done. Miller's quote illustrates the multi-level problem and challenge of trying to address sexual violence in HE.

We recognise that some university communities still seem to be evidently in denial of the extent of the problem. Worse still some do not necessarily see it as our problem. We infer this from inaction or clear under-investment. Staff working in an institution that denies the problem or disavows responsibility may wish to consider how best to influence the culture change or understandably may choose to exit the institution itself. We think that increasingly students will be even more interested in issues of personal safety when selecting their universities. In England and Wales in recent years, there has been a marked shift in who chooses who 'even in' Russell Group universities where the power has moved away from universities in selecting candidates to prospective student selecting their university. More than ever before, this gives prospective students the opportunity to apply elsewhere from those university communities who choose not to engage sufficiently in this challenging area. Prospective students may wish to consider carefully whether to go to particular universities if student safety and equality of access to education are not given a sufficiently high level of priority.

In Chapter 9, we discussed the need for first responders to believe disclosures of sexual violence, and as part of the conclusion of this book, we choose to reiterate this point, especially when in the role of first responder.

> *Even for those who do find the courage to speak out,*
> *often after a long period, being dismissed, disbelieved*
> *or silenced by their own family or friends can be a*
> *devastating experience. The refusal to believe that*
> *something has happened – from minor sexist incidents*
> *all the way up the scale to more serious harassment,*
> *assault or violence – is re-victimization. It silences the*
> *victim and often prevents them from reaching out for*
> *help. (Bates, 2014, pp. 39–40)*

As discussed in Chapter 11, we argue that it is important that those investigating sexual violence cases remain impartial and collect relevant evidence. We need to ensure that such investigations are trauma-informed and carried out sensitively mindful of intersectional power inequalities.

Sadly, there can still be problems with some denying that sexual violence occurs within the institution; failing to provide adequate resource and funding to services for victim-survivors; punishing, blaming or silencing victim-survivors; maintaining confusing or unfair reporting and adjudication procedures; gatekeeping reports of sexual violence to protect specific individuals; giving minimal sanctions and failing to find perpetrators responsible for sexual violence (Blustein, 2017). We urge institutions to recognise this behaviour and the impact it will have on the community. We praise student activists who have been the thought leaders in continuing to call out these behaviours. However, we should not have to rely on student activists to do this work. The burden should not be placed on students, who are often women victim-survivors, to create this change. It is time for us to do this work and to do it well. Again, from our perspective, this book hopefully will make some contribution as a resource to draw upon when making a difference by, e.g. prioritising this work.

One person cannot champion this alone; it needs to be owned at the highest level and student voices and external partners need to be involved in the development and delivery of this work. The consequence of not addressing sexual violence in HE means maintaining the status quo, silencing and ignoring victim-survivors, absolving perpetrators of any guilt and allowing students to continue to face trauma, drop out of university and enter into the workforce tolerating rape culture. Failure to address sexual violence in HE means that we are, for all intents and purposes, colluding with perpetrators of sexual violence.

As we have mentioned throughout this book, we have not covered sexual violence perpetrated by employees of HEIs. Staff sexual misconduct is pervasive in HEIs and even more difficult for students to report due to the inherent power imbalance present. We argue that the foundation set out in this book is relevant to addressing staff sexual misconduct; however, there are additional issues to consider due to employment law and power that we were not able to address here. We signpost readers to The 1752 Group, a research and lobbying group in the United Kingdom, working as a resource in this area.

For many readers, it may come as a surprise that it is more likely that a student will be subjected to sexual violence by a 'friend', ex/partner or associate rather than by a stranger. We have seen how 'stranger danger'-based approaches to prevention miss the point that these only account for the minority of cases of sexual violence. That is not to say that they are not important. Nonetheless, it is key to this work to base policies, procedures and practices upon premises that are appropriately grounded in the research that has been captured to date rather than simply reflecting the judgement of whoever is responsible for this area of student safety.

This work is difficult and challenging; there is an emotional labour to it especially for those in the 'frontline' of working with students who have been subjected to sexual violence. We highlighted the risks for practitioners include compassion fatigue, vicarious traumatisation, secondary traumatic stress and burnout. From a moral, ethical, legal, reputational and (even) financial basis, this work is necessary. Therefore, it needs to be done safely for all involved. Committing to addressing sexual violence will help create communities that are safer where human rights are protected and sexual violence is not ignored, minimised or tolerated. It requires change and sustained resource.

Those who take on this work, who champion it, who advocate for it, who stand up and speak out, for those active bystanders, and for those who ask the hard questions, it is expected that this work will be met with resistance. As we highlight in Chapter 6, resistance can come in many forms, from denial ('It doesn't happen here'), disavowal ('It's a police problem, not ours'), appeasement ('Yes, we need to address this, but we have other priorities right now'), all the way to aggressive backlash. We encourage practitioners, activists, students, victim-survivors and champions of this work to not be too disheartened by resistance but rather encouraged – it is a sign that the change initiative has merit. Find your allies and don't work alone. Power is rarely gifted away by those in relatively powerful positions in institutions. But we believe that we are very much at a turning point where there is more risk to denial than embracing this challenging area of work. Change will happen.

We hope that we have achieved our aim in writing this book – to provide an accessible resource for the sector which goes to a level of detail beyond the generic guidance that the sector has seen to date. Others are perhaps better placed than we are to judge the utility or otherwise of this book, but for us, it has filled a gap in the literature, and the process of writing together along with discussions on the way has helped us sharpen our understanding of our roles and contributions in this area of student safety, and it has made us think more widely about the application of this understanding to schools and prevention programmes. Moreover, in this second edition, we have moved away from simply writing a practice-based handbook – although that remains at the core of the book. We have tried to reflect the wider case for change – and invested in the provision of guidance not just for practitioners and policymakers but also for university leaders and governing bodies – let's hope they pick up the baton.

RESOURCES

RESOURCE 1: KEY RESOURCES FOR SURVIVORS AND PROFESSIONALS

Rape, Sexual Assault, & Sexual Harassment

National Ugly Mugs (NUM)

National organisation offering access to justice and protection for sex workers, with specialist ISVA support available.

uglymugs.org | Freephone (sex workers): 0800 464 7669

Rape Crisis England and Wales

Network of independent Rape Crisis Centres that provide frontline specialist, independent and confidential services to women and girls who are subjected to any form of sexual violence. To find a local rape crisis centre:

rapecrisis.org.uk/find-a-centre | 24/7 Rape and Sexual Abuse Support Line: 0808 500 2222

Rape Crisis Northern Ireland

Offers a support service through their Information and Support Line, Email Support and One to One Support Service for anyone who is 18 and over who has been subjected to rape or serious sexual assault during adulthood.

rapecrisisni.org.uk | 0800 0246 991

Rape Crisis Scotland

National office for the rape crisis movement, supporting local rape crisis centres and leading on awareness raising through campaigns, briefings and publications.

rapecrisisscotland.org.uk | National Helpline: 08088 010302

Rights of Women

Provides confidential legal advice and information to women and offers training and resources for professionals.

rightsofwomen.org.uk | Sexual Harassment at Work Advice Line: 020 7490 0152

Sexual Assault Referral Centre (SARC)

Offers advice, support, counselling, sexual health screening referrals, forensic medical examination and the support of an Independent Sexual Violence Advisor (ISVA) with or without police involvement. To find a local SARC:

nhs.uk/service-search/other-health-services/rape-and-sexual-assault-referral-centres

The Survivors Trust

Offers resources and links to services, as well as guidance for those supporting survivors. Offers support to survivors, their supporters and professionals through their national free helpline.

thesurvivorstrust.org | 0808 801 0818

Image-Based Sexual Abuse

Not Yours to Share

Scottish Government website providing information around the law on image-based abuse and how to access support.

notyourstoshare.scot

Revenge Porn Helpline

Offers confidential advice and support to individuals who have had intimate photos and/or videos distributed off/online.

vrevengepornhelpline.org.uk | 0345 6000 459

VOIC - Victims of Image Crime

Online peer support for those subjected to image-based sexual abuse

voic.org.uk

Stalking

Action Against Stalking

Provides support for those subjected to stalking in Scotland and resources and training for professionals.

actionagainststalking.org | Freephone Helpline: 0800 820 2427

National Stalking Helpline

Offers information, advice and guidance to individuals subjected to stalking.

suzylamplugh.org | 0808 802 0300

Paladin – National Stalking Advocacy Service

A trauma-informed service supporting victims of stalking in England and
  Wales through Independent Stalking Advocacy Caseworkers.
paladinservice.co.uk | 020 3866 4107

Domestic Abuse

Karma Nirvana

Offers support to victim-survivors of 'honour'-based abuse and forced
  marriage and offers training to professionals working with victim-
  survivors.
karmanirvana.org.uk | Honour Based Abuse Helpline: 0800 5999 247

Refuge and the National Domestic Violence Helpline (England and
  Wales)

Offers support to women subjected to different forms of gender-based
  violence, including access to a refuge or 'safe house' for women and
  children escaping domestic abuse.
refuge.org.uk | nationaldomesticviolencehelpline.org.uk | 0808 2000 247

Scottish Women's Aid

National charity working to prevent domestic abuse. To find a local
  women's aid group:
womensaid.scot/find-nearest-wa-group | Domestic Abuse and Forced
  Marriage Helpline: 0800 027 1234

Welsh Women's Aid

A federation of specialist organisations in Wales that provide specialist
  services to survivors of gender-based violence.
welshwomensaid.org.uk | 24/7 Live Fear Free Helpline: 0808 80 10 800

Women's Aid

National charity working to end domestic abuse against women and
  children, offering help to victim-survivors and resources to
  professionals.
womensaid.org.uk

Women's Aid Federation Northern Ireland

A federation of organisations in Northern Ireland that offer a range of
  specialist services to women and children who have been subjected to
  domestic abuse.
womensaidni.org | 24hr Domestic and Sexual Abuse Helpline: 0808 802
  1414

Culturally specific services

Ashiana Network

Refuge, counselling and advice for Black and Minority Ethnic (BME)
  women and girls (14+) who have experienced domestic abuse.
ashiana.org.uk

Halo Project

Support for victim-survivors of domestic and sexual abuse, forced marriage, honour-based abuse and female genital mutilation from Black and minoritised communities.

haloproject.org.uk | Specialist Support Hub: 01642 683 045

Imkaan

Resources and information for victim-survivors and professionals regarding Black and minoritised women subjected to gender-based violence; does not provide direct services.

imkaan.org.uk

Iranian and Kurdish Women's Rights Organisation

Offers advice to women subjected to 'honour' based violence, forced marriage, female genital mutilation, domestic abuse in Farsi, Kurdish, Arabic, Dari, Pashto, Turkish and English.

ikwro.org.uk | 0207 920 6460

Jewish Women's Aid

Offers support to Jewish women and girls subjected to domestic abuse and sexual violence.

jwa.org.uk | Helpline: 0808 801 0500

Latin American Women's Aid

Offers support and advice to Latin American and other Black and Minority Ethnic women (including trans women) subjected to gender-based violence in Spanish, Portuguese and English.

lawadv.org.uk | 020 727 50321

Muslim Women's Network Helpline

Specialist faith and culturally sensitive helpline offering information, support and guidance for those suffering from, or at risk of, abuse.

mwnuk.co.uk | 0800 999 5786

Southall Black Sisters

Offers information, advice, advocacy and practical help to Black (Asian and African-Caribbean) women subjected to gender-based violence in English, Hindi, Punjabi, Gujarati and Urdu and can arrange interpretation in Somali and other languages. Guidance for professionals also available.

southallblacksisters.org.uk | Helpline: 0208 571 0800

Services for LGBT+ People

National Helpline for LGBT+ Victims and Survivors of Abuse and Violence

Emotional and practical support for LGBT+ people experiencing domestic abuse.

galop.org.uk | Helpline: 0800 999 5428

Switchboard – Domestic Abuse
Support for LGBTQ people affected by domestic abuse
switchboard.org.uk | Helpline: 01273 204050

Services for Men

ManKind Initiative
Confidential helpline offering advice and support to all men in the UK
   subjected to domestic abuse.
mankind.org.uk | 0808 800 1170

Men's Advice Line
Helpline for men who have been subjected to domestic abuse.
mensadviceline.org.uk | 0808 801 0327

National Male Survivor Helpline
Offers support to men affected by rape or childhood sexual abuse.
safeline.org.uk/services/national-male-helpline | 0808 800 5005

SurvivorsUK
Online support for men and non-binary people subjected to sexual
   violence.
survivorsuk.org

Services for Individuals With Disabilities

Respond
Supports people with learning disabilities subjected to abuse or violence.
respond.org.uk | 020 7383 0700

SignHealth – Domestic Abuse Team
Offers practical and emotional support to Deaf people subjected to
   domestic abuse as well as training to professionals.
signhealth.org.uk/with-deaf-people/domestic-abuse | 07800 003421

Resources for Professionals

United Kingdom
Centre for Research into Violence and Abuse (CRiVA), Durham
University
A community of researchers at Durham University focused on improving
   knowledge about and responses to interpersonal violence and abuse.
durham.ac.uk/research/institutes-and-centres/research-violence-abuse

Culture Shift
A company offering digital solutions to create positive culture change.
   Creators of the Report + Support online platform designed to provide
   named and anonymous reporting options and signposting to support for
   sexual violence, harassment and bullying.
culture-shift.co.uk

EmilyTest

A non-profit working with Higher Education Institutions to end
gender-based violence through a GBV Charter, training programmes
and the resources.

emilytest.org

End Violence Against Women

Coalition of specialist support services, researchers, activists and survivors working to end VAWG through targeted campaigning and lobbying
of government.

endviolenceagainstwomen.org.uk

The 1752 Group

A UK-based research and lobby organisation aimed at ending staff sexual
misconduct in HE, publishing research in this area and building
research-informed ways forward.

1752group.com

USVreact: Universities supporting victims of sexual violence

A research project, led by Brunel University London, across six European
countries aimed at developing disclosure response training for staff.
Access to training resources and other publications are available on the
project website.

usvreact.eu

United States

Association of Title IX Administrators (ATIXA)

Professional association for Title IX Coordinators, administrators and
investigators offering training and resources to professionals.

atixa.org

**Campus Advocacy and Prevention Professionals Association
(CAPPA)**

Professional association for campus-based advocates and specialists
working in gender-based violence to share best practice, expertise and
access support. Membership is free.

nationalcappa.org

**Campus PRISM: Promoting Restorative Initiatives for Sexual
Misconduct on College Campuses**, University of San Diego

An international team of researchers, practitioners and trainers focused on
using restorative approaches to address and prevent gender-based
violence.

sandiego.edu/soles/centers-and-institutes/restorative-justice

Culture of Respect: Ending Campus Sexual Violence, NASPA

Offers tools, videos and a matrix of evidence-informed programmes aimed
at ending sexual violence.

cultureofrespect.org

End Violence Against Women International

A professional training organisation offering online training, conferences, webinars, training bulletins and a resource library for professionals.

evawintl.org

Faculty Against Rape

Voluntary collective offering resources for faculty to support survivors, help in reform efforts on campus and address retaliation for fighting sexual violence on campus.

facultyagainstrape.net

Institute on Domestic Violence and Sexual Violence, The University of Texas at Austin

A multi-disciplinary research institute focused on gender-based violence offering practical tools, education and training to practitioners, law enforcement and legal service providers in the United States.

sites.utexas.edu/idvsa

It's On Us

A prevention education campaigning programme launched by President Obama and Vice President Biden aimed at engaging young men and changing campus culture to combat college sexual violence.

itsonus.org

RESOURCE 2: TREND MONITORING AND STATISTICAL REPORTING GUIDE

Annual Trend Monitoring and Statistical Reporting From Reported Data.

Disclosure Rates

- **Number of disclosures made to staff and through online tools.** This can include any incidents that have occurred since the student or employee joined the institution regardless of the affiliation the perpetrator has with the institution to capture sexual violence impacting members of the community.
- **Number of anonymous disclosures**
- **Reasons for anonymous disclosures**
- **Types of sexual violence disclosed**, i.e., rape/attempted rape, assault by penetration, sexual assault, sexual harassment, stalking/cyber-stalking, image-based sexual abuse, sexual harassment, indecent exposure, domestic abuse, coercive and controlling behaviour, 'grooming'/boundary blurring, group misconduct, spiking, complicity, retaliation, forced marriage, honour-based abuse, female genital mutilation, etc. (N.B., you may wish to include policy definitions here, but for shorthand we are using criminal justice terms as an example.)
- **Risk markers**, e.g., use of physical violence, non-fatal strangulation, use of weapon, serial perpetration
- **Academic year of incident disclosed compared to academic year disclosure was made** to demonstrate a trend of delayed reporting as normal

Reporting Party Characteristics (If Known)

- **Demographics**, i.e., protected characteristics
- **Affiliation to institution**, i.e., student (indicating year and department), staff (type and department), visitor, other
- **Additional characteristics** may be recorded, e.g., home or international student

Responding Party Characteristics (If Known)

- **Demographics**, i.e., protected characteristics
- **Affiliation to institution**, i.e., student (indicating year and department), staff (type and department), visitor, other
- **Relationship to the Reporting Party**, e.g., peer, ex/partner, friend, stranger, lecturer
- **Additional characteristics** may be recorded, e.g., home or international student

Reporting Rates

- **Number of named reports to the institution**, may categorise as student vs. student, student vs. staff, staff vs. staff, staff vs. student
- **Number of anonymous reports to the institution** (if different from anonymous disclosures)
- **Number of reports to the police**, include criminal justice outcomes if known, e.g., guilty, not guilty, no further action, etc.
- **Types of sexual violence reported** (same as disclosure categories)

University Action (If Applicable)

- **Precautionary measure/s implemented**, e.g., no contact arrangement, partial suspension, full suspension, suspension with pay (for staff)
- **Number of investigations conducted**
- **Average length of time for investigations**
- **Outcome of investigation**, i.e., further action or no further action
- **Disciplinary outcome**, e.g., sanctions imposed, alternatives to disciplinary action
- **Number of appeals**
- **Appeal outcomes**

RESOURCE 3: NO CONTACT ORDER TEMPLATE[1]

DATE
RESPONDING PARTY NAME
ADDRESS

No Contact Order

Dear **RESPONDING PARTY NAME,**

As an outcome of breaching the **POLICY**, you are prohibited from contacting **NAME/S**, hereafter referred to as the Reporting Party. This No Contact Order takes immediate effect and stipulates that:

1. You will not make any direct or indirect contact of any kind with the Reporting Party or request that others make or attempt to contact **him/her/them** on your behalf. The following is a non-exhaustive list of examples of contact which is prohibited:
   - face-to-face contact; phone calls; voicemails; text messages; emails; letters; social media posts or messages; entering the accommodation/work/study environments of the Reporting Party.

---

[1] Based on a version originally drafted by DiSantis, C. J. for Durham University in 2016 and subsequently updated for this version (Victim Rights Law Center, 2014; ATIXA, 2019).

2. *(optional)* You are not permitted to enter or visit **LOCA-TION/DEPARTMENT**. Should there be an exceptional reason you may need to do so (e.g., an academic/work commitment) you must contact **STAFF CONTACT** well in advance to discuss if alternative arrangements can be made.

3. In the event of chance encounters on or off campus, you should not address, acknowledge or in any other way attempt to engage with **him/her/them**. If a chance encounter occurs, it is recommended that you take appropriate steps to leave the area where the contact occurs as quickly as reasonably possible.

The No Contact Order will remain in place while you and the Reporting Party are members of the university community or if the **PERSON RESPONSIBLE FOR ISSUING NCO** determines that the Order is no longer required, and this is communicated to both parties in writing.

If the university receives information that you have breached this Order and this is confirmed, **EXPLAIN CONSEQUENCES OF BREACHING NCO, e.g., temporary or permanent exclusion**.

You may appeal this decision by **EXPLAIN HOW TO APPEAL (IF APPLICABLE)**.

I take this time to remind you of the support you may access through the university **EXPLAIN SUPPORT INFORMATION**.

Please acknowledge receipt of my letter no later than **DATE**.

Regards,

Signed
cc: Student File

RESOURCE 4: DISCLOSURE RECORDING FORM TEMPLATE

DISCLOSURE INFORMATION		
Date of Disclosure		
Start Time		End Time
REPORTING PARTY the individual who disclosed they were subjected to sexual violence		
Name	*(leave blank if Reporting Party chooses to remain anonymous)*	
Gender		
Affiliation to institution	☐ Student ☐ Employee ☐ Visitor ☐ Other _____	
Department		
If student, indicate year	☐ Undergraduate ☐ Postgraduate Year_____	
RESPONDING PARTY, the individual reported to have committed sexual violence		
Name	*(leave blank if Reporting Party chooses to remain anonymous)*	
Gender		
Relationship to Reporting Party	*(e.g., friend, peer, ex/partner, stranger, lecturer, manager, etc.)*	
Affiliation to institution	☐ Student ☐ Employee ☐ Visitor ☐ Other _____	
Department		
If student, indicate year	☐ Undergraduate ☐ Postgraduate Year_____	

INCIDENT/S INFORMATION	
Date/s & Time/s of Incident/s	
Location of Incident/s	*(note specific location if known; indicate on/off campus)*
Details about incident/s as disclosed by the Reporting Party	*(Provide as much or as little information as was disclosed; use the Reporting Party's own words where possible)*
Safeguarding issues identified & actions taken to address issues	
Record the reporting & support options discussed & what, if any, decisions were taken by the Reporting Party	
Signposted to the following support options (check all that apply)	☐ Sexual Assault Referral Centre ☐ Police ☐ Student Services ☐ Specialist Counselling ☐ University Counselling ☐ Employee Assistance Programme ☐ Other: _____
INDIVIDUAL WHO RECEIVED AND RECORDED THE DISCLOSURE	
Name	
Title/Role & Department	
Contact Details	
Date Recorded	

This template is based on a version originally drafted by DiSantis, C. J. for Durham University in 2017 and subsequently updated for this edition.

RESOURCE 5: TACKLING RAPE MYTHS IN INVESTIGATIONS AND DISCIPLINE HEARINGS

Myth	Implications	Considerations to Address Myth
1. Rape is always violent or involves physical force. **(FALSE)**	• Ignores the reality of rape. • Disbelieves and invalidates the experience of the victim-survivor. • Disregards elements of power, control and humiliation in rape.	• Rape doesn't always leave visible signs on the body or the genitals. • Challenge any implication that rape involves injury. • Rapists may use manipulative techniques to intimidate and coerce their victim-survivors. • The victim-survivor may be legitimately afraid of being killed or seriously injured and so co-operate with the rapist to save their life. • Victim-survivors may become physically paralysed with terror or shock and are unable to move or fight. • Self-protection/defence can be through disassociation or freezing – any effort to prevent, stop or limit the event.
2. Rape is most commonly perpetrated by strangers in dark alleys. **(FALSE)**	• Assumes that home is always a safe place, and that rape cannot be committed by someone known to the victim-survivor. • Implies that rape can be prevented by avoiding certain places and therefore blames the victim-survivor.	• Challenge any implication that rapists only rape strangers. • Most rapes are committed by persons known to the victim-survivor, e.g. current or former intimate partner, friend, colleague. • Date or acquaintance rape is common. • Most victim-survivors are raped in their homes.

(Continued)

Myth	Implications	Considerations to Address Myth
3. Prostitutes/sex workers cannot be raped. **(FALSE)**	• Provides an excuse for sexual abuse. • Disempowers prostitutes/sex workers. • Assumes that prostitutes/sex workers consent to any and all sex under any circumstances, with anyone.	• Rape can have a lasting and devastating impact on any victim-survivor. • Prostitutes/sex workers have the same rights under the law as anyone else: the transactions they negotiate with clients are for consensual activities, not rape. • Perpetrators often deliberately target individuals on the basis that they are less likely to be believed, which can include prostitutes/sex workers. • Consider the overall context of the allegation including the vulnerability of the victim-survivor and their freedom to choose. Consider also targeting and steps to obtain consent and reasonable belief that someone was consenting.
4. You cannot be raped by your husband or partner. **(FALSE)**	• Disbelieves the victim-survivor and dismisses their experience; • Supports an ideology of male entitlement to sex and female subordination within intimate relationships and more widely.	• A significant proportion of rape occurs within an intimate relationship, against a background of domestic abuse, involving power and control. • Everyone – irrespective of their relationship status – has a right to choose.
5. The victim had previously consented to sex with the accused previously so		

(Continued)

(Continued)

Myth	Implications	Considerations to Address Myth
s/he/they must have consented. **(FALSE)**		• A person who has freely chosen to have sexual activity with another person in the past does not, as a result, give general consent to sexual intercourse with that person on any other occasion.
		• Consider the context of the overall allegation including what impact the relationship had on someone's freedom to consent, and the presence of domestic abuse and in particularly controlling or coercive behaviour. Focus on steps taken to obtain consent and reasonable belief.
6. If your culture condones, or is perceived to condone, marital rape, underage 'sex' or forced marriage, then you should not be upset about it/it does not matter as much/it's more of a grey area. **(FALSE)**	• Condones rape due to cultural reasons. • Creates further barriers to accessing support and justice.	• Everyone – irrespective of their background – has a right to choose.
		• Racial and religious stereotypes can play out in different ways in sexual violence cases.
		• Identify and challenge any racial or religious justification for rape with reference to the law/university policy.

(Continued)

Myth	Implications	Considerations to Address Myth
7. Rape is only a crime of passion. **(FALSE)**	• Romanticises rape and implies that rape is the same as sex. • Assumes that rape is impulsive, unplanned and about uncontrollable 'passion'. • Assumes men to be incapable of delaying gratification or controlling sexual urges.	• Some rapes are premeditated and planned. • Men are capable of controlling sexual urges and refraining from raping women and other men. An assertion contrary to this is sexist. • Some rapists may reframe events, even to themselves, to claim they were spontaneous and consensual, and others may claim the complainant 'knew the rules', 'they were equal' (despite any inequalities) or they 'both got carried away'.
8. When it comes to sex, men have a point of no return. **(FALSE)**	• Disregards elements of power, aggression, violence, control and/or humiliation in rape. • Deprives a victim-survivor's right to choose. • Attempts to remove the responsibility for the rape from the rapist.	• Consent is an ongoing act and can be subject to certain conditions. • In accordance with Section 79 (2) Sexual Offences Act 2003, penetration is a continuing act from entry to withdrawal. Therefore, withdrawal of consent at any point before or during the act is perfectly possible and is the right of any individual to exercise at entirely their own discretion. • Consider what consent was given for, e.g. consent to vaginal, not oral or anal sex; consent only with a condom; consent conditional upon withdrawal before ejaculation.
9. Young adult men should not be convicted as they	• Assumes that law/policy does not apply equally to all.	• Rape can have a lasting and devastating impact on victim-survivors irrespective of the age of the perpetrator.

(Continued)

(Continued)

Myth	Implications	Considerations to Address Myth
have their whole lives ahead of them/have good character references. **(FALSE)**	• Implies that the implications for the perpetrator are more important than the impact of rape on the victim-survivor as well as wider justice and safety considerations. • Implies that young adult men are less able to understand consent.	• Young offenders can be just as dangerous as older offenders and can be serial offenders. • Prosecutions will always proceed where there is sufficient evidence, and it is in the public interest. • Challenge any assumption that attempts to remove the responsibility from an adult rapist due to their age/future prospects.
10. He was satisfying demands for BDSM/choking/strangulation/aggressive sex. This cannot be rape. **(FALSE)**	• Assumes consenting to BDSM is con-senting to any type of violence, abuse or rape.	• BDSM can be explored between two consenting adults following discussion about safety and harm. • Consent is an ongoing act and even within BDSM can be subject to certain conditions. • Consider any discussion prior to the incident related to exploration of BDSM in general as well as: safety, risk, harm, the use of safe words, limits which someone might want to explore cautiously and activities which someone never wants to try. • In accordance with Section 79 (2) Sexual Offences Act 2003, penetration is a continuing act from entry to

(Continued)

Myth	Implications	Considerations to Address Myth
		withdrawal. Therefore, withdrawal of consent at any point before or during the act is perfectly possible and is the right of any individual to exercise at entirely their own discretion. • Carefully consider the context of the allegation and any role which alcohol or drugs might have on freedom and capacity to consent as well as steps taken to obtain consent and reasonable belief that someone was consenting.
11. Only gay men rape other men/only gay men get raped. **(FALSE)**	• Reinforces homophobic fears and prejudices. • Creates the illusion of safety for straight men. • Results in under-reporting of rapes on men.	• People of all sexual orientations get raped. • Men who rape other men might be heterosexual – they may have a relationship with a woman. • Rapists rape as part of their violence and need for power, dominance and control. • Consider the overall context of an allegation when assessing someone's freedom and capacity to choose, as well as steps taken to obtain that consent and reasonable belief in consent.

(Continued)

(Continued)

Myth	Implications	Considerations to Address Myth
12. The victim provoked rape and implied consent simply by their dress/ flirtatious behaviour. **(FALSE)**	• Stigmatises and blames the victim-survivor. • Assumes that if someone draws attention to themselves, they are seeking sex, consenting to sex or 'deserve to be raped'. • Asserts that women cannot dress/behave how they want – that it's for others rather than their own preferences. • Attempts to remove responsibility from the rapist by taking away their agency – that they are so provoked by clothing or behaviour they cannot help themselves.	• Challenge any implication that the victim-survivor provoked rape or automatically consenting to sex by their dress or behaviour. • Consent cannot be implied from the way a person dresses or flirtatious behaviour. • Women can be raped regardless of what they are wearing – this is just an excuse. • It would not be reasonable to believe that a person would consent to sex simply because of the way they are dressed.
13. If you send sexual images or messages prior to meeting someone, then having sex is inevitable. **(FALSE)**	• Attempts to excuse rape and blame the victim-survivor. • Assumes that if someone sends a sexual image of themselves, they are seeking sex or 'deserve to be raped'.	• Consent to sexual activity cannot be implied from flirtatious behaviour or from the sending of a sexual image or message.

(Continued)

Myth	Implications	Considerations to Address Myth
	• Assumes sencing of a message or messages automatically means physical sex is wanted any time, under any conditions. • Assumes that someone cannot change their mind, even if they had initially been interested in sexual activity.	• Challenge any implication that sexual images or messages equate to consent, explaining how normalised they are these days. • Consider steps taken to obtain consent.
14. If you voluntarily attend someone's house after a date or night out, you obviously want sex and consented to it by going there. **(FALSE)**	• Assumes that if a person goes to someone's house after a date or night out, they are looking for sex or 'deserve to be raped'. • Assumes that rape is impulsive and unplanned • Assumes that someone cannot change their mind, even if they had initially been interested in sexual activity.	• Consent to sexual activity cannot be implied simply by the act of someone going back to someone's house. • Each occasion is specific, and consent needs to be given for each occasion and can always be given under certain conditions or withdrawn entirely. • Consent can be withdrawn at any time. • Humans must understand and negotiate consent regularly in their day-to-day lives. • Many rapes are premeditated and planned. • Consent is an ongoing act and can be subject to certain conditions. • Challenge any implication that going back to someone's house equates to consent. • Consider steps taken to obtain consent.

(Continued)

(Continued)

Myth	Implications	Considerations to Address Myth
15. If you drink alcohol or use drugs, then you have made yourself vulnerable to being raped and you bear the responsibility. **(FALSE)**	• Disregards the law on consent, including capacity to consent and reasonable belief that someone was consenting. • Assumes that being under the influence of alcohol/drugs means that someone is looking for, or willing to have, sex. • Assumes that if someone is looking for sex, they therefore consent to anything that happens or are deserving of anything that happens.	• A person consents if they agree by choice and have the freedom and capacity to make that choice. • Victim-survivors of rape are never responsible, wholly or in part, for their rape or sexual assault, regardless of whether they have drunk alcohol, taken drugs are asleep or otherwise incapacitated. • Carefully consider the role which alcohol or drugs might have on freedom and capacity to consent as well as steps taken to obtain consent and reasonable belief that someone was consenting. • Some people drink alcohol, and some people take drugs. This does not provide a justification or reason for someone to rape or be raped. • Just because a person is drunk or has taken drugs does not mean that they must be looking for, or willing to have, sex. (From Crown Court Compendium). • It would also be wrong to leap to the conclusion that someone else who sees and interacts with that person could reasonably believe that person would consent to sex. (From Crown Court Compendium). • If someone is unable to give consent because they are drunk, drugged or unconscious, it is rape.

(Continued)

Myth	Implications	Considerations to Address Myth
16. If you meet men online or through hook-up apps, you are consenting to sex and should be ready to offer sex. **(FALSE)**	• Assumes that if someone goes on dating/hook-up apps or websites, then they are looking for sex or 'deserve to be raped'.	• Online dating, apps, etc. are increasingly being used to meet people. • Consent to sexual activity cannot be implied from the method of meeting. • Consent can be withdrawn at any time. • Consensual sexual interaction online does not automatically imply consent to offline sexual interaction. • Challenge any implication that online dating/apps, etc. equate to consent.
17. If you have lots of sex, including with different people, then you are promiscuous and 'deserve what you get' and are not harmed by rape. **(FALSE)** 18. If someone has truly been raped, then they would never seek, or want, sex soon afterwards. **(FALSE)**	• Assumes that if someone has multiple partners, then they are looking for sex with anyone, 'deserve to be raped' or are less impacted by rape. • Assumes that victim-survivors of rape behave in a certain way.	• Rape can have a lasting and devastating impact on victim-survivors irrespective of their sexual history. • Challenge any implication that having sex with multiple partners negates someone's right to consent. • Challenge any implication that having sex after being raped negates someone's right to consent. • Challenge any assumption that all victim-survivors behave the same way either prior to or following rape and make clear that trauma affects individuals in a huge range of ways, sometimes causing victim- survivors to behave in counter-intuitive ways.

(Continued)

(Continued)

Myth	Implications	Considerations to Address Myth
		• Sex is not confined to people who are married/co-habiting/ in long-term relationships, etc. • People have a right to have consensual sex with however many people and whenever they like. • Consent cannot be implied by the number of people someone has slept with prior to, or after, an incident. • Just because someone has consented to sexual intercourse on one occasion, it does not provide grounds for reasonably believing that they consented to sexual intercourse on other occasions – either with the same or different people. Each occasion is specific, and consent needs to be given for each occasion and can always be given under certain conditions or withdrawn entirely.
19. You can tell if someone has 'really' been raped by how they act afterwards. **(FALSE)**	• Disbelieves and re-traumatises the victim-survivor. • Invalidates the victim-survivor's experience and individuality.	• Reactions to rape are highly varied and individual. • Victim-survivors in a rape situation often become physically paralysed with terror or shock and are unable to move, resist or fight.

(Continued)

Myth	Implications	Considerations to Address Myth
20. Real rape victim are always visibly distressed when describing what happened to them. **(FALSE)**	• Assumes all victim-survivors behave in the same way/in a predetermined way, during or following rape. • Discourages the victim-survivor from seeking help.	• Many women experience a form of shock during or after a rape that leaves them emotionally numb or flat – and seemingly calm. • Rape doesn't always leave visible signs on the body or the genitals.
21. A real rape victim would never freeze when attacked; they would fight back. **(FALSE)**		• Consider the overall context of an allegation including addressing any seemingly counter-intuitive behaviour displayed by the victim-survivor. • Focus on steps to obtain consent and reasonable belief.
22. A real victim of rape would never be able to carry on with their normal life – go to work, go to lectures, etc. **(FALSE)**		• Carefully assess appropriate digital material – considering highlighting relevant evidence which supports the allegations and countering relevant evidence which points away from the allegation.
23. If the victim didn't scream, fight or get injured, then it could not have been rape. **(FALSE)**		• Victim-survivors in rape situations are often legitimately afraid of being killed or seriously injured and so co-operate with the rapist to save their lives. • Rapists use many manipulative techniques to intimidate and coerce their victim-survivors.

(Continued)

(Continued)

Myth	Implications	Considerations to Address Myth
		• When under threat, the brain will implement instinctual survival response that the victim-survivor will not necessarily have any control over. The response may not appear logical to others, or even the victim-survivor, but in the moment, the brain would choose based on basic instincts: not just fight or flight, but flop, freeze or to befriend the attacker.
24. If the victim didn't complain to the police/ university immediately, it was not rape. **(FALSE)**	• Disbelieves and re-traumatises the victim-survivor. • Discourages him/her/them from seeking help. • Assumes all victim-survivors behave in a uniform, predetermined way. • Ignores known trauma responses.	• Consider the overall context of an allegation when including reasons behind a delay. • Most victim-survivors of rape do not report the attack to the police. Some may tell a friend, General Practitioner (GP) or other individual. Many others will not tell anyone perhaps owing to feelings of shame, guilt and fear of the perpetrator and/or fear of being disbelieved. • A delayed allegation is not equivalent to a false allegation. • The time taken to make an allegation is not indicative of the level of upset.

(Continued)

Myth	Implications	Considerations to Address Myth
		• The trauma of rape can cause feelings of shame and guilt which might inhibit a victim-survivor from making a complaint.
		• The process of reporting rape itself can be traumatic, as well as an investigation process, and can deter victim-survivors from reporting the rape.
		• When under threat, the brain will implement instinctual survival response that the victim-survivor will not necessarily have any control over. The response may not appear logical to others, or even the victim-survivor, but in the moment, the brain would choose based on basic instincts: not just fight or flight, but flop, freeze or friend.
25. If you don't say 'no', it's not rape. **(FALSE)**	• Disregards elements of power, aggression, violence, control and humiliation in rape. • Goes against the legal definition of consent.	• A person consents if they agree by choice and have the freedom and capacity to make that choice. • Challenge any implication that absence of consent has to be demonstrated – consent must be actively given.

(Continued)

(Continued)

Myth	Implications	Considerations to Address Myth
		• Experience has shown that different people respond to unwanted sexually activity in different ways. • Victim-survivors in rape situations can be legitimately afraid of being killed or seriously injured and so co-operate with the rapist to save their lives. • Consent and submission are different. • Rapists use many manipulative techniques to intimidate and coerce their victim-survivors. • Victim-survivors in rape situations often become physically paralysed with terror or shock and are unable to move or fight. • When under threat, the brain will implement instinctual survival response that the victim-survivor will not necessarily have any control over. The response may not appear logical to others, or even the victim-survivor, but in the moment, the brain would choose based on basic instincts: not just fight or flight, but flop, freeze or friend. • Check also for any evidence of coercion or control.

(Continued)

Myth	Implications	Considerations to Address Myth
26. Only young/attractive people get raped. **(FALSE)**	• Assumes that only young or 'attractive' people are raped.	• There is no typical victim-survivor of rape. People of all ages, appearance, status and backgrounds can be raped.
27. Strong/independent/ powerful/older people don't get raped. **(FALSE)**	• Disregards elements of power, aggression, violence, control and humiliation in rape.	• Challenge any assertion that typifies who rapes and who is subjected to rape.

28. The victim-survivor's race/religion/background is responsible for the rape. **(FALSE)**	• Condones rape due for racial/religious/ cultural reasons.
	• Creates further barriers to accessing support and justice.
	• Can deploy racial and religious prejudices and stereotypes to blame the victim-survivor and disregard the facts of the case.
		• There is no typical victim-survivor of rape.
		• People of all races and religious backgrounds can be raped.
		• Challenge any racial or religious stereotypes and focus on the facts of the allegation.
		• Identify and challenge any racial or religious justification for rape.
		• Racial and religious stereotypes may play out in rape cases in a number of ways. For example:
		  (a) 'South East
		     Asian women are more submissive and docile'.

(Continued)

(Continued)

Myth	Implications	Considerations to Address Myth
		(b) 'African or black people are more aggressive or have "unconstrained" libido.' (c) 'Middle Eastern/Arab/Muslim women are oppressed'. (d) 'White women are more sexually promiscuous'. (e) Latina/South American women can be fetishised for their ethnic identity/sexuality.
29. A real victim would always be able to provide a clear and coherent account of being raped. **(FALSE)**	• Reinforces stereotypes of women as untruthful. • Disregards the impact that trauma has on memory. • Assumes that human beings have perfect memory recall. • Discourages him/her/them from seeking help. • Assumes intoxicated victim-survivors are inherently unreliable witnesses.	• Rape can be very traumatic, and memory can be affected in a number of ways. • Understanding the effects of fear and the psychological mechanisms that may occur during a sexual assault is vital when considering recall and memory. • Some, understandably, may try to avoid thinking about being raped or try to avoid recalling it all – this can impact upon recall. • Research conducted by Dr Heather Flowe and others has shown intoxication to impact upon the level of detail that can be recalled by the witness rather than on the accuracy
30. Inconsistencies in accounts provided by a victim always mean they lack credibility as a witness. **(FALSE)**		
31. Where a victim has consumed alcohol or		

(Continued)

Myth	Implications	Considerations to Address Myth
drugs prior to an incident, s/he/they will always be an unreliable witness as their evidence won't be accurate. **(FALSE)**	• Disbelieves and re-traumatises the victim-survivor. • Discourages victim-survivors from seeking help.	of memory. It is therefore essential that in making casework decisions, do not assume that a witness who was intoxicated at the time of the sexual assault is less reliable than a witness who was sober. • Reasons behind any inconsistencies should be addressed as part of an overall case strategy.
32. False allegations are common, and women always cry rape when they regret having sex or want to seek revenge. **(FALSE)**	• Reinforces stereotypes of the 'vindictive woman'. • Reinforces stereotypes of women as untruthful. • Re-victimises and stigmatises the victim-survivor.	• Between January 2011 and May 2012, the Director of Public Prosecutions (DPP) required Crown Prosecution Service (CPS) areas to refer to him all cases involving an allegedly false allegation of rape and/or domestic violence. During that time, there were 5,651 prosecutions for rape but only 35 for making false allegations of rape.
33. Other complaints of rape which have not resulted in successful prosecution outcomes always mean the victim lacks all credibility as a witness. **(FALSE)**	• Undermines her/his/their support for seeking justice/access to courts.	• A decision to stop a case on evidential grounds **does not** mean that an allegation is false. It means that the case does not meet the evidential standard required to put an allegation before a jury under the Code for Crown Prosecutors. • When a jury returns a not guilty verdict, it means that they were not satisfied 'beyond reasonable doubt' that the offence was committed.

(Continued)

(Continued)

Myth	Implications	Considerations to Address Myth
		• Avoid an either/or argument that allows a Reporting Party's evidence to be wholly dismissed because of a peripheral inconsistency. Don't pit it as either you believe the Responding Party OR you believe the Reporting Party for this reason.
34. Previous withdrawals of complaints, or previous reluctance to cooperate with an investigation, always mean the victim lacks credibility as a witness. **(FALSE)**	• Reinforces stereotypes of the 'vindictive woman'. • Reinforces stereotypes of women as untruthful. • Re-victimises and stigmatises the victim-survivor. • Undermines her/his/their support for seeking justice.	• Victim-survivors can face very difficult decisions when deciding to report or not to report rape. Some may decide not to report or withdraw support for an investigation for a number of reasons including intimidation by the Responding Party. • Victim-survivors come from all walks of life. Previous convictions or untruths do not automatically impact on the credibility of allegation – it is important to consider relevance and applicability. • Perpetrators often deliberately target individuals who are less likely to be believed. • Only issues of relevance should be considered when dealing with specific allegations.
35. Where the victim has previous convictions, s/he/they always lack credibility as a witness as a result. **(FALSE)**		

(Continued)

Myth	Implications	Considerations to Address Myth
36. The victim has previous convictions or had told other untruths about other matte's and so can never be relied upon to tell the truth about rape. **(FALSE)**		• Where relevant, consider context of any previous convictions. For examples, are they a result of previous victim-isation (e.g. child sexual abuse), or do they indicate a form of vulnerability?
37. Where the victim has a learnir g disability or mental health condition, s/he/they always lack credib lity as a witness. **(FALSE)**	• Disbelieves and re-traumatises the victim-survivor. • Disregards elements of power, aggression, violence, control and humiliation in rape.	• Ability or disability can be impaired by trauma. A person with a disability can become more symptomatic after trauma or during recall of trauma. • Perpetrators often deliberately target individuals that are vulnerable due to mental or physical health disabilities.
38. If someone displayed signs of sexual arousal during abuse, the only conclusion is that they	• Disbelieves the victim-survivor. • Disregards how bodies and brains can work.	• Victim-survivors themselves might believe this myth and can feel a huge amount of shame and guilt. • People can respond to any stimulation – even those which are non-consensual/traumatic/painful.

(Continued)

(Continued)

Myth	Implications	Considerations to Address Myth
wanted and/or enjoyed it. **(FALSE)**		• Focus on the definition around consent, ensure that this is dealt with proactively and sensitively with the victim-survivor and ensure a rounded assessment of the case including careful consideration of the actions and behaviour of the Responding Party.
39. Gay men who attend sex parties and/or take drugs are asking to be raped. **(FALSE)**	• Assumes gay men are promiscuous and are attracted to all men. • Assumes that sex is not romantically significant to gay men – it is all something they regularly engage in on a casual basis. • Assumes gay men do not have long-term loving relationships – for gay men, it is all about sex. • Assumes gay men always have penetrative sex. • Assumes men cannot be victim-survivors of sexual offences.	• Challenge any homophobic implications and focus on the facts of the allegation. • Forming assumptions about gay men's propensities to have multiple relationships or their sexual preferences is homophobic. • Gay men can face multiple barriers to seeking support and accessing justice. • Not just gay men attend chem sex parties (i.e. bisexual men, or 'men who have sex with men' who wouldn't define themselves as gay or bi.) • A gay man may well be promiscuous and be in a loving relationship.

(Continued)

Myth	Implications	Considerations to Address Myth
	• Assumes men who have sex with men are gay. • Denies any incidence of coercive control, i.e. if man was coerced to attend/participate	• Gay men have the same right as everyone to remove consent at any time. • There will be nuance in each situation that needs to be explored, including any power and control elements to attending a sex party – was there any underlying coercion.

Source: Crown Prosecution Service (2021); Reproduced and amended with permission under the Open Government Licence v3.0.

RESOURCE 6: INVESTIGATION REPORT TEMPLATE

Confidential Investigation Report

1. Procedural History

1.1. Include:

- Who authorised the investigation, identity of investigator/s and policy under which the investigation was conducted
- Date/s of disclosure and confirmed report to the institution
- Date/s of the reported incident/s
- Date on which investigator/s were assigned and investigation commenced
- Date when Responding Party was informed of the investigation
- Date when the investigation was completed
- Any other relevant procedural information, e.g., date of risk assessment meeting, date of precautionary measures implemented

2. Participants and Investigation Timeline

2.1. Include:

- Reporting Party name and interview date; note who accompanied them if applicable
- Responding Party name and interview date; note who accompanied them if applicable
- Witnesses Listed: name, date contacted, date received statement and interview date

(Continued)

(Continued)

Confidential Investigation Report

- Note any witnesses that did not participate or were not interviewed and why

3. Scope of Investigation

3.1. Include:

- What misconduct was reported and connect this to policy definition/s
- Any subsequent misconduct reported related to the Responding Party's behaviour after the initial report was made, e.g., a breach of a No Contact Arrangement, suspension, and/or retaliation
- Note anything submitted which was outside the scope of the investigation and therefore was not considered as part of the investigation and why

4. Standard of Proof

4.1. Include:

- Statement explaining the civil standard of proof, e.g. To determine whether an individual has breached the (relevant policy), the standard of proof required is the balance of probabilities, i.e., the evidence must demonstrate that it is more likely than not that the misconduct occurred.

5. Summary of Evidence

5.1. Include:

- List all evidence collected
- List any evidence that could not be collected and why
- Summarise the evidence presented by all parties

6. Credibility Assessment

6.1. Include:

- Assessment of validity, reliability and integrity of the Reporting Party's, Responding Party's, and witness/es' evidence, and any relevant information

7. Findings of Fact and Analysis

7.1. Include:

- State policy definition for misconduct and apply the facts based on evidence related to the policy, weighing evidence and incorporating the credibility assessment

(Continued)

Confidential Investigation Report

- Detail the facts that were established during the investigation
- Detail any areas that were inconclusive or could not be established
- Note this section may highlight if certain parts of the report are founded or not

8. Conclusion

8.1. Include:

- Whether complaint is upheld, partially upheld or dismissed
- Recommendation for further disciplinary action or no action required
- Any additional recommendations as permitted by the relevant policy, e.g., remedy for the Reporting Party if the complaint is fully or partially upheld

Investigator/s' signature/s:
Date:

ABOUT THE AUTHORS

Clarissa J. DiSantis is a practitioner, trainer and leading authority on addressing gender-based violence in higher education. She is the Education and Training Lead for Active* Consent based at the University of Galway, Ireland. She was the first person to hold a dedicated role focused on sexual violence in higher education in the United Kingdom starting in 2016–2024 as the Sexual Misconduct Prevention and Response Manager at Durham University. She is the co-author of *Addressing Student Sexual Violence in Higher Education: A Good Practice Guide* 1st Ed. (Emerald, 2020), co-editor of *Stopping Gender-based Violence in Higher Education: Policy, Practice, and Partnerships* (Routledge, 2023) and author of *Responding to Disclosures of Sexual Violence 2.0.* (Sage, 2022) online course. She is an experienced international trainer and public speaker delivering courses and presentations on a range of prevention and response topics throughout the United Kingdom, Ireland, the United States and Egypt. In 2018, she was awarded *Best Student Support* by Durham Students' Union. In 2019 and 2020, she was recognised by Durham University through *Durham Women Making a Difference* and *Inspiring Women of Durham*. She has extensive professional experience working as a forensic mental health social worker in England and as a Licenced Master Social Worker and Licenced Chemical Dependency Counsellor in Texas. She has worked clinically with survivors and perpetrators of domestic abuse and sexual violence and with individuals with acute mental illness and co-occurring substance use issues.

Graham J. Towl is a Professor of Forensic Psychology at Durham University, UK, the Chair of the Scottish Advisory Panel on Offender

Rehabilitation (SAPOR) which focuses on reducing crime in Scotland and previously a member of the Office for Students Safeguarding and Welfare Expert Advisory Panel. Formerly, he was the Pro Vice Chancellor Chair of the Sexual Violence Task Force (2015–2016) at Durham University, and he established the first full-time dedicated role focused on addressing our problems with sexual violence at Durham University in 2016. He was formerly a Senior Civil Servant and Chief Psychologist at the Ministry of Justice, UK, and a Practitioner Psychologist working with, among others, sex offenders. In his therapeutic work, he has also worked with women in prisons who have been subjected to sexual violence. He is an expert on sexual violence at universities and has worked with universities in the United Kingdom and the Office for Students on addressing sexual violence in higher and further education. He chaired the first UK conference on addressing sexual violence in both higher and further education (July 2019). He is the co-author of *Tackling Sexual Violence at Universities: An International Perspective* (Routledge, 2019), *Addressing Student Sexual Violence in Higher Education: A Good Practice Guide* 1st Ed., (Emerald, 2020) and *Stopping Gender-based Violence in Higher Education: Policy, Practice, and Partnerships* (Routledge, 2023). He was peer ranked through the British Psychological Society (BPS) as the most influential forensic psychologist in the United Kingdom.

He is the Chair of PORSCH – a multidisciplinary and multiagency research network of practitioners, policymakers and researchers interested in health and justice.

REFERENCES

AB v University of XYZ. (2020). *EWHC 2978*.

AB v University of XYZ. (2023). *EWHC 1162*.

ACAS. (2021). Sexual harassment: Handling a complaint. https://www.acas.org.uk/sexual-harassment/handling-a-sexual-harassment-complaint. Accessed on July 29, 2024.

Agócs, C. (1997). Institutionalized resistance to organizational change: Denial, inaction and repression. *Journal of Business Ethics, 16,* 917–931.

Ahmed, S. (2021). *Complaint!* Duke University Press.

Al Jazeera. (2021). Degrees of abuse. https://interactive.aljazeera.com/aje/2021/degrees-of-abuse/index.html. Accessed on July 29, 2024.

Allen, R., Elliot, K., Harvey, H., O'Callaghan, C., & Smith, K. I. (2024). Femicide census 2021. https://www.femicidecensus.org/reports/

American College Health Association. (2018). *Addressing sexual and relationship violence: A trauma-informed approach.* American College Health Association.

American Council on Education. (2024). Title IX final rule outline of key provisions. https://www.acenet.edu/Documents/Title-IX-2024-Rule-Key-Provisions.pdf. Accessed on August 29, 2024.

AMOSSHE. (2020). Support for students studying abroad: Guidelines for higher education student services. https://www.amosshe.org.uk/resources/Documents/Support-for-students-studying-abroad-2020.pdf

Archambault, J., & Lonsway, K. A. (2019). *Effective report writing: Using the language of non-consensual sex.* End Violence Against Women International.

ATIXA. (2019). *ATIXA position statement: Trauma-informed training and the neurobiology of trauma.* ATIXA.

Australian Human Rights Commission. (2017). *Change the course: The national report on sexual assault and sexual harassment at Australian universities.* Australian Human Rights Commission.

Australian Human Rights Institute. (2024). How Australian universities are responding to campus sexual violence. https://www.humanrights.unsw.edu.au/news/how-does-your-university-respond-campus-sexual-violence?mc_cid=f7af8207f5&mc_eid=51a7cdc038

Baird, H., Renfrew, K., Nash-Henry, Z., & Towl, G. (2019). *Evaluation of safeguarding students catalyst fund projects: Summative evaluation report.* Report to the Office for Students. Advance HE.

Baird, H., Towl, G., Renfrew, K., & Buckingham, R. (2022). *Evaluation of the initial impact of the statement of expectations – Final report.* SUMS Consulting.

Bates, L. (2014). *Everyday sexism.* Simon & Schuster UK.

Batty, D. (2019, December 6). Newcastle University faces student backlash over stalker's return. *The Guardian.* https://www.theguardian.com/education/2019/dec/06/newcastle-university-faces-student-backlash-over-stalkers-return

Batty, D. (2020, April 19). University of Derby suspends students over offensive group chat. *The Guardian.* https://www.theguardian.com/uk-news/2020/apr/19/university-of-derby-suspends-students-over-offensive-group-chat#:~:text=The%20University%20of%20Derby%20has,in%20an%20online%20group%20chat

BBC. (2019, December 5). Newcastle university stalker's return prompts petition. https://www.bbc.co.uk/news/uk-england-tyne-50671653

Bedera, N. (2023). I can protect his future, but she can't be helped: Himpathy and hysteria in administrator rationalizations of institutional betrayal. *The Journal of Higher Education, 95*(1), 30–53. https://doi.org/10.1080/00221546.2023.2195771

Begin, N., Hambleton, M., Scott Lewis, W., Morehead, M., Pacelli, K., Schuster, S. K., Sokolow, B. A., & Swinton, D. C. (2023). *The 2023 ATIXA guide to sanctioning student sexual harassment violations in higher education settings.* ATIXA.

Bennett, L., Gregory, M., Loschiavo, C., & Waller, J. (2014). *ASCA 2014 White paper: Student conduct administration & Title IX: Gold standard practices for resolution of allegations of sexual misconduct on college campuses.* Association for Student Conduct Administration.

Beshers, S., & DiVita, M. (2019). Changes in rape myth acceptance among undergraduates: 2010 to 2017. *Journal of Interpersonal Violence*, 1–22. https://doi.org/10.1177/0886260519867153

Black, N., Henry, M., Lewis, W. S., Morris, L., Oppenheim, A., Schuster, S. K., Sokokow, B. A., & Swinton, D. C. (2017). *The 2017 ATIXA Whitepaper: Rubric for addressing campus sexual misconduct.* ATIXA.

Blake, S., & Dickinson, J. (2023). How to involve students in work on gender-based violence. In C. J. Humphreys & G. J. Towl (Eds.), *Stopping gender-based violence in higher education: Policy, practice, and partnerships.* Routledge.

Bloom, B. E., Sorin, C. R., Oaks, L., & Wagman, J. A. (2023). Graduate students are "Making a Big Fuss": Responding to institutional betrayal around campus sexual violence and sexual harassment. *Journal of School Violence*, 22(1), 44–60. https://doi.org/10.1080/15388220.2022.2130346

Blustein, A. (2017). Student activism. In C. Kaukinen, M. H. Miller, & R. A. Powers (Eds.), *Addressing violence against women on college campuses.* Temple University Press.

Bond, E., & Phippen, A. (2019). *Higher education online safeguarding self review tool.* University of Suffolk.

Bows, H., Burrell, S., & Westmarland, N. (2015). *Rapid evidence assessment of current interventions, approaches, and policies on sexual violence on campus.* Durham University Sexual Violence Task Force.

Bull, A., Bullough, J., & Page, T. (2019). *What would a survivor-centred higher education sector look like? In a new vision for further and higher education: Essay collection.* Centre for Labour and Social Studies.

Bull, A., & Rye, R. (2018). *Silencing students: Institutional responses to staff sexual misconduct in UK higher education.* The 1752 Group and University of Portsmouth.

Bureau of Justice Statistics. (2014). *National crime victimization survey.* US Department of Justice.

Busch-Armendariz, N. B., Sulley, C., & Hill, K. (2016). *The blueprint for campus police: Responding to sexual assault.* Institute on Domestic Violence & Sexual Assault, The University of Texas at Austin.

Busch-Armendariz, N. B., Sulley, C., McGiffert, M., & Camp, T. (2018). *Compendium of resources for sexual assault (CORSA): Briefing sheets.* Institute on Domestic Violence & Sexual Assault, The University of Texas at Austin.

Busch-Armendariz, N. B., Wood, L., Kammer-Kerwick, M., Kellison, J. B., Sulley, C., Westbrook, L., Olaya-Rodriguez, D., Hill, K., Wachter, K., Wang, A., McClain, T., & Hoefer, S. (2017). *Research methods report: Cultivating learning and safe environments - An empirical study of prevalence and perceptions of sexual harassment, stalking, dating/domestic abuse and violence, and unwanted sexual contact.* Institute on Domestic Violence & Sexual Assault, The University of Texas at Austin.

Campbell, R., Wasco, S. M., Ahrens, C. E., Sefl, T., & Barnes, H. E. (2001). Preventing the 'second rape': Rape survivors' experiences with community service providers. *Journal of Interpersonal Violence, 16,* 1239–1259.

Cantor, D., Fisher, B., Chibnall, S., Townsend, R., Lee, H., Bruce, C., & Thomas, G. (2015). *Report on the AAU campus climate survey on sexual assault and sexual misconduct.* Westat.

Centers for Disease Control and Prevention. (2024, April 9). *About violence prevention.* https://www.cdc.gov/violence-prevention/about/index.html. Accessed on July 29, 2024.

Citron, D., & Franks, M. (2014). Criminalizing revenge porn. *Wake Forest Law Review, 49,* 345–391.

Clark, A. E., & Pino, A. L. (2016). *We believe you: Survivors of campus sexual assault speak out.* Holt Paperbacks.

Clery Center. (n.d.). Understanding Title IX and its intersection with the Clery act. https://www.clerycenter.org/title-ix. Accessed on July 29, 2024.

Colpitts, E. M. (2020). Addressing sexual violence at Ontario Universities in the context of rising anti-feminist backlash. *Atlantis: Critical studies in Gender, Culture, and Social Justice, 41*(1), 46–58.

Committee of University Chairs. (2022). *Tackling harassment and sexual misconduct: Guidance for chairs and governing bodies*. CUC.

Cook-Cottone, C. P., & Guyker, W. M. (2018). The development and validation of the mindful self-care scale (MSCS): An Assessment of practices that support positive embodiment. *Mindfulness, 9,* 161–175. https://doi.org/10.1007/s12671-017-0759-1

Coughlan, S. (2020, 22 October). LGBT students attacked in university Zoom meeting. *BBC News.* https://www.bbc.co.uk/news/education-54648103

Cowan, S., & Munro, V. E. (2021). Seeking campus justice: Challenging the "criminal justice drift" in United Kingdom responses to student sexual violence and misconduct. *Journal of Law and Society, 48,* 308–333.

Cowan, S., Munro, V. E., Bull, A., DiSantis, C. J., & Prince, K. (2024). Data, disclosure and duties: Balancing privacy and safeguarding in the context of UK university student sexual misconduct complaints. *Legal Studies,* 1–20. https://doi.org/10.1017/lst.2024.9

CPS. (2021, 21 May). Rape and sexual offences – Annex A: Tackling rape myths and stereotypes. https://www.cps.gov.uk/legal-guidance/rape-and-sexual-offences-annex-tackling-rape-myths-and-stereotypes. Accessed on July 29, 2024.

CPS. (n.d.). What is consent? *The Crown Prosecution Service.* https://www.cps.gov.uk/publication/what-consent. Accessed on July 29, 2024.

Crenshaw, K. (1989). Demarginalizing the intersection of race and sex: A black feminist critique of antidiscrimination doctrine, feminist theory and antiracist politics. *University of Chicago Legal Forum, 140,* 139–167.

Crenshaw, K. (1991). Mapping the margins: Intersectionality, identity politics, and violence against women of color. *Stanford Law Review, 43*(6), 1241–1299. https://doi.org/10.2307/1229039

Cruz, J. (2021). The constraints of fear and neutrality in Title IX Administrators' responses to sexual violence. *The Journal of Higher Education, 92*(3), 363–384. https://doi.org/10.1080/00221546.2020.1809268

Daniel, E., & Logsdon, K. (2015). When students' academic needs clash with behavioural sanctions. *The Journal of Campus Behavioral Intervention, 3,* 65–69.

DeKeseredy, W. S. (2017). Explaining campus violence against women: Unhealthy masculinity and male peer support. In C. Kaukinen, M. H. Miller, & R. A. Powers (Eds.), *Addressing violence against women on college campuses*. Temple University Press.

Department for Education. (2019). Relationships education, relationships and sex education (RSE) and health education: Statutory guidance for governing bodies, proprietors, head teachers, principals, senior leadership teams, teachers. https://www.gov.uk/government/publications/relationships-education-relationships-and-sex-education-rse- and-health-education. Accessed on July 29, 2024.

Department of Education. (2023). *Australian universities accord: Interim report*. Department of Education.

Department of Education. (2024, May 16). New RSHE guidance: What it means for sex education lessons in schools. https://educationhub.blog.gov.uk/2024/05/16/new-rshe-guidance-what-it-means-for-sex-education-lessons-in-schools/#:~:text=Puberty%20shouldn't%20be%20taught,the%20national%20curriculum%20for%20science. Accessed on August 29, 2024.

Dick, K., & Ziering, A. (2016). *The hunting ground: The inside story of sexual assault on American college campuses*. Hot Books.

Dickinson, J., & Blake, S. (2023). Hidden marks: The contribution of student leaders to tackling gender-based violence on campus. In C. J. Humphreys & G. J. Towl (Eds.), *Stopping gender-based violence in higher education: Policy, practice, and partnerships*. Routledge.

Dodson, S., Goodwin, R., Chambers, M. K., Graham, J., & Diekmann, D. (2020). Moral foundations, himpathy, and attitudes toward sexual misconduct claims. *Academy of Management, 2020*(1). https://doi.org/10.5465/AMBPP.2020.14553abstract

Donaldson, A., McCarry, M., & McGoldrick, R. (2018). *Equally safe in higher education toolkit: Guidance and checklist for implementing a strategic approach to gender-based violence prevention in Scottish higher education institutions*. University of Strathclyde.

Donovan, C., Bracewell, K., Changler, K., & Fenton, R. (2020). Findings from a national study to investigate how British universities are challenging sexual violence and harassment on campus. https://www.durham.ac.uk/media/durham-university/research-/research-centres/research-into-violence-and-abuse-centre-for/Universities-Responses-to-Sexual-Violence_May-2023.pdf

Donovan, C., & Roberts, N. (2023). Violence and abuse, universities and LGBTQ+ students. In C. J. Humphreys & G. J. Towl (Eds.), *Stopping gender-based violence in higher education: Policy, practice, and partnerships*. Routledge.

Drouet, F., & Gerrard-Abbott, P. (2023). EmilyTest: From tragedy to change. In C. J. Humphreys & G. J. Towl (Eds.), *Stopping gender-based violence in higher education: Policy, practice, and partnerships*. Routledge.

Edwards, K. E., Shea, H. D., & Barboza Barela, A. (2018). Comprehensive sexual violence prevention education. *New Directions for Student Services, 161*, 47–58.

Equality and Human Rights Commission. (2020). *Sexual harassment and harassment at work: Technical guidance*. EHRC. https://www.equalityhumanrights.com/equality/equality-act-2010/sexual-harassment-and-harassment-work-technical-guidance?return-url=https%3A%2F%2Fwww.equalityhumanrights.com%2Fsearch%3Fkeys%3DSexual%2BHarassment%2Band%2BHarassment%2Bat%2BWork%253A%2BTechnical%2BGuidance

EVAW (End Violence against Women Coalition). (2015). Spotted: Obligations to protect women students' safety and equality. Using the public sector equality & the human rights act in higher and further education institutions to improve policies and practices on violence against women and girls. *Legal Briefing*. https://www.endviolenceagainstwomen.org.uk/wp-content/uploads/Spotted-Obligations-to-Protect-Women-StudentsEy-Safety-Equality.pdf. Accessed on July 29, 2024.

Everyone's Invited. (2023). *Annual report July 2022-June 2023*. Everyone's Invited.

Fazackerley, A. (2023, September 17). 'It's a power game': Students accused in university rape hearings call in lawyers. *The Guardian*. https://www.theguardian.com/society/2023/sep/17/its-a-power-game-students-accused-in-university-hearings-call-in-lawyers

Feder and McCamish v Royal Welsh College of Music and Drama. (2023). County Court Central London, cases G67YJ147 and G67YJ153. https://wonkhe.com/wp-content/wonkhe-uploads/2023/10/5-10-23-Feder-and-McCamish-v-RWCMD-FINAL.pdf

Fenton, R. A., Mott, H. L., McCartan, K., & Rumney, P. (2014). *The intervention initiative*. UWE and Public Health England.

Ferguson, C. E., & Malouff, J. M. (2016). Assessing police classifications of sexual assault reports: A meta-analysis of false reporting rates. *Archives of Sexual Behavior, 45*(5), 1185–1193.

Fletcher, G. (2014). Just how do we create change?: Sites of contradiction and the 'black box' of change in primary education. In N. Henry & A. Powell (Eds.), *Preventing sexual violence: Interdisciplinary approaches to overcoming a rape culture*. Palgrave Macmillan.

Flood, M., Dragiewicz, M., & Pease, B. (2018). *Resistance and backlash to gender equality: An evidence review*. QUT Crime and Justice Research Centre.

Flood, M., Dragiewicz, M., & Pease, B. (2021). Resistance and backlash to gender equality. *Australian Journal of Social Issues, 56*, 393–408.

Flood, M., O'Donnell, J., Brewin, B., & Myors, B. (2021). *Engaging men: Reducing resistance and building support*. Eastern Health, Eastern Domestic Violence Service (EDVOS), and Queensland University of Technology (QUT).

Franklin-Corben, P., & Towl, G. (2023). Responding to gender-based violence in higher education: Changes as a function of COVID-19. *Journal of Aggression, Conflict and Peace Research, 15*(3), 216–220. https://doi.org/10.1108/JACPR-06-2022-0721

Funnell, N. (2017, February 24). Sixteen of my students at the University of Sydney told me they were raped. *The Sydney Morning Herald*. https://www.smh.com.au/opinion/sixteen-of-my-students-at-the-university-of-sydney-told-me-they-were-raped-20170224-gukz30.html

Gamez-Guadix, M., Almendros, C., Borrajo, E., & Calvete, E. (2015). Prevalence and association of sexting and online sexual victimization among Spanish adults. *Sexuality Research & Social Policy, 12*(2), 145–154. https://doi.org/10.1007/s13178-015-0186-9

Garvey, J. C., Hitchens, J., & McDonald, E. (2017). Queer-spectrum student sexual violence. In J. C. Harris & C. Linder (Eds.), *Intersections of identity and sexual violence on the college campus: Centering minoritized students' experiences*. Stylus.

Ghani, H., & Towl, G. J. (2017, April 7). Students are still afraid to report sexual assault. *Times Higher Education.* https://www.timeshighereducation.com/blog/students-are-still-afraid-report-sexual-assault

Greathouse, S. M., Saunders, J., Matthews, M., Keller, K. M., & Miller, L. L. (2015). *A review of the literature on sexual assault perpetrator characteristics and behaviors.* RAND Corporation.

Griffin, S. (1971, September). Rape: The all-American crime. *Ramparts Magazine,* 26–35. https://nyheritage.contentdm.oclc.org/digital/collection/p16694coll58/id/4725/

Griffin, R. A. (2017). Foreword. In S. Carrigan Wooten & R. W. Mitchell (Eds.), *Preventing sexual violence on campus: Challenging traditional approaches through program innovation.* Routledge.

Guttmacher Institute. (2023). Sex and HIV education. *Guttmacher Institute.* https://www.guttmacher.org/state-policy/explore/sex-and-hiv-education. Accessed on July 29, 2024.

Guy, L. (2006). Re-visioning the sexual violence continuum. *Partners in Social Change, IX*(1), 4–7. https://www.pcar.org/sites/default/files/resource-pdfs/revisioning-the-sexual-violence-continuum.pdf. Accessed on July 29, 2024.

Hales, S. (2023). Sexual violence in higher education: Prevalence and characteristics of perpetrators. In C. J. Humphreys & G. J. Towl (Eds.), *Stopping gender-based violence in higher education: Policy, practice, and partnerships.* Routledge.

Halliday, J. (2020, September 23). Durham University withdraws fresher's place over 'abhorrent' online posts. *The Guardian.* https://www.theguardian.com/education/2020/sep/23/durham-university-withdraws-freshers-place-over-abhorrent-online-posts#:~:text=Durham%20University%20has%20withdrawn%20a,poorest%20student%20they%20could%20find

Hannan, S. M., Zimnick, J., & Park, C. (2021). Consequences of sexual violence among college students: Investigating the role of PTSD symptoms, rumination, and institutional betrayal. *Journal of Aggression, Maltreatment & Trauma, 30*(5), 586–604. https://doi.org/10.1080/10926771.2020.1796871

HarassMap. (n.d.). https://harassmap.org/cn/

Harrin, E. (2023). RAG and (BRAG) status and how to use them on projects. *Rebels Guide to Project Management.* https://rebelsguidetopm.com/understanding-rag-in-project-management/. Accessed on July 29, 2024.

Harris, J. C. (2017). Centering women of color in the discourse on sexual violence on college campuses. In J. C. Harris & C. Linder (Eds.), *Intersections of identity and sexual violence on the college campus: Centering minoritized students' experiences.* Stylus.

Henry, A. (2023). *Regulatory responses to addressing and preventing sexual assault and harassment in Australian university settings.* PhD Doctorate, UNSW. UNSW. https://doi.org/10.26190/unsworks/24894

Henry, M., Lewis, W. S., Morris, L. K., Schuster, S. K., Sokolaw, B. A., Swintom, D. C., & Brunt, B. V. (2016). *The 2016 ATIXA whitepaper: The seven deadly sins of Title IX investigations.* ATIXA.

Henry, M., Sokolaw, B. A., Swinton, D. C., Oppenheim, A., Lewis, W. S., & Schuster, S. K. (2018). *ATIXA 2018 whitepaper: The ATIXA guide to sanctioning student sexual misconduct violations.* ATIXA.

Hodgins, M., & O'Connor, P. (2021). Progress, but at the expense of male power? Institutional resistance to gender equality in an Irish university. *Frontiers in Sociology,* 6, 1–14. https://doi.org/10.3389/fsoc.2021.696446

Hollander, J. A. (2016). The importance of self-defense training for sexual violence prevention. *Feminism & Psychology,* 26(2), 207–226. https://doi.org/10.1177/0959353516637393

Hong, L. (2017). Digging up the roots, rustling the leaves. In J. C. Harris & C. Linder (Eds.), *Intersections of identity and sexual violence on the college campus: Centering minoritized students' experiences.* Stylus.

Hong, L., & Marine, S. B. (2018). Sexual violence through a social justice paradigm: Framing and applications. *New Directions for Student Services,* 161, 21–33. https://doi.org/10.1002/ss.20250

Hotchkiss, J. T., & Lesher, R. (2018). Factors predicting burnout among chaplains: Compassion satisfaction, organizational factors, and the mediators of mindful self-care and secondary traumatic stress. *Journal of Pastoral Care & Counseling,* 72(2), 86–98. https://doi.org/10.1177/1542305018780655

Humphreys, C. J. (2021). Technology-facilitated sexual violence in higher education: Impact on victim-survivors and recommendations for universities. In N. Akdemir, C. Lawless, & U. Türkşen (Eds.), *Cybercrime in action: An international approach to cybercrime*. Nobel.

Humphreys, C. J. (2022). *Responding to disclosures of sexual violence 2.0 (UK version)*. Oxford University Press.

Humphreys, C. J., & Towl, G. J. (2023a). Comprehensive institution-wide approach: What is means to be comprehensive. In C. J. Humphreys & G. J. Towl (Eds.), *Stopping gender-based violence in higher education: Policy, practice, and partnerships*. Routledge.

Humphreys, C. J., & Towl, G. J. (2023b). We should do something (someday): Identifying and working through resistance to gender-based violence prevention. In C. J. Humphreys & G. J. Towl (Eds.), *Stopping gender-based violence in higher education: Policy, practice, and partnerships*. Routledge.

Humphreys, C. J., & Towl, G. J. (Eds.) (2023c). *Stopping gender-based violence in higher education: Policy, practice, and partnerships*. Routledge.

IACP. (2005). Sexual assault incident reports: Investigative strategies. http://www.theiacp.org/portals/0/pdfs/SexualAssault Guidelines.pdf. Accessed on July 29, 2024.

Jeffreys, B. (2019, 3 October). Student rape survivor – 'It felt like I was being interrogated'. *BBC News*. https://www.bbc.co.uk/news/education-49893389

Jeffreys, B. (2021, 10 December). Student stalked at university calls for change. *BBC News*. https://www.bbc.co.uk/news/education-59587275

Kamal, M., & Newman, W. J. (2016). Revenge pornography: Mental health implications and related legislation. *The Journal of the American Academy of Psychiatry and the Law*, 44(3), 359–367.

Karp, D., Shackford-Bradley, J., Wilson, R., & Williamsen, K. (2016). *Campus PRISM: A report on promoting restorative initiatives for sexual misconduct on college campuses*. Skidmore College Project on Restorative Justice.

Keenan, M. (2018). Notes for the field: Training for restorative justice work in cases of sexual violence. *The International Journal of Restorative Justice*, 1(2), 291–302.

Kelly, L. (1987). The continuum of sexual violence. In J. Hanmer & M. Maynard (Eds.), *Women, violence and social control. Explorations in sociology*. British Sociological Association Conference Volume Series. Palgrave Macmillan.

Kelly, L. (1988). *Surviving sexual violence*. Polity Press.

Kelly, L., Lovett, J., & Regan, L. (2005). *A gap or a chasm? Attrition in reported rape cases*. Home Office Research Study No. 293. Home Office Research, Development and Statistics Directorate.

Kelly, L., & Sharp-Jeffs, N. (2016). *Knowledge and know-how: The role of self-defence in the prevention of violence against women*. Report prepared for the Directorate General for Internal Policies, Citizen's Rights and Constitutional Affairs. Women's Rights and Gender Equality, European Union.

Khan, R. (2021). *Domestic abuse policy guidance for UK universities*. Honour Abuse Research Matrix (HARM), University of Central Lancashire.

Khan, R., Morris, P., Hall, B., & Alam, A. (2023). *Evaluation of domestic abuse policy guidance for UK universities*. Honour Abuse Research Matrix (HARM), University of Central Lancashire.

Kimble, M., Neacsiu, A., Flack, W., & Horner, J. (2008). Risk of unwanted sex for college women: Evidence for a red zone. *Journal of American College Health*, 57(3), 331–332.

Klein, L. B. (2016). Fostering compassion satisfaction among college & university Title IX administrators. *Journal of Campus Title IX Compliance and Best Practices*, 2, 58–75.

Koss, M. P., Wilgus, J. K., & Williamsen, K. M. (2014). Campus sexual misconduct: Restorative justice approaches to enhance compliance with Title IX guidance. *Trauma, Violence, & Abuse*, 15(3), 242–257.

Krebs, C., Lindquist, C., Berzofsky, M., Shook-Sa, B., & Peterson, K. (2016). *Campus climate survey validation study final technical report*. Bureau of Justice Statistics.

Latane, B., & Darley, J. M. (1969). Bystander "Apathy". *American Scientist*, 57(2), 244–268.

Li, Y. L., Evans, K., & Bond, M. A. (2023). Allies as organizational change agents to promote equity and inclusion: A case study. *Equality, diversity and inclusion*, 42(1), 135–156. https://doi.org/10.1108/EDI-12-2021-0308

Linder, C., Grimes, N., Williams, B. M., Lacy, M. C., & Parker, B. (2020). What do we know about campus sexual violence? A content analysis of 10 years of research. *The Review of Higher Education, 43*(4), 1017–1040.

Linder, C., & Myers, J. S. (2017). Intersectionality, power, privilege, and campus-based sexual violence activism. In J. C. Harris & C. Linder (Eds.), *Intersections of identity and sexual violence on the college campus: Centering minoritized students' experiences*. Stylus.

Lisak, D., Gardinier, L., Nicksa, S. C., & Cote, A. M. (2010). False allegations of sexual assault: An analysis of ten years of reported cases. *Violence Against Women, 16*, 1318–1334. https://doi.org/10.1177/1077801210387747

Lisak, D., & Miller, P. M. (2002). Repeat rape and multiple offending among undetected rapists. *Violence & Victims, 17*, 73–84.

Lonsway, K. A., & Archambault, J. (2016, September). *Start by believing: Participation of criminal justice professionals*. End Violence against Women International.

Lonsway, K. A., & Archambault, J. (2019). *Statement on trauma informed responses to sexual assault*. End Violence against Women International.

Lorenz, K., Hayes, R., & Jacobson, C. (2023). "Title IX Isn't for You, It's for the University": Sexual violence survivors' experiences of institutional betrayal in Title IX investigations. *Journal of Qualitative Criminal Justice & Criminology, 12*(1). https://doi.org/10.21428/88de04a1.2794dde3

Loschiavo, C. (2017). An academic credit model for training hearing panels. In S. C. Wooten & R. W. Mitchell (Eds.), *Preventing sexual violence on campus: Challenging traditional approaches through program innovation*. Routledge.

Lynch, R. J., & Glass, C. R. (2020). The cost of caring: An arts-based phenomenological analysis of secondary traumatic stress in college student affairs. *The Review of Higher Education, 43*(4), 1041–1068. https://doi.org/10.1353/rhe.2020.0030

MacNeela, P., Dawson, K., O'Rourke, T., Healy-Cullen, S., Burke, L., & Flack, W. F. (2022). *Report on the national survey of student experiences of sexual violence and harassment in irish higher education institutions*. Higher Education Authority.

Manne, K. (2021). *Entitled: How male privilege hurts women*. Penguin Books.

Marine, S. B. (2017). For Brandon, for justice: Naming and ending sexual violence against trans* college students. In J. C. Harris & C. Linder (Eds.), *Intersections of identity and sexual violence on the college campus: Centering minoritized students' experiences*. Stylus.

McGlynn, C., & Johnson, K. (2020a). Criminalizing cyberflashing: Options for law reform. *The Journal of Criminal Law*, *85*(3), 171–188. https://doi.org/10.1177/0022018320972306

McGlynn, C., & Johnson, K. (2020b). Criminalising cyberflashing: Options for law reform. *The Journal of Criminal Law*. https://doi.org/10.1177/0022018320972306

McGlynn, C., Johnson, K., Rackley, E., Henry, N., Gavey, N., Flynn, A., & Powell, A. (2021). 'It's Torture for the Soul': The harms of image-based sexual abuse. *Social & Legal Studies*, *30*(4), 541–562. https://doi.org/10.1177/0964663920947791

McGlynn, C., & Rackley, E. (2017). Image-based sexual abuse. *Oxford Journal of Legal Studies*, *37*(3), 534–561. https://doi.org/10.1093/ojls/gqw033

McGlynn, C., Rackley, E., Johnson, K., Henry, N., Flynn, A., Powell, A., Gavey, N., & Scott, A. J. (2019). Shattering lives and myths: A report on image-based sexual abuse. https://durham-repository.worktribe.com/output/1605209. Accessed on July 29, 2024.

McGlynn, C., & Westmarland, N. (2019). Kaleidoscopic justice: Sexual violence and victim-survivors' perceptions of justice. *Social & Legal Studies*, *28*(2), 179–201.

McPhail, B. A. (2017). A question of consent: Engaging men in making responsible sexual decisions. In S. C. Wooten & R. W. Mitchell (Eds.), *Preventing sexual violence on campus: Challenging traditional approaches through program innovation*. Routledge.

Miller, C. (2019). *Know my name: A memoir*. Viking Press.

Ministry of Justice. (2024). Statutory guidance the code of practice for victims of crime in England and Wales and supporting public information materials. https://www.gov.uk/government/publications/the-code-of-practice-for-victims-of-crime. Accessed on July 29, 2024.

Ministry of Justice, Home Office, and the Office for National Statistics. (2013). An overview of sexual offending in England and Wales: Statistics bulletin. https://assets.publishing.service.gov.uk/media/5a7ca66d40f0b65b3de0a47d/sexual-offending-overview-jan-2013.pdf. Accessed on July 29, 2024.

Möller, A., Söndergaard, H. P., & Helström, L. (2017). Tonic immobility during sexual assault – A common reaction predicting post-traumatic stress disorder and severe depression. *Acta Obstetricia et Gynecologica Scandinavica, 96*, 932–938.

Moore, J., & Mennicke, A. (2020). Empathy deficits and perceived permissive environments: Sexual harassment perpetration on college campuses. *Journal of Sexual Aggression, 26*(3), 372–384. https://doi.org/10.1080/13552600.2019.1651913

Morgan, S. (2018). Working together for wellbeing. https://civilservice.blog.gov.uk/2018/12/20/working-together-for-wellbeing/. Accessed on July 29, 2024.

Murphy, A., & Van Brunt, B. (2017). *Uprooting sexual violence in higher education: A guide for practitioners and faculty.* Routledge.

National Police Chief's Council. (2024). *Tackling violence against women and girls – Framework for delivery publication February 2024.* College of Policing.

Nolan, J. J. (2019, July). *Fair, equitable trauma-informed investigation training.* Holland & Knight. https://www.hklaw.com/en/insights/publications/2019/07/fair-equitable-trauma-informed-investigation-training. Accessed on July 29, 2024.

NUS. (2011). *Hidden marks: A study of women students' experiences of harassment, stalking, violence and sexual assault.* National Union of Students.

NUS. (2013). *Confronting 'lad culture' in higher education: Summary of responses to the consultation and call for evidence.* National Union of Students.

NUS. (2018). *Power in the academy: Staff sexual misconduct in UK Higher Education.* National Union of Students.

NUS. (2019). *Sexual violence in further education report: A student of students' experiences and perceptions of sexual harassment, violence and domestic abuse in further education.* National Union of Students.

Office for Civil Rights. (2007). Questions and answers on Title IX and sexual violence. *United States Department of Education.* https://www2.ed.gov/about/offices/list/ocr/docs/qa-201404-title-ix.pdf. Accessed on July 29, 2024.

Office for Civil Rights. (2011, April 4). Dear colleague letter from assistant secretary for civil rights. *US Department of Education.*

Office for Health Improvement and Disparities. (2022). Working definition of trauma-informed practice guidance. https://www.gov.uk/government/publications/working-definition-of-trauma-informed-practice/working-definition-of-trauma-informed-practice. Accessed on July 29, 2024.

Office for National Statistics. (2017). Focus on violent crime and sexual offences, England and Wales: Year ending Mar 2016. https://www.ons.gov.uk/people populationandcommunity/crimeandjustice/compendium/focusonviolentcrimeand sexualoffences/yearendingmarch2016. Accessed on July 29, 2024.

Office for National Statistics. (2020). Sexual offences victim characteristics, England and Wales: Year ending March 2020. https://www.ons.gov.uk/peoplepopulationand community/crimeandjustice/articles/sexualoffencesvictimcharacteristicsenglandand wales/march2020. Accessed on July 29, 2024.

Office for National Statistics. (2021). The lasting impact of violence against women and girls. https://www.ons.gov.uk/peoplepopulationandcommunity/crimeand justice/articles/thelastingimpactofviolenceagainstwomenandgirls/2021-11-24. Accessed on July 29, 2024.

Office for National Statistics. (2023). Sexual offences victim characteristics, England and Wales: Year ending March 2022. https://cy.ons.gov.uk/people populationandcommunity/crimeandjustice/articles/sexualoffencesvictim characteristicsenglandandwales/latest. Accessed on August 29, 2024.

Office for Students. (2021). Office for students statement of expectations for preventing and addressing harassment and sexual misconduct affecting students in higher education. https://www.officeforstudents.org.uk/advice-and-guidance/student-wellbeing-and-protection/prevent-and-address-harassment-and-sexual-misconduct/statement-of-expectations/. Accessed on July 29, 2024.

Office for Students. (2022). NSS data archive. https://www.officeforstudents.org.uk/data-and-analysis/national-student-survey-data/nss-data-archive/. Accessed on December 2024.

OIA. (2018a). Good practice framework: Disciplinary procedures. https://www.oiahe.org.uk/resources-and-publications/good-practice-framework/disciplinary-procedures/. Accessed on July 29, 2024.

OIA. (2018b). OIA briefing note: Complaints involving sexual misconduct and harassment. https://www.oiahe.org.uk/resources-and-publications/learning-from-our-casework/sexual-misconduct-and-harassment/oia-briefing-note-complaints-involving-sexual-misconduct-and-harassment/. Accessed on July 29, 2024.

Our Watch. (2021). *Change the story: A shared framework for the primary prevention of violence against women in Australia* (2nd ed.). Our Watch.

Packer, H. (2024, July 30). Firing of Chinese professor renews sexual misconduct concerns. *Times Higher Education.* https://www.timeshighereducation.com/news/firing-chinese-professor-renews-sexual-misconduct-concerns

Padmanabhanunni, A., & Gqomfa, N. (2022). "The Ugliness of It Seeps into Me": Experiences of vicarious trauma among female psychologists treating survivors of sexual assault. *International Journal of Environmental Research and Public Health, 19,* 3925. https://doi.org/10.3390/ijerph19073925

Page, T. (2022). Sexual misconduct in UK higher education and the precarity of institutional knowledge. *British Journal of Sociology of Education, 43*(4), 566–583. https://doi.org/10.1080/01425692.2022.2057924

Perez, R. J., & Bettencourt, G. M. (2023). Exploring compassion fatigue and community care in student affairs. *Journal of Student Affairs Research and Practice, 61*(2), 266–278. https://doi.org/10.1080/19496591.2023.2176774

Phippen, A., & Bond, E. (2023). Working with schools to tackle online harms and gender-based violence. In C. J. Humphreys & G. J. Towl (Eds.), *Stopping gender-based violence in higher education: Policy, practice, and partnerships.* Routledge.

Phipps, A., & Young, I. (2012). That's what she said: Women students' experiences of 'lad culture' in higher education. *National Union of Students.*

Pincident. (n.d.). https://www.durhamsu.com/pincident

Pinciotti, C. M., & Orcutt, H. K. (2021). Institutional betrayal: Who is most vulnerable? *Journal of Interpersonal Violence, 36*(11–12), 5036–5054.

Powell, A. (2011). *Review of bystander approaches in support of preventing violence against women*. Victorian Health Promotion Foundation (VicHealth).

Powell, A., & Henry, N. (2014). Framing sexual violence prevention: What does it mean to challenge a rape culture? In N. Henry & A. Powell (Eds.), *Preventing sexual violence: Interdisciplinary approaches to overcoming a rape culture*. Palgrave Macmillan.

Powers, R. A., & Leili, J. (2017). Engaging men in anti-violence against women efforts on college campuses. In C. Kaukinen, M. H. Miller, & R. A. Powers (Eds.), *Addressing violence against women on college campuses*. Temple University Press.

Preston, P. J., Sanchez, D., & Preston, K. S. J. (2022). Exploring mindful self-care as a potential mediator between compassion satisfaction and compassion fatigue among student services professionals. *Trauma Care, 2*(4), 535–549. https://doi.org/10.3390/traumacare2040044

Preventing Sexual Violence in Higher Education Act 2016 (ILCS). (n.d.). https://illinoisattorneygeneral.gov/Page-Attachments/Preventing_Sexual_Violence_in_Higher_EdAct.pdf

Prince, K., & Franklin-Corben, P. (2023). Case management as a dedicated role responding to gender-based violence in higher education. In C. J. Humphreys & G. J. Towl (Eds.), *Stopping gender-based violence in higher education: Policy, practice, and partnerships*. Routledge.

Project Callisto. (2024). https://www.projectcallisto.org. Accessed on December 2024.

Quadara, A. (2014). The everydayness of rape: How understanding sexual assault perpetration can inform prevention efforts. In N. Henry & A. Powell (Eds.), *Preventing sexual violence: Interdisciplinary approaches to overcoming a rape culture*. Palgrave Macmillan.

Raimondi, T. P. (2019). Compassion fatigue in higher education: Lessons from other helping fields. Change. *The Magazine of Higher Learning, 51*(3), 52–58. https://doi.org/10.1080/00091383.2019.1606609

Rennison, C. M., Kaukinen, C., & Meade, C. (2017). Sexual violence against college women: An overview. In C. Kaukinen, M. H. Miller, & R. A. Powers (Eds.), *Addressing violence against women on college campuses*. Temple University Press.

Revolt Sexual Assault and The Student Room. (2018). Sexual violence at universities statistical report. https://revoltsexualassault.com/research/. Accessed on July 29, 2024.

Rogalin, C. L., & Addison, S. M. (2023). "He Is Not a Monster": Himpathy and sexual assault. *Midwest Social Sciences Journal, 26*(1). https://doi.org/10.22543/2766-0796.1115

Sall, K., & Littleton, H. (2022). Institutional betrayal: A mixed methods study of college women's experiences with on-campus help-seeking following rape. *Journal of Trauma & Dissociation, 23*(5), 584–601. https://doi.org/10.1080/15299732.2022.2079795

SAMHSA. (2014). *SAMHSA's concept of trauma and guidance for a trauma-informed approach.* HHS Publication No. (SMA) 14-4884. Substance Abuse and Mental Health Services Administration.

Saungweme, F. J. S., Ngang, C. C., & Towl, G. J. (2024). Mapping future directions in addressing sexual harassment in Africa. In F. J. S. Saungweme, C. C. Ngang, & G. J. Towl (Eds.), *Sexual harassment and the law in Africa: Country and regional perspectives.* Routledge.

Towl, G., & Humphreys, C. (2021, April 22). *How to do more than the bare minimum on harassment and sexual misconduct.* WONKHE. https://wonkhe.com/blogs/how to-do-more-than-the-bare-minimum-on-harassment-and sexual-misconuct/

Schnurr, J. (2016, October 19). U o O newspaper editor receives backlash after expose on pub crawl. *CTV News.* https://ottawa.ctvnews.ca/u-of-o-newspaper-editor-receives-backlash-after-expos%C3%A9-on-pub-crawl-1.3122435. Accessed on July 29, 2024.

Schulz, J. S., Forster, C., & Diesfeld, K. (2022). The discipline of, and failure to sanction, sexual misconduct by Australian legal practitioners. *Legal Ethics, 25*(1–2), 88–108. https://doi.org/10.1080/1460728x.2022.2146965

Scott, C. V., Singh, A. A., & Harris, J. C. (2017). The intersections of lived oppression and resilience: Sexual violence prevention for women of color on college campuses. In J. C. Harris & C. Linder (Eds.), *Intersections of identity and sexual violence on the college campus: Centering minoritized students experiences.* Stylus Publishing.

Sen, P. (2019, September). *What will it take? Promoting cultural change to end sexual harassment*. UN Women.

Senn, C. Y., Saunders, K., & Gee, S. (2008). Walking the tightrope: Providing sexual assault resistance education for university women without victim blame. In S. Archand, D. Damant, S. Gravel, & E. Harper (Eds.), *Violences faites aux femmes*. University of Quebec.

Sexual Violence Task Force. (2016). *Durham University's sexual violence task force: A higher education initiative to address sexual violence and misconduct on campus*. Durham University.

Shannon, E. R. (2022). Protecting the perpetrator: Value judgements in US and English university sexual violence cases. *Gender and Education, 34*(8), 906–922.

Shannon, E. R., & Bull, A. (2024). Unwilling trust: Unpacking the assumption of trust between sexual misconduct reporters and their institutions in UK higher education. *Sociology Compass*, e13197. https://doi.org/10.1111/soc4.13197

Sherriff, L. (2013a). Durham University rugby club under fire for 'it's only rape if' drinking game. *The Huffington Post UK*. https://www.huffingtonpost.co.uk/2013/10/31/durham-university-rugby-club-rape-drinking-game_n_4181729.html

Sherriff, L. (2013b). Oxford University rugby club sends repulsive 'Free Pussy', drink spiking, email. *The Huffington Post UK*. https://www.huffingtonpost.co.uk/2013/11/01/oxford-university-rugby-club-free-pussy-email_n_4189455.html

Sidelil, L. T., Cuthbert, D., & Spark, C. (2022). Institutional betrayal and sexual harassment in STEM institutions: Evidence from science and technology universities of Ethiopia. *Gender and Education, 34*(2), 231–246. https://doi.org/10.1080/09540253.2021.1952935

Smith, C. P., & Freyd, J. J. (2013). Dangerous safe havens: Institutional betrayal exacerbates sexual trauma. *Journal of Traumatic Stress, 26*, 119–124.

Sokolow, B. A., Swinton, D. C., Morris, L. K., Price, M. E., & Issadore, M. N. (2015). *Investigations in a box: A toolkit from the association of Title IX administrators*. ATIXA.

Stalking Prevention Awareness and Resource Center. (2022). Identifying stalking: SLII strategies. https://www.stalkingawareness.org/wp-content/uploads/2022/04/Identifying-Stalking-as-SLII-Strategies.pdf. Accessed on August 29, 2024.

Starmer, K. (2013, March 13). False allegations of rape and domestic violence are few and far between. *The Guardian.* https://www.theguardian.com/commentisfree/2013/mar/13/false-allegations-rape-domestic-violence-rare#:~:text=In%20the%20period%20of%20the,both%20rape%20and%20domestic%20violence

Sundaram, V., Shannon, E., Page, T., & Phipps, A. (2019). *Developing an intersectional approach to training on sexual harassment, violence and hate crimes: Guide for training facilitators.* University of York.

Swartout, K. M., Koss, M. P., White, J. W., Thompson, M. P., Abbey, A., & Bells, A. L. (2015). Trajectory analysis of the campus serial rapist assumption. *Journal of the American Medical Association: Paediatrics, 169*(12), 1148–1154. http://doi.org/10.1001/jamapediatrics.2015.0707

Tan, Y., Vandebosch, H., Pabian, S., & Poels, K. (2024). A scoping review of technological tools for supporting victims of online sexual harassment. *Aggression and Violent Behaviour, 78,* 101953.

Thomas-Card, T., & Eichele, K. (2017). Blending victim advocacy and violence prevention when training student volunteers on college campuses. In S. C. Wooten & R. W. Mitchell (Eds.), *Preventing sexual violence on campus: Challenging traditional approaches through program innovation.* Routledge.

Tillapaugh, D. (2017). The wounds of our experience: College men who experienced sexual violence. In J. C. Harris & C. Linder (Eds.), *Intersections of identity and sexual violence on the college campus: Centering minoritized students experiences.* Stylus Publishing.

Towl, G. (2016). Tackling sexual violence at UK universities: A case study. *Contemporary Social Science, 11*(4), 432–437.

Towl, G., & Paske, K. (2017, November 7). The Weinsteins of academia can no longer be tolerated. *Times Higher Education.* https://www.timeshighereducation.com/opinion/weinsteins-academia-can-no-longer-be-tolerated

Towl, G. J., & Walker, T. (2019). *Tackling sexual violence at universities: An international perspective*. Routledge.

UN Women. (2018a). Guidance note on campus violence prevention and response. https://www.unwomen.org/sites/default/files/Headquarters/Attachments/Sections/Library/Publications/2019/Campus-violence%20note_guiding_principles.pdf. Accessed on July 29, 2024.

UN Women. (2018b). Towards an end to sexual harassment: The urgency and nature of change in the era of #metoo. https://www.unwomen.org/sites/default/files/Headquarters/Attachments/Sections/Library/Publications/2018/Towards-an-end-to-sexual-harassment-en.pdf. Accessed on July 29, 2024.

UN Women. (2020). *Online and ICT facilitated violence against women and girls during COVID-19*. UN Women.

United Educators. (2021). Title IX from the UE toolbox: Checklist for conducting student sexual assault investigations. https://www.ue.org/risk-management/sexual-assault-and-misconduct/sexual-harassment-investigations/. Accessed on July 29, 2024.

Universities UK and Pinsent Masons. (2016). *Guidance for higher education institutions: How to handle alleged student misconduct which may also constitute a criminal offence*. Universities UK.

Universities UK. (2016). *Changing the culture: Report of the universities UK taskforce examining violence against women, harassment and hate crime affecting university students*. Universities UK.

Universities UK. (2017). *Changing the culture: Responding to cases of violence against women, harassment and hate crime affecting university students – Directory of case studies*. Universities UK.

Universities UK. (2019a). *Changing the culture: Tackling gender-based violence, harassment and hate crime: Two years on*. Universities UK.

Universities UK. (2019b). *Changing the culture: Tackling online harassment and promoting online welfare*. Universities UK.

Universities UK. (2020). *Continuing the conversation: Responding to domestic violence and technology mediated abuse in higher education communities during the Covid-19 pandemic*. Universities UK.

Universities UK. (2022a). *Changing the culture: Sharing personal data in harassment cases. Practical guide for universities.* Universities UK.

Universities UK. (2022b). *Changing the culture: Sharing personal data in harassment cases. Strategic guide for universities.* Universities UK.

Universities UK. (2022c). *Changing the culture: Tackling staff-to-student sexual misconduct. Practical guide for universities.* Universities UK.

Universities UK. (2022d). *Changing the culture: Tackling staff-to-student sexual misconduct. Strategic guide for universities.* Universities UK.

Universities UK. (2022e). *Spiking: What universities can do. A practice note to support universities' response to spiking.* Universities UK.

Universities UK. (2023). *Our response to the Office for Students' consultation on a new approach to regulating harassment and sexual misconduct in English higher education.* Universities UK.

Universities UK, Pinsent Masons, & Coventry University Group. (2024). *How to handle alleged student misconduct: Case studies. Supplemental note to UUK-Pinsent Masons guidance.* Universities UK.

University of Pennsylvania. (2012). Adjudicating complains of sexual misconduct: 17 tips for adjudicators of student discipline. https://view.officeapps.live.com/op/view.aspx?src=https%3A%2F%2Fwww.legalmomentum.org%2Fsites%2Fdefault%2Ffiles%2Freports%2FGuide%2520for%2520Discipline%2520Panels%2520on%2520Sexual%2520Violence%2520for%2520Distribution_0.doc&wdOrigin=BROWSELINK. Accessed on July 29, 2024.

USVreact. (2016). Review of best practice in 'first response' training internationally. *Universities Supporting Victims of Sexual Violence.* https://usvreact.eu/wp-content/resources/USVSV_best_practice_review_sep2016.pdf. Accessed on July 29, 2024.

USVreact. (2020, February). Training resources. https://usvreact.eu/resources/training-resources/. Accessed on July 29, 2024.

Vera-Gray, F. (2018). *The right amount of panic: How women trade freedom for safety.* Policy Press.

VicHealth. (2018). *(En)countering resistance: Strategies to respond to resistance to gender equality initiatives.* Victorian Health Promotion Foundation.

Victim Rights Law Center. (2014). Where to start: Drafting and implementing no contact orders for sexual violence victims on college campuses. https://victimrights.org/wp-content/uploads/2021/02/Where-to-Start-Drafting-Implementing-and-Enforcing-No-Contact-Orders-for-Victims-of-Gender-Based-Violence-on-Campuses-1.pdf. Accessed on July 29, 2024.

Warrick, D. D. (2023). Revisiting resistance to change and how to manage it: What has been learned and what organizations need to do. *Business Horizons*, *66*(4), 433–441.

Weaving, M., Haslam, N., & Fine, C. (2023). Himpathy and status: Attitudes to social hierarchy predict reactions to sexual harassment. *PLoS One*, *18*(12), e0292953. https://doi.org/10.1371/journal.pone.0292953

White House Task Force to Protect Students from Sexual Assault. (2017, January). Preventing and addressing campus sexual misconduct: A guide for university and college presidents, chancellors, and senior administrators. https://changingourcampus.org/resources/not-alone/VAW-Event-Guide-for-College-Presidents.PDF. Accessed on July 29, 2024.

Wiggins-Romesburg, C. A., & Githens, R. P. (2018). The psychology of diversity resistance and integration. *Human Resource Development Review*, *17*, 179–198.

Wilson, C., Lonsway, K., & Archambault, J. (2016). Understanding the neurobiology of trauma and implications for interviewing victims. *End Violence against Women International*. https://evawintl.org/wp-content/uploads/2016-11_TB_Neurobiology1.pdf

Wiseman, T. (1996). A concept analysis of empathy. *Journal of Advanced Nursing*, *23*(6), 1162–1167. https://doi.org/10.1046/j.1365-2648.1996.12213.x

World Health Organization. (2019). *International statistical classification of diseases and related health problems* (11th ed.). https://icd.who.int/

Worthington, K. (2021, 17 May). What to do when your content cannot be removed. https://revengepornhelpline.org.uk/news/what-to-do-when-your-content-cannot-be-removed/. Accessed on July 29, 2024.

INDEX

www.ingramcontent.com/pod-product-compliance
Lightning Source LLC
Chambersburg PA
CBHW050329270326
41926CB00016B/3373